SCREW
WORK
BREAK
FREE

'We have two lives, and the second begins when we realise we have only one.'

—Confucius

JOHN WILLIAMS

Bestselling Author of *Screw Work, Let's Play*

SCREW
WORK
BREAK
FREE

How to launch your own
money-making idea in 30 days

Vermilion
LONDON

1 3 5 7 9 10 8 6 4 2

Vermilion, an imprint of Ebury Publishing,
20 Vauxhall Bridge Road,
London SW1V 2SA

Vermilion is part of the Penguin Random House group of companies
whose addresses can be found at global.penguinrandomhouse.com

Penguin
Random House
UK

First published in the United Kingdom by Vermilion in 2016

www.penguin.co.uk

A CIP catalogue record for this book is available from the British Library

ISBN 9781785040832

Printed and bound by Clays Ltd, St Ives PLC

MIX
Paper from
responsible sources
FSC® C018179

Penguin Random House is committed to a sustainable
future for our business, our readers and our planet.
This book is made from Forest Stewardship Council®
certified paper.

Contents

Introduction

'We're here to put a dent in the universe.
Otherwise why else even be here?'

—Steve Jobs, co-founder of Apple

You hold in your hands the handbook for the Idea Age. Today, an idea can change the world, an idea can make you famous and an idea can make you a millionaire or even billionaire. Whatever it is you want to do – find something to get you out of your job, do something with a burning idea you have, have a positive impact on the world or launch a business to make you rich – follow the process contained here and within 30 days you'll have launched something real into the world (even if you don't have an idea yet). And you can start something on the side, without quitting your job and with near-zero investment.

You'll be in good company because you'll be joining a movement of people all over the world taking the opportunity to make ideas happen in ways that were impossible just a few years ago. This movement takes many forms:

- It's thousands of people every week stepping out of their jobs to go freelance or consult under their personal brand, using online tools to work when and where they choose – and contributing an estimated $715 billion in freelance earnings to the economy in the US alone.
- It's 1.5 million people selling $2 billion of handmade goods and vintage items on the online marketplace Etsy.com every year.
- It's the rise of a maker culture of enthusiasts designing their own products, making objects with home 3D printers and

hacking together $5 computers and open source software in what's been called a second Industrial Revolution.

- It's an army of passionate authors publishing their books directly to Amazon Kindle and earning around $300 million in royalties.
- It's ordinary people using crowdfunding to raise as much as $30 billion from fans excited by their idea.
- It's every person making their ideas a reality – launching their own online shop, creating and marketing their own events, courses and workshops, developing mobile apps or taking a shot at creating the next big startup.

And now it's you too.

You're about to discover a process that's been proven with thousands of people who have used these techniques to create acclaimed blogs, publish bestsellers, launch businesses, win media attention, make a positive impact on others' lives, quit their jobs and create a life-changing financial return.

Your call to adventure

You'll be discovering shortly how to start something that will make you money. One of life's greatest freedoms is to realise you can make a living without a job or a boss and without doing work that bores you.

But there is more than just money at stake here.

This unique process you are about to embark on of finding ideas and making them happen is one of life's greatest adventures. It's about finding what you're capable of, expressing yourself, having an impact on the world. It's about coming alive.

This is your chance to become the main protagonist in the story of your life, rather than a bit-part player in someone else's.

It's also about finding out what you can give to the world. This might seem a strange way to think for those of us who have been convinced by the education system to believe we have no great gifts. Fortunately, confidence is not required for this process. Right now I probably have more belief in what you're capable of than you do.

Starting something new is one of those things that's all too easy to put off. Perhaps you've been putting it off for some months or even years already. Once you see how easy it is to start, you won't want to wait a moment longer.

Become the main protagonist in the story of your life, instead of a bit-part player in someone else's

---

This is our moment

So why is this movement happening now? Throughout history people all over the world have had good ideas – for services, products, books, businesses, events, brands and innovations. But within just the last ten years, something has happened that has changed the world forever.

The difference is that now it's easy to make those ideas happen – and to make some real money out of them as well. The World Wide Web is only a little over 9,000 days old and yet it has already changed our lives irrevocably. We live in a world today where you can publish your own book, sell your own music or create your own online shop in an hour or two. You have access to incredibly powerful tools to create whatever you want and to reach a global market.

Saskia Nelson launched her photography business for online dating profiles in just 30 days when she found her first paying customer online. Wolfgang Wild started his blog of remarkable historical photos using the free WordPress system and ended up with a site getting 200,000 hits a day and an exclusive licensing deal with Mashable.com. Jody Day started a blog called Gateway Women to support childless women like herself and within 30 days it was already on its way to becoming the international movement it is now – with a global reach of 2 million people and a bestselling book to support it.

Matt Inman, creator of the webcomic The Oatmeal, raised a million dollars in crowdfunding in one day for a card game he helped design. Even more extreme, Elon Musk pre-sold over $10 billion worth of Tesla's new Model 3 electric vehicle in just two days. None of these things would have been possible even a few years ago. (You'll read more about these stories and many others later.)

You don't need to wait for anyone's permission anymore. You don't need to win a book deal to publish your book. You don't need to sign a record deal to publish your music. You don't need to convince a bank to invest in you to try out a business idea. You don't need to give a big cheque to an advertising agency to spread the word. This is a revolutionary shift of power to the individual.

Yet too few of us are taking advantage of it. We've been handed the most powerful toolbox in history and yet many of us still use it for nothing more than retweeting other people's ideas and LOLing around on Facebook. It's like we've been given a free Ferrari and we're driving everywhere in first gear. How can you squander even one more day sitting on the sidelines of the biggest opportunity in history?

Those that continue to do so might be in for a nasty surprise ...

Get ready for the post-job world

While technology has given us enormous personal power, it brings other seismic shifts too, ones that are critical to understand for anyone who wants to make a good living. It's time to get wise to where it's all heading if you don't want to be a victim of it.

The animal called The Job is on the endangered list. Now that everyone can work remotely and on an ad hoc basis, there is no longer the imperative to have an office full of permanent staff so companies are increasingly turning to the freelance market or 'gig economy' to fulfil their needs. Good jobs are also being outsourced to smart, well-educated people in other countries. And they're even being automated by software.

So far, much of this is just below the radar but the rate of technological change driving it all is accelerating rapidly. There are big shockwaves heading our way over the next few years that we are very poorly prepared for. A report by Oxford University predicts that 47 per cent of occupations in the US will be automated within fewer than 20 years. The World Economic Forum predicts robots will take 5 million jobs in the US in the next 4 years alone. And that's before machine learning (or Artificial Intelligence) really takes off.

The jobs that remain are squeezing employees harder and harder – to work longer and for less money. The squeeze is even greater for those under 35; 1 in 3 millennials graduating today has no job and many of those who do are in low-wage or even unpaid positions.

Even some hard-won skills and professions are becoming commoditised. If you don't know how to make ideas happen there's a danger you'll end up the minimum-wage employee of someone who does. The single most useful skill in the twenty-first century is to know how to find a good idea and execute it successfully – a skill you're going to learn over the next 30 days.

If you don't know how to make ideas happen you might end up the minimum-wage employee of someone who does

---

Many of us have a psychological block about alternatives to the job; we think they are more risky – somehow forgetting that as an employee we can be made redundant at any moment without warning.

It's interesting that so many don't even consider the alternatives to the job and yet the job is a concept that is only a few generations old. A little over a hundred years ago nine out of ten people didn't have a job. Then the Industrial Revolution came and people moved to the cities to take jobs in factories. The factory evolved into the modern office, but with largely the same principles – to engage people at the lowest possible cost to perform a narrowly defined role. By the end of the twentieth century, nine out of ten people were in a job and couldn't imagine anything else.

Now it's starting to swing back the other way.

Today nearly 30 per cent of the global work force is self-employed. And in many Western countries it's growing. Self-employment in the UK is now higher than at any point over the past 40 years and in 2015, 7,700 people in the UK became self-employed every week.

The dominance of the job, therefore, is a hundred-year blip in the 8,000-year story of human civilisation. The job won't disappear overnight but the changes in the world of work are dramatic and gathering speed. The shift that defined the twentieth century – the Industrial Revolution – is over and we're entering the next stage in human civilisation. I want to show you how to be ready for it.

What's stopping us?

So given all this, why haven't you started something of your own already? Well, I don't believe it's laziness or lack of ability. It's because you were trained not to. And the training started on your first day at school. Here's how business guru Seth Godin describes it:

> Years ago, when you were about four years old, the system set out to persuade you of something that isn't true. Not just persuade, but drill, practice, reinforce and, yes, brainwash. The mission: to teach you that you're average; that compliant

work is the best way to a reliable living; that creating average stuff for average people, again and again, is a safe and easy way to get what you want – Entrepreneur and business author Seth Godin in his manifesto 'Brainwashed: 7 ways to reinvent yourself' on changethis.com

School trains you for a job. It sets your expectations on employment and encourages you to work on becoming the kind of all-rounder valued by companies. Life in school even looks like the office – sitting at a desk with your peers following instructions from your superior. School teaches us to expect to get a job and that anything we do for fun is a hobby.

The education system trains us to be passive: sit still, wait for instructions, seek approval from others and ask permission before doing anything. This is good training for an employee, terrible training for making your own dreams happen.

The similarity between school and employment is no coincidence – school was designed during the Industrial Revolution to produce compliant workers for the factory. Now it's for the office.

We have been brainwashed to become 'workerbots' – we look to others for instructions, we try to fit into the opportunities offered to us rather than create our own and we vastly underestimate our own unique talents. Given all this, it's no surprise that most of us grow up without considering self-employment or entrepreneurship a possibility.

And here's the real kicker: because this workerbot mindset is the dominant one surrounding you, it doesn't even look like you've been brainwashed. It looks like normality. It looks like sanity. But as psychologist and philosopher Erich Fromm said, 'That millions share the same forms of mental pathology does not make those people sane.'

What's really crazy is it doesn't even work anymore. Today, if you really are a replaceable cog, just slotting into a standard role, the chances are some well-educated person in another country can fill that slot remotely, much more cheaply than you. Soon it might even be possible for technology to do it.

You were built for this

Remember that being a workerbot is not your natural state. Barbara Winter, author of *Making a Living Without a Job*, has said:

> I read about a study that found that nearly all kindergartners are naturally entrepreneurial. They exhibit the very qualities that make for successful self-employment. They're curious, adventurous, and extraordinarily persistent. They regularly come up with creative ideas and are eager to share their discoveries. Sadly, this same study found that only a few years later, by the fourth grade, these qualities had begun to diminish. This wasn't entirely news to me, of course. I've been watching people struggle with their own doubts and fears for decades.

Our natural state is to be 'players'. A player in my terms is someone who seeks out the most exciting opportunities, is willing to experiment and have fun with them and to get *into* play – not to just sit and think about ideas but to get their hands dirty by trying the ideas out in the real world.

My job over the next 30 days is to return you to your true nature. They made you a worker but you were *born* a player:

> All human beings are entrepreneurs. When we were in the caves, we were all self-employed ... finding our food, feeding ourselves. That's where human history began. As civilization came, we suppressed it. We became 'labor' because they stamped us, 'You are labor.' We forgot that we are entrepreneurs – Muhammad Yunus, Nobel Peace Prize-winner and microfinance pioneer

The potential upside today of launching your own idea is incredible but if you approach it with a workerbot mindset you *will* fail. Everyone's model of work, of value creation in its broadest sense, is the job. But workerbot thinking from the world of jobs won't help you make ideas happen. The workerbot mindset will have you planning instead of experimenting, holding off on going public in a quest for perfection and wasting your time on unnecessary side issues.

In the fast-moving world we live in now you need an entirely new approach.

Introducing the New Entrepreneurialism

What if everything you'd been told about starting a business was wrong?

Eleven years ago I started working with creative people on their careers and I quickly found that the conventional career and business strategies did not work well for my clients. I developed a new approach centring not on rumination, research and planning but on real-world experimentation.

What if everything you'd been told about starting a business was wrong?

In recent years I have been delighted to find experts in other fields were coming to similar conclusions. The field of project management was adopting 'agile methods' to cope with the unpredictability of the modern business environment. Tech startups were adopting 'Lean Startup' principles pioneered by Silicon Valley entrepreneur Eric Ries to launch more quickly, cheaply and successfully. And Tim Brown of international design firm IDEO was helping to popularise the term 'Design Thinking' to show that the methods designers used to create products could be extended to solve a whole range of complex problems, from business challenges to public health initiatives.

Everywhere it seemed people were waking up to the fact that the world was moving too fast for making long-term plans, too many ventures were failing and it was no longer possible to push your solution onto people with the brute force of advertising.

My response was to develop an approach that is radically different to that described in conventional business books. It's designed for people who are taking their very first steps in making their creative and business ideas happen. And yet it mirrors the techniques used by some of today's most successful global brands to get started. I call it 'The New Entrepreneurialism'.

In 30 days' time when you've absorbed and experienced the New Entrepreneurialism for yourself, you'll see the world in a new light – a world full of possibilities for what you can create – and you'll be amazed how quick and easy it can be.

There are three huge benefits you'll get from this new approach:

Speed

From what I've seen, people starting their own thing for the first time waste 90 per cent of their time. They spend months researching and analysing, googling how to write a business plan or fiddling with every detail of a logo or website that they abandon soon after. This book will show you how to avoid all these rookie mistakes and save a massive amount of time.

When you first witness how an experienced entrepreneur operates it might well shock you. Recently I was in Bali sitting next to a serial entrepreneur from the Philippines. We were discussing a new business idea he had just had. I gave my input and he immediately put it into action. He reached for his phone, called someone who could help with the project and arranged to work with him on it. Then, as we sat in a bar overlooking the ocean, he registered a domain name and created a simple one-page website with the ability for people to register their interest by giving their email.

This 'cut-the-crap' mode of operating is not so surprising to me as it is how I work now. But back when I was an employee I never imagined that starting a new business could be done in a few minutes with an iPad in a bar.

Once you've really absorbed the New Entrepreneurialism over the next 30 days you'll move just as quickly. For now, just trust that most things can be done a lot faster than you think.

Reduced risk

There's no need to quit your job, spend your life savings or risk making yourself look a fool just to get an idea off the ground. The New Entrepreneurialism avoids any of that by starting small in your spare time, getting something out quickly and then adjusting your direction based on the results. This also saves you from the number one cause of startup failures – making something nobody wants.

Fun!

While other 'how to start a business' books make you wade through tedious admin before you take a single step and leave you with nothing at the end but a business plan, this book will throw you straight into the most exciting part – doing the thing people are going to pay you for! This also helps you learn quickly what kind of projects you actually enjoy doing so you don't waste time starting something you hate.

After you've been through the 30-day process once you'll understand how to make any idea happen from scratch. And that makes the world a more exciting place than you could possibly imagine right now.

The seven hacks of the New Entrepreneurialism

At the heart of the New Entrepreneurialism are seven hacks I've developed – revolutionary strategies, formulas and tools you can use to dramatically save time and money, reduce risk and start creating something successful faster than you ever thought possible.

1. VALUE-FOCUS

Instead of chasing money right from the start, put your focus on creating something of real value to others – something interesting or useful. Because once you've done that there will pretty much always be a way to make money out of it. Focusing too much in the early stages on when and how you're going to get paid can cause you to give up on good ideas that would have paid off later down the line. And it pulls your focus away from where it is best placed – creating something people love.

The CEOs of Facebook, Google and Apple, to name just three, have publicly declared their focus on value not money. It's easy to dismiss such talk as mere window-dressing but remember that Mark Zuckerberg turned down a billion-dollar offer for Facebook from Yahoo at the age of 25. It seems likely if money was his first concern he would have taken it. After the first billion, there isn't much in the world that you can't buy.

CEO of Amazon, Jeff Bezos, has said that it's this focus on creating something valuable over just making money as soon as possible that ultimately wins the greatest rewards. Here's how he evaluates a company he's thinking of acquiring:

> I'm always trying to figure out: Is this person who leads this company a missionary or a mercenary? The missionary is building the product and building the service because they love the customer, because they love the product, because they love the service. The mercenary is building the product or service so that they can flip the company and make money. One of the great paradoxes is that the missionaries end up making more money than the mercenaries anyway –
> As reported in the book *Bold* by Peter H. Diamandis and Steven Kotler

Value-focus also means skipping enormous amounts of time that most beginning entrepreneurs waste in fiddling with websites, logos, business names and the other trappings of business. Instead, you put all your time and energy into creating something people love. As you start to understand this approach over the next few days you will be amazed at the speed you can move compared to others.

We'll dive deeper into this topic on Day 9.

2. THINK BIG, START SMALL

Grand missions are great but you also need to be able to find a tangible first step. Follow this process over the coming days and, no matter how big your vision, you'll find a starting point – a first product, project, event, blog post series or whatever it might be – something that represents what you're trying to do. Then you can start straight away on making it happen.

This is one of the most fun parts of my business – showing someone how to take a huge vision they've been sitting on because they don't know how to start it without a big investment in time, energy and money and in a few minutes pulling something out of it that they can start on immediately. In the 'Lean Startup' movement this is called the Minimum Viable Product. And once they've proven their minimal version works, they can build on it.

3. THE 30-DAY PLAY PROJECT

Even a Minimum Viable Product could take a few months to create. In the meantime, how can you know you're on the right track? How do you know you'll enjoy this kind of work? The solution is the 30-day Play Project. Why 'Play Project'? Firstly, because you're choosing something that excites you and will look forward to working on. Secondly, because this isn't about spending 30 days writing a business plan or choosing the colours for your logo. It's jumping straight into playing out your idea – doing something you're excited about, out in the world, with a tangible result to share at the end. In the process you'll immerse yourself in the world you want to impact and you'll find out what you do and don't enjoy about it.

Don't imagine that doing a 30-day project is somehow too inauspicious a start to amount to anything significant. Mark Zuckerberg developed the first version of Facebook in just 30 days at the start of 2004 in the time set aside for study before taking his finals. And it wasn't part of a grand plan to take over the world or become a billionaire. He has said himself, 'We didn't actually care about it being a business early on.'

4. THE POWER OF ITERATION

How do ideas become a reality? Well, if you believe the dominant myth, you have an idea, you do some research that confirms that it will definitely work, then you write a plan to make it all happen. If you execute the plan well enough it is a success; everyone lives happily ever after.

Unfortunately this no longer works, if in fact it ever did.

The real process to produce something successful today is *iterative*; it's a cyclical process of taking your best shot at what you think *should* work, noticing what happens and, if it seems to be working, building on it from there. If the results are not what you expected, you adjust your approach before trying again. It's about exploring, experimenting and testing – and then reacting to what happens.

This iterative, more playful process is the most accessible, reliable, low-risk way to launch any idea – whether building a new career, starting a business, writing a winning blog or discovering the work you love.

The good news for you is that you don't need to know all the answers before you start. If you focus on creating something of value to people and keep iterating, adapting and improving, you pretty much can't fail. That might even mean a complete change of direction when it becomes obvious that your market or audience wants something else. In the startup world that's called a *pivot* and some of the most successful companies in the world have been through it.

On Day 6 you'll discover what I've termed the 'Play Cycle' – a simple way to try something out and then keep adapting it to make it better until it's a hit.

5. PLAY IN PUBLIC

Instead of keeping secrets and going for the big reveal once everything is finished, put perfectionism aside, open up your process and invite people in to get involved. Blog out the themes of your book and see how people respond in the comments, write a talk to summarise your mission and spread the word, release beta versions of your app and invite people to contribute to your project.

You'll get great feedback much earlier in the process and be able to iterate faster towards a killer product. You'll also be building an engaged audience who can later become your paying customers, clients or fans.

You'll have a chance to practise this throughout the book by sharing what you're doing with others.

6. THE PLAYCHEQUE FORMULA

What makes the right idea for you to pursue? How can you choose one that will be successful and you'll enjoy doing? My answer is the Playcheque Formula, putting together the five essential elements your idea needs to be meaningful to you and also to be successful.

As you progress you can also use the Playcheque Formula to check whether you're on track. Find out more on Day 10. You can also find a free online assessment to find out how close you are to unlocking the Playcheque Formula at www. screwworkbreakfree.com.

7. THE KILLER IDEA CRASH COURSE

Don't worry if you don't yet have an idea for something to start. That's quite normal for people at the beginning of this process.

But you don't need to spend weeks researching and analysing to find something. Instead, use the Killer Idea Crash Course and in just a few hours find an idea that both excites you and will be popular with others.

The sooner you start working on something the faster you'll learn.

What can you use this book to create?

The 30-day process and principles contained in the book can be used to make pretty much any idea a reality: a new freelance career, a book, a blog, a physical product, an art exhibition, an event, a club night, a membership programme, a lifestyle brand, a music career, a mobile app, an online service, consulting to corporations, launching yourself as a coach, therapist, advisor or mentor, selling handmade art and crafts, setting up an online shop.

The book's primary focus is on helping you start something quickly on the side, with little investment and without a large team. This might be a one-off creation like a book, product or art exhibition or it could be what's called a 'lifestyle business'. A lifestyle business is something that provides a good lifestyle: it's doing something you care about that makes you an income to replace your job, up to six (and sometimes even seven) figures. But it doesn't require investing the kind of time and money usually required to build something with limitless potential to scale.

However, a good proportion of what you'll learn also applies to fast-growth businesses, like an Internet startup. In addition, if you have never had any experience working for yourself it can be very beneficial to flex your entrepreneurial muscles for the first time on something easier to get off the ground, such as working as a freelancer or consultant. And anything that puts you in direct contact with a particular niche market (such as running events or working freelance for them) will give you a wealth of information you can use to come up with your killer startup idea later down the line.

Although the book is primarily focused on an idea you can make money out of, it also works very well for both non-profit projects (such as raising awareness of a cause) and creative projects (like making your first album) where financial return is not the primary goal.

You can even use the book for intrapreneurship – launching an innovative project within your current company. This might be focused internally, experimenting with a better way to do something or launching an entirely new initiative (like one of my clients who is helping fellow dyslexics in a national retailer to recognise their strengths and overcome their reading issues). Or it could have an external focus – providing something new for customers.

The book therefore has a broad scope and you'll notice I quote from a wide range of creative people – well-known authors and artists, clients with lifestyle businesses, recognised experts in startups and leaders of multi-billion-dollar companies. That's because the process of making an idea happen is universal.

Who am I?

I've had the kind of widely varied career that would give a recruiter nightmares – working in multiple industries and fields in varying formats. I've been an employee, a freelancer, a consultant on contract and I am now the founder and director of The Ideas Lab.

I started my career as a software developer in special effects for TV and film, then moved into streaming video and then became a senior managing consultant at one of the largest consultancies in the world. I left to work as an independent consultant advising broadcasters in several countries on technical strategy, then after a couple of years I qualified as a coach, took seven years of professional development courses in psychotherapy and counselling and shifted completely to helping people launch creative ideas and make money out of them.

I've enjoyed making many of my own ideas happen – making experimental music that was played on radio stations around the world, helping create an exhibit for the London Science Museum, launching a London event for creative people which got into the national press, writing a bestselling book, designing and running life-changing programmes and building a business I can run from anywhere in the world. My ideas and projects have been featured in *The Times*, *The Daily Mail*, *The Financial Times*, *Marketing Week* and other magazines, and BBC Radio.

My first book, *Screw Work Let's Play: How to do what you love & get paid for it*, was a UK bestseller, recommended by *The Sunday Times* and has since been translated into nine languages.

After the book came out I led the creation of programmes such as The Screw Work 30-day Challenge, with hundreds of people around the world making an idea happen in 30 days. The new ideas and techniques in the 30-day Challenge have had a profound impact on the participants, with many telling me the experience was life-changing. When you include my live events, Mastermind and Mentorship programmes and consulting to corporations, several thousand people have road-tested the strategies you'll learn here.

The results have been a joy to witness as participants of my programmes have ...

- Launched award-winning blogs
- Won clients and freelance projects
- Got book deals and launched bestsellers
- Attracted high-profile writing opportunities online and offline
- Run sell-out comedy, music and speaking events
- Seen their ideas go viral on social media
- Sold one-to-one advice sessions
- Launched networking groups and membership programmes that make them six-figure recurring income

- Created and sold out group programmes, workshops and experiences
- Launched apps that got featured on the Apple App Store
- Attracted national and international press, radio and TV
- Launched global movements and been named a thought leader in their field
- Quit their jobs
- Attracted funding for their business
- Met, and even collaborated with, celebrities and personal heroes

And if you think these people are some kind of separate breed of super-entrepreneurs, believe me, the vast majority of them are not! Many of them started with only the vaguest of ideas (or none at all), no website and no sales.

So I decided to take these strategies and techniques that had such an impact, update and develop them and make them into a step-by-step process anyone could follow. The result is the book you're holding in your hands now.

The Screw Work mission

What does 'Screw Work' really mean? Well, it's not about living an empty life of doing nothing. Quite the opposite. It's saying 'screw it' to the outdated ideas of work as something you drag yourself to every day just to earn a paycheque, that work is something empty, dry and lacking any fun.

Say 'screw it' to the outdated idea of work as something unfulfilling and lacking any fun

Instead, it's joining the global movement to take control of your own life, create something that excites you and has a positive impact on the world and get well rewarded for it.

My first book, *Screw Work Let's Play*, was an introduction to this new way of thinking about work as something you do for the love of it. But I noticed that some people read the book and reported that they were still stuck – they didn't know how to start something quickly that would actually get them paid.

That's why I wrote this book, *Screw Work Break Free*. This is about breaking free of workerbot thinking and jumping straight into finding and playing out an idea in a step-by-step 30-day process that anyone can follow and that really works. It contains everything I've discovered over the last six years since my first book was published, including the very latest thinking about websites, marketing, social media and making money.

How to use the book

The book starts with the Killer Idea Crash Course, a quick and simple way to find an idea for your first project. Even if you have no clue right now what you could start, you will do once you've followed the simple three-step process of the Crash Course. (If you already have an idea, do read the Killer Idea Crash Course anyway because it will introduce important concepts of the New Entrepreneurialism and make your idea even better.)

If you want even more guidance on ideas, download the Idea Cheatsheets from www.screwworkbreakfree.com – these give details on five possible projects that are particularly good if you're still in the exploration stage and want to choose something that leaves your options open and helps you come up with other ideas you can follow on with.

The rest of the book is laid out in 30 days. Start each day by reading that day's lesson and follow the suggested tasks to progress your project. Even if you can only squeeze 20 minutes on your project into your day, you can make real progress by following the process in the book.

The 30 days are divided into sections:

Week 1 is kickoff: jumping in, finding your feet and learning some fundamental principles on the go. This includes where to put your focus, how to make progress in just 20 minutes a day, your instant business, setting up your kitchen-table global HQ and more.

Week 2 is about going deeper: we get into some of the deeper understanding of how the New Entrepreneurialism really works: the value of being a curator, what really makes something successful, the Playcheque Formula, how to discover and grow your inner genius and superniching (or the shortcut to instant brilliance).

Week 3 is about dissolving obstacles: dealing with doubts, setbacks and critics, beating perfectionism, creating yourself a website in one evening and what to do if it really isn't working.

Week 4 is about making your idea take off: this is when we'll get into the nitty gritty of getting stuff finished, working out how you'll make money, telling your story, getting others to send you lots of web visitors and customers, a beginner's guide to social media, how to make your idea go viral and how to sell something before you've even finished creating it.

Finally **the Launch Zone** covers the last two days of thirty which are about how to launch the results of your project to the world, how to make a lot of money very quickly by running a promotion and finishing up with a celebration and instructions on what to do to keep growing what you've created.

Each day has tasks for you to put what you've learned into action. Some of the daily lessons include one or more 'worker-bot thoughts' that are likely to get in the way of your progress on that particular day. Get ready to unlearn some things and find surprising truths about how creativity and entrepreneurship really work. In some of the 30 days you'll also see 'Player pointers', providing an extra level of detail for using what you've just learned.

How do you know you're on track? Well, each week ends with a simple check-in so that you can spot if you need to change your approach (there is no check-in in the final week, instead there is a review of your whole project after the end of the 30 days). You can also take the chance to share your progress with others working through the book.

On page 324 you can read about Kiva. I donate ten per cent of ongoing royalties from this book to Kiva, an organisation that makes microloans to entrepreneurs in the developing world. Even a $25 loan can be life-changing for someone needing to buy a sewing machine to make clothes to sell or buy stock for a small shop in a remote location. You can read about the amazing work Kiva does, how your purchase of this book will help and how you can make your own small loans.

Grab the free resources on the website

Before you kick off, take a moment to grab the Break Free toolkit at www.screwworkbreakfree.com free of charge. This includes project choice worksheets, the Idea Cheatsheets, a ticksheet to track your progress and my recommendations and guides on how to create your website.

Elsewhere on the website you'll find more information about the people and case studies mentioned in this book, some audio and video interviews with people featured in the case studies, the interactive Playcheque Formula assessment, the latest updates to this book, news of Kiva loans to entrepreneurs in the developing world ... and even my music playlist for getting you charged up for doing your project!

Connect with others in the movement

This is not just a book; it's a movement. My intention is that this book spreads the strategies, tools and approaches we so badly need in this Idea Age, empowering people all over the world to break free of the old world of work and create something they really care about. So when you find benefit from the things you're learning over the next 30 days, do pass them on.

It's good to connect with other like-minded people for your own benefit too. Knowing you're not alone can make all the difference to your project. To that end, you'll find prompts at several points in the book to share what you're doing with others for encouragement and feedback, whether it's with one like-minded buddy or all your friends on Facebook.

You might also choose a buddy to meet up with once a week to do the check-ins contained in the book and help each other stay on track. Or you could get a group of friends together to meet weekly – online if necessary.

Even better, you can connect with others following through this book on social media using the hashtag #screwworkbreak-free. And you'll be able to check in to see what they're doing too.

To help enlist your playmates (or simply to spread the word and grow the movement) you can download a quickstart guide to this book and find the best ways to connect with me and other readers at www.screwworkbreakfree.com.

Ready to start?

OK then, fasten your seatbelt and get ready for the adventure ...

The Killer Idea Crash Course

Not got an idea? Don't even know what you would enjoy doing? Got several ideas but don't know how to choose between them? The Killer Idea Crash Course will find you a money-making idea you love in a simple three-step process.

Introduction to the Killer Idea Crash Course

Your adventure to find a money-making idea you love starts here with the Killer Idea Crash Course. In three steps lasting as little as an hour each you're going to discover a unique, counterintuitive method for finding killer ideas that you love and that others appreciate and will pay for.

Once you've taken the Killer Idea Crash Course, you'll not only have an idea ready to put into action in your own 30-day project, but you'll never look at the world the same again – because you'll know the secrets to coming up with great ideas that you love putting into action.

Don't be surprised if you start to see new ideas everywhere you look!

If you already have an idea, do still read this section to learn some of the fundamental concepts of the New Entrepreneurialism and to help you make your idea even better.

Warning

What is presented here will contradict commonly held beliefs about how you find winning ideas and turn them into a business. (But, then, if the commonly held beliefs worked, everybody would be doing it, right?)

Stay the course and be prepared to discover a far easier and more natural way to success. This process models the latest thinking in fast-moving companies such as Facebook, Google, Zappos, Dropbox and Toyota.

It is also the process I used to achieve my own career goals: first escaping the nine to five to become a highly paid independent technology consultant, then writing a bestselling book and building my own six-figure business from scratch in a completely different field with plenty of competition.

And these techniques have since been proved over and over again with thousands of people who have attended my events and programmes.

Idea myth-busting

Now, before we get into the process of finding an idea you love, we need to do a little myth-busting otherwise you're likely to put yourself under so much pressure to find the right idea that it might just stop you in your tracks.

Let's take the pressure off. When you're new to the world of launching ideas, it's easy to imagine that your success hangs entirely on the quality of the idea with which you choose to kick off. And that commonly held but inaccurate belief stalls a lot of people right at the starting line, thinking that they shouldn't take a single step until they have found an idea that is brilliant and original and yet somehow guaranteed to work. Since these things are mutually exclusive you could spend the rest of your life looking for such an idea!

The reality is quite different; the idea you start with is not nearly as important as you might imagine. Here are two reasons why:

Firstly, how you execute your idea is just as important (if not more) than the idea you choose. Apple's first iPod was a commercial hit that signalled the start of a new era of success for the company. And yet there were plenty of other MP3 players around at the time. The iPod wasn't even the first MP3 player with a hard disk. Nor was it the first digital product to use a wheel to control it. Even the name iPod had already been trademarked by someone else and had to be purchased by Apple.

What really made the first iPod such a success was how well Steve Jobs, Jonathan Ive and the rest of the Apple team *executed* on the idea to make the very best product they could.

Secondly, your idea will, and must, change as soon as you start executing it. Ideas change in response to the reactions of your audience or market or to get around the obstacles that come up along the way or just because you get new inspiration (and new, better ideas) in the process of playing it out. Once you give life to an idea it develops an intelligence of its own – you might be surprised where it takes you. As a result, the idea you start with is rarely the idea you end up succeeding with. Often times, your resulting book, product or business is unrecognisable from your original idea – which is kind of ironic if you spent months agonising over your idea before starting!

Even if your idea is a winner, the game doesn't end there. Apple didn't reinvent the music industry by designing one iPod. They continued to innovate and evolve the product. Today's iPod bears almost no similarity to the original white model with the hard disk. Now the iPod uses ram instead of hard disk, has a touch screen and can do many things other than play music. The iPod functionality is also wrapped into the iPhone and even the Apple Watch. If Apple had created the first iPod and then rested on their laurels the device would be a footnote in the history of technology rather than a product line that was instrumental in Apple becoming the most valuable company in the world.

So remember that your first idea is just that – your *first*.

The secret of the killer idea

So now you know that you don't need the perfect idea before you start, but some part of you is probably still wishing for that killer idea to drop into your lap. Well, I'm going to let you into the secret of how brilliant entrepreneurs and creatives find winning ideas – and how you can too.

You see the truth is that people in the know don't sit around waiting for inspiration to strike. That's because they know the secret of the killer idea. It's this: the best ideas come to you when you're in the fray, making another idea happen. So if you want to find great ideas, start with *an* idea. Take your best shot at a good idea and put it into action in a 30-day project. Immerse yourself in your subject of choice and make something happen. You'll be learning rapidly, you'll meet people, discover new organisations, new models, useful books and handy shortcuts. And as a result you'll get a bunch *more* ideas that you can sift through and try out in another 30-day project.

Smart people don't sit around waiting for inspiration to strike

---

The 3M corporation was trying to create a super-strong adhesive when they accidentally made the opposite, a low-tack reusable adhesive. This directly led to the invention of Post-it Notes, one of their most successful products ever. Richard Carlton, their CEO said, 'Our company has indeed stumbled onto some of its new products. But never forget that you can only stumble if you're moving.'

Whether you want to create products, books, paintings or businesses, you just need to start somewhere. As artist Chuck Close explains:

Inspiration is for amateurs; the rest of us just show up and get to work. If you wait around for the clouds to part and a bolt of lightning to strike you in the brain, you are not going to make an awful lot of work. All the best ideas come out of the process; they come out of the work itself.

Things occur to you. If you're sitting around trying to dream up a great art idea, you can sit there a long time before anything happens. But if you just get to work, something will occur to you and something else will occur to you and something else that you reject will push you in another direction. Inspiration is absolutely unnecessary and somehow deceptive. You feel like you need this great idea before you can get down to work, and I find that's almost never the case – Chuck Close, American artist appointed by Barack Obama to the President's Committee on the Arts and Humanities, quoted in *Wisdom: The Greatest Gift One Generation Can Give to Another* by Andrew Zuckerman

You never know where an idea will lead you

When you're new to finding ideas and making them happen, don't be afraid to choose something that excites you even if it seems small, trivial or a bit of fun.

In 2003 Harvard student Mark Zuckerberg had an idea for a website called facemash that he built in one afternoon. It grew in popularity so quickly it crashed the Harvard servers. Facemash, along with some other Play Projects centring on online collaboration, inspired him in the creation of theFacebook in 2004. In the intervening ten years the site has changed massively and even changed its name to become Facebook as we know it today, with over a billion users worldwide. But if Mark hadn't created facemash he might never have seen the potential in creating Facebook.

So for your first 30-day Play Project, don't be afraid to choose something simply because it excites you – even if it seems somewhat trivial or you can't see how it can ever make money. Follow it through for 30 days and then see how it inspires you to bigger and more commercial ideas.

Here's the bottom line: your success does not live or die on this idea. Your success depends on you becoming a 'player' – someone who knows how to go out into the world, play out an idea and have fun with it.

So let's find you your first idea.

KILLER IDEA CRASH COURSE STEP 1

Generate Dozens of Ideas in Record Time

There are two distinct and very different processes involved in finding an idea for your Play Project. The first is to generate options and the second is to choose between them. Most people make the mistake of merging these together and as a result get stuck. If you think you've got no ideas, that's because you're doing this too – evaluating and discarding ideas at the same time as trying to generate them. This just ties your brain in knots and leaves you confused and frustrated. To ensure that doesn't happen this time, we're going to separate the different processes into two steps with a break in between. First we'll generate ideas and later, in the second step, we'll evaluate them. In the third step of this Crash Course we will then turn the best idea into a manageable project you can start right away.

Shouldn't I wait to find my passion first?

No! Here's why. Most people don't have a single, clear passion. I don't. And yet I have constructed a successful working life made of things I love doing. If I won the lottery tomorrow and never had to make any money ever again, I would still be doing much of what I do now – reading, writing, giving talks, running events, learning, teaching fascinating ideas to people, running courses, playing with technology and doing online projects. And those are the things I get paid for. That's what I call 'getting paid to play'. The way I got there is how most people get there – by choosing one project that I was excited about at a time and following it through. After each project I would reflect on how well it worked and how much I enjoyed it and use that to choose my next project.

Even if you are one of the minority with a singular passion, the only way you can find it is by trying stuff out. The only way to know if you really enjoy something is to experience it.

So if you want to find your passion or just find work you love, here is the single most important message in this book for you:

Don't think it out.
***Play* it out.**

Don't sit around hoping to find your calling; go out into the world and explore. Be willing to experiment with some ideas. And that starts with generating some.

Let's generate a couple of dozen ideas

That might sound like a lot but in fact it's easier to generate *lots* of ideas than try to come up with one *right* idea.

It's easier to generate lots of ideas than try to come up with one right idea

---

Today is all about possibilities. Your aim is simply to generate as many ideas as you possibly can for businesses, events, services, products, courses, workshops, websites, books, freelance/consulting careers and so on that you think you might enjoy pursuing.

IMPORTANT: Your focus today is *quantity* not quality. That means generating as many ideas as you can without worrying whether they are possible or can make money, whether you can do them in 30 days or whether you have the skills or talent or connections or funds to make them happen. We will look at all that later.

And put aside any workerbot thoughts about finding a career for the rest of your life. In fact, don't even think about a business at this point. Today is just about projects and ideas you'd like to make happen.

We're going to approach idea generation from five different angles. Some might work better than others for you. That's fine.

Don't evaluate your ideas at all. Just write anything down that you think might be interesting, exciting or fun to do. Today is about brainstorming and the first rule of brainstorming is *no judgement*. Remember, premature evaluation results in disappointment for everyone.

1. The braindump

Let's start with a braindump of all those projects you've wanted to do for a while – creative projects you've thought of doing but haven't got round to, the book you haven't had time to write, the business idea you couldn't see how to start. Write them all down.

#	Idea (in 10 words or fewer)
1	
2	
3	
4	
5	
6	
7	

If you can't come up with seven, that's OK. See if you can write down at least one or two, then move on to the next category.

2. If you've got it, use it

Ideas that use your talents, skills, knowledge or even just your personality traits are usually quicker to get off the ground than the ones that are in a completely new field. So let's think of a few ideas that make use of what you already have.

- What skills from your work or personal life would you enjoy using in a new business or project?
- What topics do you have expertise in that you would enjoy sharing with others? What ideas does this give you for books, blogs, courses or consultations?
- What are three aspects of your personality that could be really useful to others? For example, ability to connect with anyone, a natural with technology, detail focused, great ideas person, good at making people laugh. What ideas could make good use of these things?
- If you don't enjoy your current work, it's easy to assume that you need to do something completely unrelated in your next career move. And yet sometimes it's just the format or environment that you have been using them in that isn't enjoyable. When I left the world of IT, I assumed I wouldn't be using my technical skills anymore. In fact, I love using my tech skills to create online programmes and they give me a huge advantage over less technical people. Are there some ideas that could channel your existing skills or knowledge into something more exciting for you?
- Need some income quickly? What is low-hanging fruit for you? How could you quickly and easily offer something you know there is demand for and you have experience in? For instance, could you do freelance work using your skills and knowledge from your recent career?

#	Ideas using my talents, skills, knowledge, personality
1	
2	
3	
4	
5	
6	
7	

3. Organic ideas

'Behind almost every frustration, inconvenience and lack lies a new business waiting to be born.'

—Alain de Botton, author, TV presenter
and co-founder of The School of Life

Paul Graham of Y Combinator (one of the most well-respected startup investment companies in the world and named the top startup incubator and accelerator by *Forbes*) says that the most successful startup ideas are organic ones – meaning ones that grow organically out of your life experience. These succeed more often than ideas people choose in an area they have no experience of just because it looks like it has potential. The iPhone for instance is an organic idea – it's the phone that Steve Jobs wanted to exist so he created it.

Sara Blakely, inventor of the innovative body-shaping pantyhose Spanx, told CNBC in 2013 that, 'My own butt was the inspiration.' One night, she couldn't find the right hosiery to wear under white trousers, so she decided to invent her own. She named it Spanx and turned it into a business that made her, at the age of 41, the youngest self-made female billionaire.

'Why doesn't this exist?'

This question has driven the creation of businesses throughout history. Here's an example from Sweden.

A little fewer than ten years ago, sound designer Alex Ljung and artist Eric Wahlforss got frustrated trying to exchange music files. They told *Wired* magazine in 2009 that

> It was just really, really annoying for us to collaborate with people on music – I mean simple collaboration, just sending tracks to other people in a private setting, getting some feedback from them, and having a conversation about that piece of music. In the same way that we'd be using Flickr for our photos, and Vimeo for our videos, we didn't have that kind of platform for our music.

So Alex and Eric built one. They called it SoundCloud and it now has 175 million registered users worldwide.

Necessity could be the mother of invention for you too. What do you wish existed? It might be an app you can't find, a guidebook you'd like to read, a support group you would join or a club night that doesn't yet exist.

You'll often find that some version of what you're considering already exists but it has been poorly implemented or just doesn't work the way you'd like it to. If it's a book or blog you'd like to write, you could approach the same topic with your own distinctive style and still create something successful.

Think of all the things you wish existed or an area where the existing solutions frustrate you and write down any ideas for projects.

#	Organic ideas (in 10 words or fewer)
1	
2	
3	
4	
5	
6	
7	

4. Let's dream

OK, let's add in a few wild cards. Let your imagination rip for a while and see if we can top the list up with some dream ideas. What do you dream of doing? What did you dream of doing as a child? What would you do if you won the lottery? After you'd had a couple of months off work, sitting on the beach drinking cocktails, what projects might you take on?

Let's write down some dream ideas: things you would do if you had all the money, time, confidence and contacts you could ever want. What would you do? Write that novel? Build your own house from scratch? Design your own car? Put on a one-person show at the Edinburgh Festival? Write a killer app that dominates your field? Get your own TV show?

Write down seven dream ideas below, the more outrageous the better.

#	Dream ideas (in 10 words or fewer)
1	
2	
3	
4	

5	
6	
7	

Now, in order that we can do something useful with these wonderfully outlandish dreams of yours, all we need is a simple little rule from the wonderful US author, Barbara Sher. As Barbara says, 'You can always have the part you love most about any dream.'

So for each of your seven dreams above, fill in the following table by writing down the part of the dream that you most love or find most exciting. For example, if you wrote down a dream of having your own prime-time chat show, what is the most exciting part of that dream for you? It might be being the centre of attention in front of an audience or spreading a message with your choice of topics and guests or a chance to meet your heroes on your own show or having a vehicle for indulging your passion for comic performance.

If you dream of creating the killer app that trounces Adobe or Facebook, the exciting part for you might be to finally immerse yourself in a project you have complete control over or a chance to indulge your passion for technology or good design or a chance to finally prove how awful the current solutions are and show them how it should be done. Of course the idea of getting rich and quitting your job could be a big part of the appeal, but what we're looking for is a dream that's exciting to be *doing*, not just one with an exciting paycheque. That's because if you don't enjoy doing it, you're unlikely to have much success at it.

What we're looking for is a dream that's exciting to be doing, not just one with an exciting paycheque

For each of your dream ideas above, write down the part you find most exciting.

Dream #	The part that excites me most about this dream is ...
1	
2	
3	
4	
5	
6	
7	

Your next step for each dream is to think of some idea that seems more doable but that retains the part of the dream you wrote down as being the most exciting. If the exciting bit of the chat show example was meeting your heroes, you could simply try and meet several of your heroes and interview them for a blog. If the most exciting bit was the chance to be funny, you could launch your own chat show as a podcast for free right now and develop your comedy skills.

If you want to create a new social network that you think would be better than Facebook but you don't have millions of dollars of funding, then your more doable idea might be to write posts on LinkedIn Pulse critiquing the good and bad of current leading social networks and laying out your vision of a better way. Or it might be to develop an add-on to an existing social network that addresses your concerns.

Write down the more doable versions of your dream ideas below.

Dream #	Doable version of my dream idea
1	
2	

3	
4	
5	
6	
7	

5. And finally ...

You should have a good few ideas written down now but let's chuck in one last idea. This is your 'Ah what the hell!' idea that you throw into the hat at the last moment.

#	My 'ah what the hell!' Idea (in 10 words or less)
1	

(It's funny, but sometimes it's the thing you throw in at the last minute that turns out to be the one closest to your heart.)

Need some more prompting?

I've detailed five ready-to-go ideas for you in the Idea Cheatsheets which you can download for free from www.screwworkbreakfree.com – these give details of five possible projects that are particularly good if you're still in the exploration stage and want to choose a project that leaves your options open and helps you come up with other ideas you can follow on with: write a book (or blog), start an online business, run an event or workshop, sell arts, crafts or physical products, and sell your services as a freelancer, consultant or advisor. If you struggled to come up with your own ideas, download the Idea Cheatsheets now and pick one or two to add to your list here before we move on. I guarantee that there will be something that will work for you.

In the next step we'll look at how to evaluate your ideas and then make a choice. Then in the final step, we'll take your chosen idea and turn it into something you can do in just 30 days. But for now, take a break: have lunch, go for a walk or sleep on it.

Choosing the Right Idea

I n this step we're going to choose which of your ideas to turn into a project first. Before we start, if any additional ideas have occurred to you in your break, add them to your list. Then it's time to start sorting through your ideas.

Evaluating your ideas

You've got a whole bunch of ideas. Now we can start evaluating them.

Here's what people most often do when trying to choose ideas. They come up with an idea, then find a possible problem with it and discard it. Then they come up with another one and find a problem with that and discard it. And then they claim they don't have any ideas at all. In reality they've had several; they're just throwing them away too quickly.

You're already one step ahead of these people because you've generated several ideas without succumbing to the dreaded problem of 'premature evaluation'.

Now I'll show you how to process the ideas to make them work and choose the best one of the bunch to take forward into the next 30 days.

Create your shortlist

Firstly, out of all the ideas you wrote down yesterday, choose four that seem particularly exciting and put them on the shortlist below. If you only have two or three that really interest you, that's OK; just write them down.

Then for each idea complete the table as follows:

What excites me about this idea? Write what appeals to you about doing this. Which parts seem like they'd be enjoyable? Choosing an idea that you think will be enjoyable to work on is important.

What might I *not* enjoy about this? Is there any part of pursuing this idea that you might not enjoy? For example, does it require selling face to face, using technology a lot, working alone a lot of the time or something else you don't like? If so, write it down.

What are the obstacles? What practical things might get in the way of making this idea a success? For example, you need a key contact to make it work, you need a book deal, it would require an expensive website build that you don't have funds for. Write it down.

What do I bring to this project? List anything about you that could help in doing this project – experience, skills, contacts, industry knowledge, even relevant personality traits such as being a natural techie or being brilliant at making friends and new contacts wherever you go.

Who might find this interesting or useful? Write down who you think this idea might appeal to if you went ahead and did it. You might not know right now but if you think there is a particular demographic, type of person or niche, write it down. Alternatively if this idea would appeal to people who have a particular problem, need or desire, write it down. For example, 'This should appeal to people who have chronically low energy' (addresses a problem). Or 'This should appeal to the kind of people who like The Oatmeal webcomic' (niche). Don't worry too much if you don't know the answer to this question at this stage.

Idea #1	Idea #2
Idea in 10 words or fewer:	Idea in 10 words or fewer:
What excites me about this?	What excites me about this?
What might I *not* enjoy about this?	What might I *not* enjoy about this?
What are the obstacles?	What are the obstacles?
What do I bring to this project?	What do I bring to this project?
Who might find this interesting or useful?	Who might find this interesting or useful?

Idea #3	Idea #4
Idea in 10 words or fewer:	Idea in 10 words or fewer:
What excites me about this?	What excites me about this?
What might I *not* enjoy about this?	What might I *not* enjoy about this?
What are the obstacles?	What are the obstacles?
What do I bring to this project?	What do I bring to this project?
Who might find this interesting or useful?	Who might find this interesting or useful?

Download a printable version of this exercise at www.screwworkbreakfree.com.

Idea tune-up

Hopefully you're already having some interesting insights just from filling in the table. But the real power is that breaking your ideas down like this allows you to fix or tune up ideas that you might previously have discarded.

So let's look at the parts of this idea that don't appeal and the practical obstacles and address them. Firstly, can you modify the idea to minimise the part that doesn't appeal? So if you wanted to write a book but the solitariness of it didn't appeal, could you write it as a blog and get input and comments as you go along from your readers? Could you make it a book of interviews with experts in your chosen area?

If you had a practical obstacle such as needing a book deal, could you self-publish it? Or talk to friends to see if any of them have contacts in publishers? If you're stuck on how to get around an obstacle start thinking about who might be able to help you with it.

So instead of discarding ideas, see how you can modify them and tune them to make them a better fit.

Problems are part of the game

Whatever you do, there will always be obstacles while you're playing out your idea.

If there was a straightforward way of making your idea happen that would go as smoothly as clockwork, you can bet that someone out there would have done it already. There are 7 billion people on Planet Earth and 40 per cent of them are online (and therefore have access to the same resources and global markets as you). The likelihood that your idea has never flitted across the mind of one of those billions of people is extremely small. *Most* people however won't do anything with the idea or, if they do, they give up the moment they see it isn't going to be a walk in the park.

You're different. You're a *player*.

So expect there to be obstacles to work around. That's part of the adventure. That's what makes it exciting. And that's what makes *you* something special when you deliver it at the end.

Turning obstacles into assets

When Anita Roddick opened the first Body Shop in Brighton in 1976, two neighbouring funeral parlours initially objected to the shop's name. Rather than give up on her distinctive brand name or go hunting for new premises, Roddick fought back by suggesting to a local newspaper that she was a woman entrepreneur under siege. The publicity attracted lots of visitors to the shop and helped her on her first step towards the global success she later attained.

Forget searching for the effortless idea and get on with the one that's most exciting to you now.

It is unlikely that you will be able to see how you are going to make every part of your idea happen before you start. You almost certainly don't have all the knowledge and skills necessary either. But that's one of the best reasons for doing a project – for what you will need to learn along the way. Most gaps in your knowledge can be worked out when you reach them. In those rare situations when Google isn't enough, there'll always be someone else who knows the answer who you can go and ask. Or you can invite others with complementary skills to get involved in your project.

Get ready to choose your idea

Now it's time to pick your best idea out of your shortlist of four.

At this point it's not unusual to experience some 'choice anxiety'. This happens when you tell yourself you have to pick the right idea that you're definitely going to enjoy and is definitely going to work and definitely make you money.

But that's not true.

Firstly, the only way to tell for sure whether you enjoy something is to *do it*. So stop wondering *if* you will like writing, freelancing, programming, coaching or whatever it might be, and just go do some as a project.

Secondly, you're not choosing a career to dedicate your life to. You're not even choosing a business at this stage. You are choosing an idea to do for *30 days*. That's it. You can change it afterwards and pick another one.

> *You're not choosing a career*
> *or business to dedicate your life to.*
> *It's just 30 days.*

Thirdly, if you get a week or two into the idea and realise you've picked something that's a terrible fit for you, I'll be showing you how to turn it into something you love. But you have to get into action before you can actually find out. As the old naval adage goes, you can't steer a ship until it's moving.

Fourthly, if you're worried about choosing an idea that won't make money, I suggest you put that concern aside for now. More on why in a moment.

Finally ... your success does not depend on *this* idea. So don't focus on finding some magic idea right now. Your job here is learning how to become a *player* – someone who is capable of coming up with ideas and making them happen in the real world. This skill, strangely lacking from our education system, is the single most valuable skill you can have right now, with the global economy in a state of enormous change and flux.

Can I do more than one project?

The simple answer is no! Don't try to do two or more projects in the thirty days. If you run two projects simultaneously they'll both progress at half the speed. But worse than this, when one project gets tricky, you'll be tempted to jump to the other one if it looks easier. And when that one hits any kind of setback, you'll want to switch again. This lack of focus (which is actually a fear of committing) makes it far less likely to succeed at any of your projects.

I'm sure you will have other things going on in your life while you're doing your project, but make sure there is only one thing you're applying this process to for the next 30 days. Of course, once 30 days is over you can do your next project.

You might find more ideas than usual coming into your mind now you've started this process. This happens because when you take your ideas seriously for the first time and take action on them, your brain wakes up and goes, 'Oh wow we're actually going to make an idea happen, so how about this one too? And this one?' That's why Nobel Prize-winning author John Steinbeck said that, 'Ideas are like rabbits. You get a couple and learn how to handle them, and pretty soon you have a dozen.' The solution is just to make sure you capture all the ideas so that you can come back to them later and then carry on with your chosen project.

Are you choicephobic?

If the thought of narrowing your options and making a choice is causing you something close to panic then perhaps you are a 'scanner'. The scanner personality type, as identified by Barbara Sher, is one who has a lot of ideas and many interests, loves learning for the sake of learning and is great at starting things but not so great at finishing them. Making a choice of project (and therefore putting some options aside) is like Kryptonite for scanners – it makes us go weak at the knees.

If that's you, the principles and processes you'll learn in this book might very well change your life. Because as a scanner myself, I developed them based on a model of operating that I know works for us. You don't have to dedicate yourself to anything for too long. Pick a project, follow through on it to produce tangible results and then decide whether to build on it or just start something completely different. I've built my whole business this way and you can too.

You can also choose a scanner-friendly project. That means one that harnesses your love of idea generation and learning new things. Instead of writing a blog on one narrow topic, write a blog that looks at a subject area from many different angles. Instead of starting a live event based on a fixed topic, start an event that is focused on the very latest thinking and research delivered by a diverse variety of interesting guest speakers.

But ... you must make a choice of a single project for the next 30 days. If you want to do other things as well over the next 30 days, that's possible but relegate them to the status of a hobby. That means you commit to making daily progress on your Play Project but anything else you want to do has to be fitted in if and when you have the time and energy.

It's essential that you follow through to produce something to show for your project. I ran my live event, Scanners Night, for six years and the critical difference between the scanners who moved their lives forward (producing successful books, blogs, websites, events and businesses) and those that went nowhere is this: the successful scanners chose a project and delivered on it. And then chose another project and delivered on that.

You need to make a decision today on which kind of scanner you want to be: one with lots of dreams but who does nothing or one who makes things happen, impacts the world with their creativity and makes money from the things they love.

So let's now choose your first 30-day Play Project.

How to choose your idea

Look back at your shortlists of four ideas and consider these three parameters for choosing.

1. Does it excite you?

Look at what you wrote under 'What excites me about this?' and 'What might I not enjoy about this?' Which one of your four ideas excites you most? Which do you think you would enjoy doing the most? This is the starting point for any Play Project. Don't expect every moment of your project to be fun but even the most brilliant and lucrative idea won't succeed unless you get some enjoyment, excitement or fulfilment in the process of doing it. Go where the energy is.

Beware choosing a 'should' project – one that makes logical sense, that is in a supposedly lucrative area, even though it holds no real interest for you. I see plenty of people do this in their first project and guess how well it turns out? It takes plenty of energy to make an idea happen so choose something that you think will energise you. Billionaire CEO of both SpaceX and Tesla, Elon Musk, has said that:

> Whatever area that you get into, given that even if you're the best of the best, there's always a chance of failure, so I think it's important that you really like whatever you're doing. If you don't like it – life is too short. And also if you like what you're doing, you think about it even when you're not working; it's something that your mind is drawn to. And if you don't like it, you just really can't make it work

Remember that there is a difference between liking an idea and liking making it happen. I've always liked the idea of a bookshop focused entirely on supporting people's creativity but I don't think actually running a bookshop would be much fun for me.

Imagine starting your Play Project tomorrow. Are you excited (and maybe a little nervous)? Good. If it feels like a drag, pick another one and see how it feels to know you get to work on it tomorrow. When it feels like a treat or feels really exciting (and maybe a little scary), that's the one.

Don't let the obstacles put you off too much; you'll be surprised how easy they might be to get around when you're willing to think creatively about them and get help from others.

Tweak your project idea as you want to. How can you minimise or remove the unappealing aspects of it? In my example of the bookshop, I might not enjoy running a bookshop but I do enjoy running courses on creativity, writing reviews of books on the topic and even creating a simple online bookshop of my favourite creativity books.

What we are seeking here is not some bland state of happiness. You'll know you're doing the right project when it excites you, frustrates you, delights you and scares you from one day to the next. Your goal is not to feel blissfully happy but to feel truly *alive*.

2. Do you bring something to it?

A project is even better if it includes *you* in it. That means you bring something to it: your skills, your knowledge, your talents, your contacts, the stuff you're good at, your interests, your life experience or just your particular personality traits. Look at what you wrote under 'What do I bring to this project?' and anything else that you just thought of.

If you like the idea of doing something but you don't bring anything to the table that will help make it a success, it's probably not the right one for you. Let someone else do it. Or change the project to use more of your talents.

It's particularly important if you want to turn your idea into your main source of income that it's one you can bring real experience and skills to even if you've never used them in this kind of project before.

3. Does it have value to others?

It's even better if you can see how your project could be inter-esting or useful to other people, creating value for a specific audience. Value can be experience, inspiration, amusement, education, entertainment, a service, a new perspective, a solu-tion to a problem etc.

Now of course, when you're starting out, you might have no idea who your audience or market is. And it's all too easy to underestimate how valuable someone might find your idea. For example, if you're going to write a blog for the first time, it might even seem arrogant to consider how valuable people are going to find it. But if there are other popular blogs on a similar topic, that's a pretty good sign that there is at least a demand for your topic area.

Ultimately, creating value for others is something you can't predict before you start. You have to play it out, looking for what people seem to respond to best about your project as you start sharing it with others. Once your project is underway you can modify it according to the response you get.

What about making money?

Trying to assess the commercial potential of your project before you begin it can be problematic, particularly if this is your first Play Project. Here's why:

Firstly, if you want to be successful it is essential to have some clarity on what kind of work you enjoy doing and where your talents (in the broadest sense of the word) lie. It's worth running one or two 30-day Play Projects at the start simply to explore this. Trying to evaluate your ideas on potential income at the same time just gets in the way.

Secondly, it is very unlikely that you are up to speed right now on the amazing variety of ways available for making money out of your ideas. Thirdly, the amount of money you can make is often simply a product of how clever you can get at monetisation and marketing. That's a skill anyone can learn (as I did) and you'll get a good intro in the latter part of the next 30 days.

So if you try to qualify your ideas by how much money you can see them making, the danger is you'll throw away some great ideas you'd love doing that could, in fact, be turned into something that makes money.

If you're a Play Project virgin, you will get better results if you focus on value creation at this stage. If you know how to create something valuable to others, you can bet there'll be some way to monetise it – even if you have to modify or deliver it to a different market than you originally intended. We'll look more at monetisation in Week 4.

Not your first project?

Once you've run through this process at least once, taking a 30-day Play Project to completion and sharing the results with others, then you'll have got some clarity on the kind of projects you enjoy and you'll have some practice at making them happen. Now you can start to consider the commercial value of your ideas as well as the other three criteria in your choice (it excites you, you bring something to it, it has value for others).

Imagine your first project is a blog. After writing it for 30 days or perhaps several cycles of 30 days, you establish that you like the topic and are getting some interest from your readers in the shape of blog comments and Facebook or Twitter shares. However you know that you can't charge someone simply for reading your blog. You *can* however charge someone for an online course, a mobile app, attending a live event you organise, buying physical or digital products you create or having a one-to-one consultation with you. So your spotlight for finding your next project is focused on these kinds of ideas for which you can charge money.

When you're at this stage, you can explore the commercial potential of your ideas simply by asking two questions:

Firstly, is there a pre-existing market for this idea? Rather than trying to find an idea no one has ever made work before, it is much better to choose one that you can see there is already demand for. Is this a problem or need that people are already paying to address? Look for whether people are running successful careers and businesses in this area.

Secondly, what are the best people in this area charging? This will help assess the potential income for you if you pursue it long term.

Five Lousy Reasons to Ditch an Idea

If there is an idea you're excited about but you've just ruled out for other reasons, check this list to make sure you're not being too hasty and ruling out an exciting idea for one of these five misguided reasons:

1. Someone else is already doing it (i.e. you have competition)

An idea without competition is extremely rare and, if you do find one, it might not be a good thing. If there's no competition, there's probably no demand. An entrepreneur on the UK TV programme *Dragons' Den* ended their pitch for a rather curious invention by saying, 'We believe there's a gap in the market for this product'. One of the Dragons drily replied, 'Yes, but is there a *market* in the *gap*?' Often the answer is 'no' when there isn't any competition for it.

So if someone has done it before or there are a number of players in the same area, this doesn't necessarily mean you should give up on it. It's the way that you execute the idea that matters: your unique voice that appears in the process of writing your blog or your book, your obsessive attention to detail in running your business, your genuine care for your customers or your creativity for finding solutions for clients.

So when you're choosing your Play Project (particularly your first one), don't worry too much about competition and don't waste your time with endless 'competitor analysis' – this is often really just you searching for a reason *not* to do it.

2. It's too obvious or it's not original

You don't need to invent a new kind of vacuum cleaner or the next Facebook. In fact you don't need an original idea at all to make a fortune. Richard Branson's Virgin Group is worth billions and yet the bulk of that has come from businesses no more exotic than a record label, an airline and a cable TV service.

Programmes like *Dragons' Den* and *American Inventor*, while fascinating, do tend to encourage the belief that we need some never-seen-before concept in order to be successful. But if that were true, no one would ever open another Italian restaurant or write another romcom. And as you'll see later, even the most innovative ideas are in truth a derivation, evolution or combination of other ideas.

Evan Williams, co-founder of Twitter, went so far as to name his company 'Obvious'. When *Fast Company* magazine asked him why, he explained that

> The best ideas are always those that are obvious in retrospect. It's not about being clever, it's having the breakthrough to see the obvious thing that wasn't obvious to everybody. We want all our products to be very obvious.

Twitter set out to do one simple thing very well: take the idea of status updates, in the style of Facebook, LinkedIn and many other social networks, and allow anyone to follow them. This seemingly simple, obvious idea led to a user base of 300 million monthly active users sending over 500 million tweets daily.

3. It looks harder than I first thought

Problems are part of the game as we saw earlier. If it turns out your idea is too huge to fit in 30 days, we'll fix that tomorrow.

4. It's kind of scary

Good! The right project should generate a nice mix of excitement and nervousness. If it's so scary that you're in danger of not taking action, find an easier way in. If you want to launch a speaking career you don't have to volunteer to go give your first public speech at a big conference. You could join a Toastmasters public speaking club and make your project to deliver a five-minute speech there.

On my Screw Work 30-day Challenge we ask two important questions when people choose their project: 'What excites you the most about this project?' and 'What scares you the most about this project?'

And a surprising number of times, the answer to the two questions is exactly the same thing:

> 'What excites you the most about this project?'
> *'Sharing my writing publicly for the first time.'*

> 'What scares you the most about this project?'
> *'Sharing my writing publicly for the first time!'*

So while some butterflies in the stomach are to be expected, you'll be glad to know that over the next few days and weeks I'm going to be showing you a step-by-step process that makes any project more manageable.

5. I can't see how it will make money

As we've seen, if you can create something people really like, there will almost certainly be a way to make money out of it. Remember that Facebook costs nothing to use but it still made $18 billion in 2015. Over 2,000 wonderful TED talks are all free to watch online at TED.com but the costs are all covered by the TED conference tickets.

If you still need some convincing on this, I refer you to Paul Graham, founder of startup investment company Y Combinator. Their successes have included Dropbox, Airbnb, Reddit, Scribd and Disqus (all of which I use regularly and which you may well have used yourself) and the average valuation of the companies they have backed is $45 million.

Despite the remarkable success of their investments, Paul Graham's most important guidelines for their new startups boil down to two lines:

1. Make something people want
2. Don't worry too much about the money at the beginning

The reason for this is that if you can make something people want, the money part is relatively easy to work out.

And the way you make something people want is by taking your best guess, getting started and being willing to change and improve it along the way.

What if I need my idea to make me money straight away?

If you've just lost your job or are otherwise without an income and need something quickly to keep you afloat financially, it's not a good idea to depend on the completely new venture you're launching. If you do, it puts too much stress on you about your project and puts your focus on monetisation ahead of creating something people really value. Paradoxically, this often kills any possible prospect of return.

Instead, my recommendation is to think about your work situation as two parallel tracks. The first track is whatever work you've been doing until now. This is your easiest way to earn money in the short term because you have a CV or résumé to back it up. It may not be the work you love but you can at least earn from it for the time being.

The second track that runs in parallel is the new thing you are starting on the side. For a while they're going to need to run alongside each other, but if you can build a successful, solid second track, you will at some point be able to switch tracks completely.

Our goal within these 30 days is to prove you can do something that people value. Yes, you could even make your first Playcheque – money for doing something you love – but it's likely to take a fair bit longer to turn that into a sustainable income you can depend on.

Are you suffering from Researchitis?

Researchitis is a serious affliction that may present itself once you've found an idea you're excited about. You might recognise its primary symptom: endless googling, reading and researching in an attempt to scratch a 'What if it doesn't work?' itch.

For some people Researchitis is a chronic condition that causes considerable trouble. If you look long enough for a reason why your idea won't work, you'll find it. Researchitis can therefore keep you stuck for years in a state of deadlock.

If this is you, you'll be glad to know you're holding the cure in your hands. Close your Google search tab, follow the process laid out here and you'll come to understand that the only research you can trust is putting your idea into play.

And finally …

If you're still struggling to choose your project, then discard everything else and just follow this one rule:

CHOOSE ANY PROJECT THAT EXCITES YOU

Your excitement, even if paired with some trepidation, will help carry you through your project. And the things you find enjoyable or exciting to do are often things that you have some natural ability for too.

If none of the projects in your list excites you that's probably because you've chosen 'sensible' or 'worthy' projects. Add some new ones that seem frivolous or purely enjoyable to the list. Even seemingly frivolous projects can lead somewhere interesting when you put your energy into them.

In 2012, 24-year-old Elise Andrew started a Facebook page called 'I Fucking Love Science' because, as she told *The Chemical Blog*, 'I was always finding bizarre facts and cool pictures and one day I decided to create somewhere to put them – it was never supposed to be more than me posting to a few dozen of my friends.' After the first day of being on Facebook, the page already had over 1,000 'Likes'. It now has over 24 million.

This simple Facebook page led to Elise collaborating with Discovery Communications to create an online video series and attracted speaking engagements for her around the world.

Don't spend too long choosing your project. Remember: this is not the rest of your life in the balance. It's just 30 days. So if you spend more than a couple of days choosing you're wasting your time.

I met a woman at a workshop I was running who seemed stuck. She said, 'I've got some ideas I like but nothing I want to spend the rest of my life doing' and my response was, 'Why would you want to give yourself a life sentence?'

The job for life is over. No one expects you to spend your entire life in one career or business if you don't want to.

If you create something that works, you can always hand it over to someone else to run. If it's a business, you can either sell it or find someone else to manage it, retaining an overseeing role and a portion of the ongoing profits. If you've created a successful blog or website, you might be able to sell it on a website marketplace like Flippa.com or package it up and sell it as an e-book. Or if you've created something people appreciate but isn't about making money, someone else will be happy to take it over and continue it for you.

But just because you start an idea doesn't mean you even have to go this far. You might just start an idea to see if you like doing it. So, the pressure's off.

Your success does not depend on which idea you choose for these first 30 days. Your best ideas and your best insights into how to make money out of them will all come out of the process itself once you're in play. You just have to start even if your idea looks fundamentally flawed right now.

Even if you end up going in a completely different direction after you've finished the 30 days, you will have learned some very important stuff about what you do and don't enjoy doing, what other people respond to best, and the value you have to offer. You will also have learned how to operate as a player for the first time – someone who can generate ideas and put them into action.

The only way to fail is not to choose.

OK, got an idea? Good. Take another break and when you come back we're going to turn your idea into a project you can start right away – even if right now it looks too big to tackle.

Idea Alchemy – Turn Any Idea, No Matter How Big, Into a 30-Day Project

*'Everyone who's ever taken a shower has an idea.
It's the person who gets out of the shower, dries off
and does something about it who makes a difference.'*

—Nolan Bushnell, co-founder of Atari, Inc.

So you've got an idea – perhaps with a lot of doubts and questions to go with it – but an idea nonetheless. Now what? Well, you can't actually *do* an idea but you can do a project that realises that idea. And what we're looking for specifically is a project you can do in 30 days, because that's a project that you won't put off. With a 30-day project, you can find out quickly whether this idea suits you and whether it's of interest to other people, all without spending months of your time (or your life savings).

If you're secretly wishing you could just get paid for having ideas, unfortunately that doesn't really work. Ideas in themselves are not that valuable. You have to turn them into something tangible of value to people so that you can get paid for it. It's the execution that matters.

The technique you're about to learn for how to turn any idea into a 30-day Play Project is a deceptively powerful one because it makes almost any kind of idea doable and testable in the shortest time possible.

*This makes almost any idea
doable and testable in the
shortest time possible*

What to do when your idea's too big

What if you've got an idea you want to put into action but it's big … too big? Perhaps you want to open a chain of restaurants or create your own fashion label or build the next Facebook or revolutionise the school system?

These are the kind of things you might imagine requiring you to quit your job or to get some serious funding, hire a whole team of people, rent some premises or build a huge software platform. Or that simply require masses of time and energy, which you don't have right now.

So how do you even start something like that? And without quitting your job, finding a pot of money or magically clearing your diary?

Chances are that your answer till now has been not to start it at all – to put your idea back in a drawer and get on with your life. Well, not today. While other people let their good ideas fade away, we're going to find out how to make them doable – so that you can start today.

To be clear, there's nothing wrong with having big ideas – a multi-million-pound business, a series of bestselling books, a national movement or just making a great living from something you love. It's a useful skill to be able to take an idea and envision just how huge it could become. But … you also need to be able to do the opposite; to take your big idea and chunk it down into a project you can start *right now*.

The power of thinking small

Imagine you wake up tomorrow morning to find an envelope on your doorstep stuffed with enough cash to allow you to quit your job and launch your biggest possible idea.

Even then you would be better off starting small.

Why?

Because starting small gives you the greatest possible chance of making something people really want – and therefore the greatest chance of being successful and making money. You might think you know right now what your intended audience or market will like, but the only way to know for sure is to create it, give it to them, and find out what they make of it. And that's best done with something small.

History is littered with stories of people and organisations who think they know exactly what is going to be popular, so they launch it on a grand scale to be met with nothing but the sound of crickets. Even the biggest companies with the best market research in the world get this wrong. New Coke, anyone? Segway?

Get your idea right while it's still small and it will grow quickly

---

Don't make the same mistake. Start something small, test it out with people, improve it, then grow it and scale it towards your original big vision. Get it right while it's still small and it will grow quickly. That's the snowball effect. And some of the most successful companies today started in the very same way. As the founder of CDBaby, Derek Sivers says, 'Even elephants are born small.'

The multi-billion-dollar company Dell started as a college experiment

Michael Dell's parents wanted him to become a doctor so, despite a growing interest in computers, he enrolled as a pre-medical student at the University of Texas. Michael's passion for computers proved too irresistible though and he started buying old PCs, upgrading them and selling them to other students. Before long he was also selling them to small businesses in the city.

With an emphasis on affordability and good customer support, his dorm-room business boomed (and his shared room started to look like a computer lab). His parents were furious when he told them he wanted to drop out of college so he agreed that if he couldn't make it work as a serious business over the summer he would go back to studying.

He registered a formal company and in his first month of business Dell sold $180,000 of PCs. He never returned to university. By the end of his first full year of business he had made $6 million in sales. Fifteen years later he was a billionaire. Dell told *Forbes* in 2011 that when people ask him today, 'How do I be an entrepreneur?' his answer is simply, 'Go experiment and do something.'

Starting small has two additional big advantages: firstly, it allows you to check you actually enjoy this project before throwing everything you have into it – no point selling your house to open a café to realise that, while you love sitting in cafés, you hate running one! Secondly, unlike trying to realise your original grand vision in one step, starting small avoids the kind of overwhelm that makes you want to put your project off for another day.

The best way to start small is to use a little trick from the tech startup world that will change the way you think about starting a business forever. It's called the 'Minimum Viable Product', or MVP.

The ultimate startup hack: the Minimum Viable Product

The Lean Startup movement, spearheaded by entrepreneur and author Eric Ries, is a method for rapidly creating successful startups on a minimal budget. Its advocates include tech start-ups, such as Dropbox, Instagram, Etsy and Airbnb, and some more traditional businesses, like Toshiba and General Electric.

Having been through two failed startups of his own before reaching success with a third, Ries realised that conventional business approaches didn't work well for startups because of the innovative nature of their products and the fast-moving world they operate in. Planning out your business for years in advance and investing considerable time and money in creating a complete product before customers get to try it too often resulted in failure. A new approach was needed.

Lean Startup focuses at the beginning on the concept of a Minimum Viable Product. And the MVP is a really useful idea for you even if you have no interest in software, the startup world or creating a company. The principle works just as well for freelancing, writing, stand-up comedy or launching your own event. What Lean Startup suggests is that at the start of a business, you focus on creating the minimum product (or service) that someone could find useful, then you get it out into the world as fast as possible and get feedback from people that you can use to go back and make it better. Try to choose an audience who are willing to give helpful feedback and will be forgiving if they find glitches in what you've created. Even Google does this when they release new software as a beta version and ask for feedback before they go any further.

This avoids you slaving away for months or years on something that completely misjudges what people want. Instead, create something as fast as possible, get it out there and see how you can improve it.

How minimal can you get? Take a lesson from the story of Zappos

Zappos shoes is one of the world's largest online shoe retailers and was bought by Amazon in 2009 in a deal worth around $1 billion. But the founder Nick Swinmurn didn't start in the way you might imagine, by building an expensive ecommerce system and buying a huge stock of shoes.

Instead, he went to local shoe shops and asked the owners' permission to take photos of shoes and put them online on a simple shop (originally called shoesite.com). When an order came in he took payment, emailed the receipt manually, went to the shop, bought the pair that was ordered and boxed it and shipped it himself by hand.

This of course does not make for a profitable, scalable business but it was a great MVP. And it allowed Nick back in 1999 to prove that people were willing to buy shoes online without trying them on. Once he'd done that, he could show investors that the principle worked and get the funds to buy stock and build the automated systems he needed to make the business work.

That same year Nick left a voicemail for young entrepreneur Tony Hsieh to ask for $500,000 funding from his investment firm Venture Frogs. Tony reports on Inc.com that when he heard Nick's message he nearly deleted it until he heard Nick mention that shoes are a $40 billion dollar market and 5 per cent of that was already being sold by mail order. Nick got his investment and the rest is Internet history.

So your focus in the next 30 days is to create and release the Minimum Viable Product for your idea – your first speech, your first project with a client, your first training programme, your first live event, your first version of an app with just the features that make it special, your first ten blog posts (that could turn into a book), your first five-minute stand-up routine.

Most importantly, focus your effort, and any money you're spending, primarily on the things that are valuable for your user, reader, customer or client. Don't waste time at the start on a beautiful logo, complex website or getting some details right that your first users won't even notice. That's what makes it 'lean'.

Buy, don't build

If you're technically minded or just like to go large on any project, be wary about jumping into building an enormous dedicated site or app. First, prove that there is demand for the thing you want to create. And the best way to do that is to create it using someone else's platform. If you want to create the ultimate social network for stay-at-home dads, start by creating a group on Facebook and inviting people in. Or use one of the configurable social networking systems like Ning.com.

Or, if you want to build a niched dating website, you can use a white-label dating site system. White-label systems allow you to use their platform, configure it to suit your own needs and apply your own branding so that it looks like your own dedicated platform. Many of the national newspapers' own dating sites are run in this way. It's much easier than diving into the technicalities of building your own. And it avoids an expensive investment before you can even start.

If you want to run a retreat in some exotic location, you don't have to build your own retreat centre. Partner with a hotel or resort. And if you have no experience running retreats but you have some great content to share with people, partner with someone who has run retreats before and is looking for someone to bring fresh subject matter.

Building the ultimate electric car

When Elon Musk decided to build the coolest electric car ever made, the Tesla Roadster, he partnered with British manufacturer Lotus to help create the body. Building the world's fastest electric engine was a difficult enough task without the additional work of designing a good-looking body for it to power too. Tesla created its initial prototypes by modifying models of the legendary Lotus Elise. Then, as Tesla worked on creating the model of car they could sell, they worked with Lotus Engineering to create their own unique body for the car. The end result was a car so remarkable it won multiple awards and brought the young company into profitability for the first time.

Let's nuggetise your idea

So what do you do if your idea is to open a restaurant or a coffee shop or write a book or release your own line of clothes or change the world? How do you do that in 30 days, even as an MVP?

Well, you don't attempt the whole thing in 30 days. Instead, find the heart of your project idea – the nugget that really matters – and do that as a Play Project. Here's the key though: make sure your project centres on the part you love most about your idea that will also be interesting or useful to others. Strip away the rest.

Do something that excites you – the part of your idea that matters most to you. Often people think they need to create all the trappings around their project first. For instance, people who want to start a business will spend 30 days setting up a website or writing a business plan or designing a nice logo when what you really should be doing is the actual work that excites you.

So, for example, if you dream of being a professional declutterer, your project shouldn't be to set up your website in the hope of getting clients. If you've not done this work before, your project is to go do some decluttering for someone. Call up a friend and say, 'You know that messy room of yours? Can I come round and sort it out with you in one day in exchange for lunch and a testimonial?' If they say no, keep calling friends until one says yes. It won't take long.

This means you jump right into the thing you love and start doing it. You're getting experience, you're finding out what you like and don't like about it, you're building your confidence in it and you're walking away with your first testimonial. Better than spending 30 days fiddling with your logo, right?

Note: if writing business plans, building websites or designing logos is the most fun thing you can imagine, then make your project all about that! Go write business plans for five friends or design ten logos for people and see if you can get paid for it; you could start by offering your services on fiverr.com.

Let's look at some other examples so that you can get the feel for how to nuggetise your idea:

- **Want to start a restaurant?** Develop a menu first and invite your friends round to sample it. You could also try running a 'supper club'. Then later you can try a food stall or even a pop-up restaurant.
- **Got a grand website idea?** If it's based around content you're creating, create the site first in WordPress. If it's more interactive than that, see if there's a commercial system you can use to test the idea out. For example, if you want to create an immersive training programme, use one of the many online training platforms before you spend a fortune on custom building your own system.
- **Writing a non-fiction book?** Start writing about your topic on a blog, post by post. Explore your topic and your particular take on it. Later you can use the posts as part of your book. (More on this in the Idea Cheatsheet for

writing a book or blog which you can download at www. screwworkbreakfree.com.)

- **Want to write a novel?** Write the outline and two to three chapters. Or start off by writing a short story or two first. Share it with some friendly readers.

- **Want to explore a new business idea?** Start blogging about the area or the problem you want to help with. Interview people, experiment with possible solutions. If you're selling your own services, aim to get your first piece of work within 30 days, even if it's at a reduced fee for a friend or colleague.

- **Want to be a public speaker?** Go to Toastmasters, learn some of the basics and set a deadline to give your first talk of five–ten minutes at one of their meetings to a friendly and supportive audience of fellow speakers.

- **If you want to be a stand-up comic,** don't just go to see a stand-up show – do a course where you stand up and perform! **If you want to launch a national campaign or change the world,** create a Facebook group for your cause and then create an event that people can take part in to build a buzz.

- **Want to create a mobile app?** Try the free Pop App which allows you to sketch out the layout of your app on paper and then make it into an interactive prototype on your phone. Or google 'app building software' for systems that can create your app without any programming.

The humble beginnings of one of the most influential books of all time

Dale Carnegie's classic book *How to Win Friends and Influence People* has sold 30 million copies but it started as a short talk. That talk expanded to 90 minutes and Carnegie gave it multiple times to students urging them to, 'go out and test it in their business and social contacts, and

---

then come back to class and speak about their experiences and the results they had achieved'. This was Carnegie's MVP.

Using everything he learned, Carnegie created a 'Set of rules printed on a card no larger than a postcard. The next season we printed a larger card, then a leaflet, then a series of booklets, each one expanding in size and scope.' This led eventually to the international bestselling book and also his company Dale Carnegie Training, which has lasted over a hundred years and trained 8 million people in more than 90 countries.

You can read the whole story in a chapter titled 'How this book was written – and why' in *How To Win Friends and Influence People.*

Of course, jumping straight into action like this might be a bit more scary than just playing around with your logo! Hmm, I wonder if that's why most people don't do it.

That's why it really helps to connect with others who are going through the same process (you can find ways to do that at screwworkbreakfree.com).

Declaring your 30-day Play Project

OK, it's time for you to write down your project. A 30-day Play Project is a deceptively powerful thing. Put your focus on creating something valuable in 30 days, use the deadline to keep you focused, share your results at the end and you'll be amazed what can come out of it.

An important part of this is to produce something tangible from your project that you can share. That might be an online sales page for the first product you've created, a report on your first project, client or event or a blog with a dozen new posts exploring your topic. Building this habit of sharing what you're creating is a key part of the New Entrepreneurialism. We'll look at this in more depth on Day 5.

So now, fill in the boxes below to declare your project.

My Play Project
My 30-day Play Project is:
What I will be sharing on the thirtieth day of my project:
What's most exciting about this for me is:

Share what your project is!

Throughout this book you'll see prompts to share what you're working on with others. When you give up the myth of the lone entrepreneur striving against the world and instead get into the habit of connecting with others for mutual support and learning, you multiply your chances of success.

Who can you share your project with that you know will give you some encouragement (i.e. someone supportive, not that super-critical friend or family member who likes to pick holes in everything)? Take a moment to tell them now. Alternatively, you could share your project with friends on Facebook or elsewhere. Making a public commitment makes it more likely you'll follow through and you might even get some encouraging words or tips for your project right away.

You can also share your project with others following this book: simply post it to Twitter or Instagram with the hashtag

#screwworkbreakfree. (You can follow me on Twitter as @johnsw and on Instagram as @johnwlondon.)

You're ready!

You now know how to generate ideas, choose the best ones for you and turn them into something you can launch in 30 days. You're already way ahead of most people. You're ready to make something happen.

Tomorrow we get started for real. You'll find out how to get started quicker than you would ever think possible and after that you'll see how to make progress on your project in just 20 minutes a day.

WEEK 1

Kickoff!

In our first week you'll be discovering how to get started and make progress when you have very little time, the power of sharing your project as you go and how to keep your project on track for success.

Getting Started Faster Than You Ever Thought Possible

'The secret to getting ahead is getting started.'

—Mark Twain, author and humorist

Day one. Big day, huh? Better get this right – start by planning the whole thing out properly …

Screw that!

Don't make a big deal out of getting started. If you are obsessing over exactly how to take that first step or you're making meticulous plans before you make a move, you're stuck in workerbot thinking. Starting a life-changing – or even world-changing – project need be no more momentous than making breakfast.

Don't worry about a five-year plan. The world today moves too fast for detailed and long-term planning and, besides, there is so much up in the air at this stage of your journey that any plan you do make will need to be thrown out within a few days.

You don't need to know your next hundred actions. You just need one – your first action. Then get on and do it. As award-winning novelist E. L. Doctorow put it, 'It's like driving a car at night: you never see further than your headlights, but you can make the whole trip that way.'

Your first step

'We have a "strategic" plan. It's called doing things.'

—Herb Kelleher, co-founder of SouthWest Airlines

Pick one simple thing that you can do today in 20 minutes or fewer, something that's at the heart of your project. Make a call, write an email to someone, join Blogger to start your blog, make something, write something, grab the nearest scrap of paper and sketch a rough design for your app or your book chapter list or the course you'd love to teach. Did you know the original idea for the iconic Mini that went on to sell 5 million cars was sketched on a restaurant tablecloth by Alec Issigonis of the British Motor Corporation?

The original idea for the Mini that went on to sell 5 million cars was sketched on a restaurant tablecloth

---

Whatever you choose to do, do it right now if you possibly can. It's only 20 minutes. We'll dive deeper into this trick of breaking your time into small blocks tomorrow.

The things you don't need

'How wonderful it is that nobody need wait a single moment before starting to improve the world.'

—Anne Frank, diarist and writer

Whatever your project, even if it's part of some eventual world-domination plan, there is a whole bunch of stuff you might think you need, but you almost certainly don't at this early stage. I'm talking about things like:

- The perfect business or blog name
- A business plan

- A logo
- A fancy business card
- A killer website design
- 57 clever blog widgets
- A high search-engine ranking
- Loads of web traffic
- Copyright protection for your blog posts
- More Twitter followers or Facebook 'Likes'
- Yet another training course
- A year-long software development plan
- Investors and funding
- Your own company set-up

What you *do* need is to cut to the chase and get to the heart of your project. Find the nugget that matters to you and make it happen. Then keep playing every day to create something of value: put something of yourself into it, make it as good as you can and keep making it better and better until people can't wait to 'Like' you, follow you, subscribe to you, steal from you (they will!) and, yes, buy from you.

> If you're opening a hot dog stand, you could worry about the condiments, the cart, the name, the decoration. But the first thing you should worry about is the hot dog. The hot dogs are the epicenter. Everything else is secondary – Jason Fried, co-founder of Basecamp, in the book *Rework*

Where to put your focus

What really matters in these 30 days is your mission to create something of value to other people. Do that and the rest is relatively straightforward. Don't waste time on all the trappings of business when you're still finding out what you want to do and how to make it into something other people like.

If your project is about writing, put your focus on writing every day. If your project is to try making money from a skill you enjoy using, go use this skill right away. See if you can do it for a friend or colleague even if it's free the first time. Go teach them what you know or put this skill into action for them – design their website for them, coach them on their wedding speech or whatever it may be. If you want to be a public speaker, focus on writing and practising speeches. If you want to develop an app, focus on the design and coding. Leave the other stuff for later.

Start with one

All successful businesses, websites, blogs or events must start somewhere. You might be trying to build something big, something that will make consistent and significant income. But when you're starting out, this can feel overwhelming. Remember that you can start with just one thing – your first product, first event, first blog post, first client – without worrying too much about what's going to happen afterwards.

Delivering your first whatever-it-is makes a big difference. You can have the grandest plans in the world for, say, a series of original themed events, but it's difficult to get people excited about a concept. You can, however, get people excited about a real event that you're organising when they know where it is, what the theme is and who is speaking or performing. Start with the first one and build it from there.

Jeff Bezos did this with Amazon when he started out. Although Amazon now sell everything from PCs to MP3s to saucepans, Amazon started with just one product – books. They picked books because of their worldwide popularity, low price point and because Amazon's virtually limitless shelf-space would be particularly beneficial to book buyers. Amazon sold their first book on 3 April 1995 to a Mr John Wainwright; the catchily titled *Fluid Concepts and Creative Analogies: Computer Models of the Fundamental Mechanisms of Thought* by Douglas R. Hofstadter. Within two months, Amazon's sales were up to $20,000 a week. Now they make that amount every six seconds. But they never forgot customer number one. In fact they named a building on the Amazon campus after him – the Wainwright Building.

So for now, put all your thinking and energy during your Play Project into creating the first instance of what you're doing and make it happen.

It's OK not to know

I know you've been told all your life that you should know where you're heading and how you're going to get there before you set off but that's not how entrepreneurship and creativity works. As Picasso said, 'To know what you're going to draw, you have to begin drawing.'

The interesting thing about any significant creative project you undertake – whether it's a book, blog or business – is that, while you might have a title (and even some kind of outline), you don't really know what it's about until you dive into making it.

Sometimes you think you know at the start, but it always changes along the way. For my first book, *Screw Work Let's Play*, it was only when I'd finished the whole of the first 60,000-word draft that I turned to my agent and said, 'I think I know what this book is about now.' It had taken that long for the core message to evolve and become crystal clear to me.

Essayist and venture capitalist, Paul Graham says, 'expect 80% of the ideas in an essay to happen after you start writing it, and 50% of those you start with to be wrong' – and the same can be said of most creative projects, including starting a business.

So don't be alarmed if your idea seems kind of half-baked and you're not really clear how you're going to make it happen. Trust that the process you'll learn over the next 30 days will fill in the gaps in ways that will surprise and delight you.

'If the path before you is clear you're probably on someone else's.'
—Joseph Campbell, writer and mythologist

Today's task

- Do your first action! Just make a start.

Workerbot thoughts to challenge

Each day, I'll be covering the kind of thoughts that are likely to pop up that could get in your way. These are thoughts arising from the training we have all had to become workerbots – and you'll need to be able to spot them and challenge them.

'I haven't got the headspace to make a proper start so I'll do it tomorrow when I have more time.' Don't wait to be in the right mood to get started and don't make a big deal out of it. Just do 20 minutes today if nothing else.

'If this is my first thing it had better be perfect!' It's easy to think of your first blog post, event or offering as the decider of your whole future. But that's not helpful. Think of it instead as your first experiment. I see people get very hung up on publishing their very first blog post, for instance, but it might help you to know that in reality very few people will see it! So, in one sense, it's your least important blog post. That doesn't mean you should be slipshod about it. It's important to do the best you can do at the moment. Just remember that you will get better every time you finish something and put it out into the world. You have to start somewhere. So start now.

'I don't know where to start.' Then start anywhere. Choose anything on your project and do it for 20 minutes.

Microblocking or 'How To Change the World in 20 Minutes a Day'

'You can do so much in ten minutes' time. Ten minutes, once gone, are gone for good. Divide your life into ten minute units and sacrifice as few of them as possible.'

—IKEA founder and multi-billionaire, Ingvar Kamprad

Today, we are all busier than we've ever been. Technology was supposed to bring us a life of leisure and relaxation and yet somehow it seems to have done the opposite – encouraging us to be always on, responding immediately to every notification and update. When you have so many calls on your attention how do you make your project happen, even when you're short of time?

The answer is microblocking. It's an essential skill for your 30-day project. If you learn how to microblock and practise it daily, your life will change forever. You'll make progress on your projects despite everything else that's happening around you.

Microblocking is my mashup of the best ideas from the time-management experts of the last four decades, including David Allen, Mark Forster and Alan Lakein. I first wrote about microblocking in *Screw Work Let's Play*, but even I have been surprised by just how powerful it has been when I have taught it to thousands of participants of my programmes, so I've included the technique again here. Users report that microblocking has a transformational effect on their ability to make things happen, even when they don't have much time. As one 30-day Challenge participant told me: 'My productivity in the past month has shattered any previous expectations. The way prolific people work now makes sense in a way that it never had before.'

If you get nothing else from this book other than giving up waiting to 'find' time and instead start microblocking every day, it will have been worth it.

Microblocking is all about super-focusing for small blocks of time. Most of the time our attention is divided between the task in hand, incoming emails, texts, Twitter notifications and other interruptions. When you exclude everything else and focus on one task, your productivity is multiplied. The standard length of a microblock is 20 minutes, but you'll be surprised when you find out what you can get done in even 10 minutes if you're prepared and you're completely focused on the task in hand.

For today and the following 28 days, I'm asking you to commit to doing one microblock of 20 minutes a day, 6 days a week. This allows you one day off a week. You can make your microblocks longer – and some of them should be if you want to make good progress on your project – but one 20-minute microblock for 6 days a week is the bottom-line commitment. This will give you over eight hours of super-focused time over the course of the thirty days. That might not seem very much, but when was the last time you spent eight hours of real focus on your own creative project? For a lot of people, the answer is 'not for a very long time'.

You'll find you make a lot more progress doing little and often than waiting for hours of time to magically free themselves up in your diary.

You'll make a lot more progress doing little and often than waiting for hours of time to magically free up in your diary

---

Today's task: learn to use microblocking for your project

- Think about today; when can you fit in a microblock? How about right now? For your first microblock just do 20 minutes. At other times you might choose to do 30, 60 or 90 minutes.

- Decide what is your 'Best Next Action'. This is the thing that will move your Play Project forward and that will have the biggest impact for the least amount of time spent. Don't choose something just because it's quick – it's far better to choose something important that you may not finish in this microblock than to choose a simpler but less important task. Remember to focus on creating something valuable to others, not on the stuff around it like adding yet another widget to your website.

- Get out your diary and book it in as a real appointment with a description of the task you'll do in that microblock:

  7:00–7:20pm Sign up with blogger

  It's important to be specific. Don't write 'Plan business' or 'Start blog'– write 'Sign up with blogger' or 'Write rough draft of first blog post'.

- Turn up for your appointment. Make this as real a commitment as if you had a doctor's appointment. If something critical comes up you might move it, but otherwise you stick to it. You never just skip it.

- Switch off your phone, your email, Facebook notifications and anything else you don't need that might distract you. Tell others who might interrupt that you are busy.

- Get a kitchen timer or some kind of digital timer that counts *down* and set it to 20 minutes. Place the timer right in front of you and set it counting down. This will help keep you focused. For a free timer app, go to my dedicated website www.microblocking.com.

- Start the timer and do exactly what you wrote in your diary.

- When the timer goes off, you can stop – even if you haven't finished the task. If you're feeling motivated, you can continue.
- Before you file your notes or close your document, decide what you will do in your next microblock and write it down as your Best Next Action so that, when you pick up again tomorrow, you know exactly what you're doing.
- Put your project away somewhere that you can pick it up again quickly.
- Get out your diary and write in the appointment for tomorrow's microblock and the Best Next Action you will take.
- Find and book time in your diary for a daily microblock. If you can do your microblock at the same time every day, why not put a recurring appointment in your calendar?
- Go and relax!

Track your daily progress

'Isn't it funny how day by day nothing changes, but when you look back, everything is different ... '

—C. S. Lewis, author of the *Chronicles of Narnia* series

It's one thing to make a promise to yourself that you're going to stick to a schedule, it's another to actually keep it. It's all too easy to 'forget' to complete your microblock one day and not really flag it. To help you with this, I've created a 30-day ticksheet; you can download it now from www.screwwork-breakfree.com.

Place the ticksheet on your wall where you'll see it every day. Every time you do your microblock of 20 minutes or more, place a big tick on the corresponding day's square. When you take your rest day once a week, write 'R' in the square. Your aim is to fill every square!

Remember that doing 40 minutes one day does NOT make up for doing nothing on another day. The point is to keep your promise to yourself and build the habit of daily action and progress.

The ticksheet is another simple technique that is surprisingly powerful; it externalises your commitment to yourself. Now when you consider skipping your microblock you'll picture the blank space on the ticksheet on your wall – bringing your decision into sharper focus. You'll also have the childlike satisfaction of seeing your ticks fill in the sheet day by day. Try it and see how addictive it can be!

Player pointers

Try doing a microblock first thing in the morning before you start anything else. It's a great way to start your day and ensures nothing can get in the way of doing it. If you can grow the block of time to an hour every day, you can make a huge amount of progress on your project.

Six or seven days a week? I normally recommend a maximum of six days of microblocking a week. This allows for one day a week when you just can't get to your project. And it can be good to deliberately not think about your project for a day (even God rested on the seventh day!). Strangely, this time off when you weren't even trying can sometimes generate the freshest insights into your project. However if you find it easier to keep a daily habit without breaks, go for it. That's what Jerry Seinfeld did when he started his stand-up comedy career as you'll see in the story below.

If you like to go for the burn and pull an all-nighter once you've got started, here's a word of warning: this behaviour of not stopping goes hand in hand with not starting. That's because part of you knows that, once you do start, you're likely to work yourself to the point of exhaustion. Develop a kinder and more sustainable way of working with microblocking and you'll almost certainly make more progress.

It's OK to stop in the middle of your task when the timer goes off. Nobel Prize-winning writer Ernest Hemingway would deliberately stop mid-sentence in order to make it more enticing to come back to his writing the next day:

> The best way is always to stop when you are going good and when you know what will happen next. If you do that every day ... you will never be stuck ... Always stop while you are going good and don't think about it or worry about it until you start to write the next day. That way your subconscious will work on it all the time – *Esquire* magazine, 1935

Don't use up your creative energy in managing your time. The secret of very focused people is that they don't waste their will-power and energy choosing whether and when to work on their projects. Instead they set up structures and habits that become automatic and save their energy for creating. The key to success is not stronger willpower or using more energy to avoid the distracting stuff, but to remove the distractions and formularise good habits – so that you actually have to think *less*.

Jerry Seinfeld's productivity secret

Blogger and software developer Brad Isaac once ran into Jerry Seinfeld on the stand-up comedy circuit and he took the chance to ask him for his success tips. Brad reports in a blog post on Lifehacker.com what Seinfeld told him:

He said the way to be a better comic was to create better jokes and the way to create better jokes was to write every day. But his advice was better than that. He had a gem of a leverage technique he used on himself and you can use it to motivate yourself—even when you don't feel like it.

> *He revealed a unique calendar system he uses to pressure himself to write. Here's how it works.*
>
> *He told me to get a big wall calendar that has a whole year on one page and hang it on a prominent wall. The next step was to get a big red magic marker.*
>
> *He said for each day that I do my task of writing, I get to put a big red X over that day. 'After a few days you'll have a chain. Just keep at it and the chain will grow longer every day. You'll like seeing that chain, especially when you get a few weeks under your belt. Your only job next is to not break the chain.'*
>
> *'Don't break the chain,' he said again for emphasis.*

Workerbot thoughts to challenge

'Microblocking is pointless; I'll never write a whole book/start a real business in 20 minutes a day.' The fact is you can make real projects happen in 20 minutes a day and many people have done so – from writing books to learning new skills to launching an online business. Of course the more time you can dedicate the faster you'll make progress, but 20 minutes should always be your fallback position. On busy days and at times you lack motivation, if you keep your promise to do your 20-minute microblock without fail, you will be amazed by what you achieve. Award-winning novelist and blogger Cory Doctorow wrote in a *Locus* magazine essay titled 'Writing in the Age of Distraction':

> When I'm working on a story or novel, I set a modest daily goal—usually a page or two—and then I meet it every day, doing nothing else while I'm working on it. It's not plausible or desirable to try to get the world to go away for hours at a time, but it's entirely possible to make it all shut up for 20 minutes. Writing a page every day

gets me more than a novel per year—do the math—and there's always 20 minutes to be found in a day, no matter what else is going on.

'**I'm tired and I'm not in the mood.**' This is often fear, procrastination or perfectionism in disguise. Think how many times you have felt like this and then went on to Facebook or YouTube for 20 minutes or more, clicking enticing links and watching videos. Wasting time online is not actually very relaxing for your brain and body, so you might as well do something useful and then relax properly. Remember also that motivation often comes after you start something, not before. So start anyway.

As American basketball player Julius Erving put it, 'Being a professional is doing the things you love to do even on the days you don't feel like doing them.'

You've probably had that deflating experience of putting something important to you on your 'To Do' list and then seeing weeks go by without doing anything on it at all. Once you start microblocking you need never have that feeling again because you'll always be making progress.

Your Instant Business

'Soon is not as good as now.'
—Seth Godin

You can now set yourself up to promote something to the whole world in just an hour or so – whether it's your skills, writing, ideas, products, events or art. That's because there is a huge range of online tools available to help you start your business faster than you ever imagined possible. And many of them are very affordable or even free. It's like a giant toybox just waiting for you to dive in!

No website yet? No traffic? No problem!

If you don't yet have a website – or you have one but its total weekly visitors would all fit in a London cab – it's easy to see this as a roadblock to getting started. But today we're going to sidestep that entire issue by looking at how you can start playing out your project without needing your own site with lots of traffic. (Later, when you're further into your project and have a clearer picture of what it's about, we'll look at the quickest way to create your own site.)

Imagine having a huge audience ready and eager to buy exactly what you can offer. Sound good? Well that's what is available for you right now. Here's the trick: go where your buyers are. Instead of marketing yourself on your own site that attracts nothing but tumbleweeds, promote yourself on a third-party marketplace which people are visiting every minute of every day searching for what you're providing.

Go *where your buyers are*

There are marketplace and community sites for every possible kind of product, service or experience you can offer. So if your idea revolves around using a skill you've developed or marketing a product or art form you have available already, here are some ways to get started.

There is more information on several of these in the Idea Cheatsheets on screwworkbreakfree.com.

Selling your skills as a freelancer

If your business idea revolves around skills you already have from your previous career (or that you've been developing on the side) you can promote them on a freelance marketplace today. Sites like Freelancer.com, PeoplePerHour.com and elance.com make an ideal showcase for any skills you have in design, photography, translation, web development, social media, marketing and business support. You can post a profile and then search for projects needing help and submit proposals. Freelancer.com has 16 million users who have posted a total of 8 million projects so far, so there's no shortage of work, but you'll need to show that you have something of real value to bring to a project to win it.

For a more playful take on selling services check out fiverr. com. People registered on the site will record a movie-trailer-style voiceover, draw a cartoon, design a logo, transcribe an interview or sing a personalised ring tone for $5 and up. As the bargain basement of freelance marketplaces, Fiverr can be a fun place to experiment with charging for something you've only previously done as a hobby. It's also a good way to practise your skills on projects where the stakes are not too high.

If you want to sell your services to other businesses (for example, as a consultant or trainer) and you don't have a website yet, just create a profile on LinkedIn so that you can give its address to people interested in your work. You can also invite others into your network, write blog posts within the site to share your expertise and join groups to communicate with others in your field.

Running events

If your idea is for a live event, meetup.com is designed exclusively for that very task and has 25 million users across 180 countries. That means there could be up to a million people searching meetup.com for events on any one day. The site is ideal for launching a free or low-cost event for the general public and can even take ticket payments for you. There is enormous value in running an event that places a whole group of your target market in the same room with you, even if the event itself makes little money. You can build a community and get to know their concerns and desires, you'll be seen as a leader in your field and you'll have opportunity to promote your work.

If you want to start really low key – for example, just to get some people together who might be interested in getting involved with your project – just post an event on Facebook and invite all your contacts to RSVP.

Selling arts, crafts and physical products

If you have handmade or vintage arts or crafts you can set up a store front on Etsy.com, which handles an estimated $2 billion in total annual transactions. Or, even easier, just try selling your first items on eBay. What's great about eBay of course is that you can see how much people are willing to pay for your product in an auction. That's a great way to test pricing. You can also search the site for completed auctions to see what similar products finally sold for.

Alternatively, it's possible for you now to get a product manufactured in China (using a supplier listed on alibaba.com, the portal to Chinese manufacturing companies) and sell it on Amazon or other online marketplace. You can even have your products shipped directly from China to Amazon's facility and then delivered to buyers using the Fulfilled By Amazon service. There is more information on this in the Idea Cheatsheets.

At the opposite end of the scale, you can have a lot of fun creating T-shirts, mugs, magnets and cards with just a few clicks by uploading your design to a site like CafePress or Zazzle. Visitors can buy your product off the site and it is then printed and shipped to them.

Books

If you want to sell your book, Amazon is without doubt the number one place to make it available, whether that's a digital version on Kindle or a printed version delivered by Amazon direct to your reader. Search 'Kindle direct publishing' to get started.

What if you don't have anything to sell?

It's equally likely of course that at this stage you are still developing something and not yet ready to sell it. That's OK. You might not be able to create instant income but there might be a way to provide instant value – something interesting or useful to others. This after all is the bedrock of a good business.

Here are a few examples:

Go help someone. Start with someone you know who you think you can help. Call them up and ask them if you can use your skills to help them in some way. Be honest that you're just starting out but that you are keen to help them. You may be able to use the skills from your career history in a new field. For example if you're a natural with numbers and have worked in finance you might find yourself drawn to helping small businesses or individuals. Try it out with someone.

You can also help people online. If you have expertise in a topic you can answer questions on the excellent Q&A site, Quora. com or look out for forums, online groups and Twitter discussions where people are asking for help.

Curate the latest news in your chosen area and share it on Twitter, Facebook, LinkedIn, a blog or elsewhere (see Day 8).

Connect people, online or in person. Connecting a community with a shared interest is a very valuable thing to do in itself. This can be as simple as setting up a Facebook or LinkedIn group and inviting people to join. You can then post the most interesting articles you're reading every day in this field and encourage conversation.

Or you could go one further and get people together in a room for a free event. For example, you could run a monthly meet-up for a particular niche. This can very naturally lead on to a paid membership programme, a money-making conference event or other opportunities.

If your project is to write a non-fiction book but you're only just starting out, you might be better off blogging out your book idea by idea. This allows you to engage readers along the way and you can still compile it into a book with additional content later. (See the Idea Cheatsheets for more on this.)

If you're a geek into open-source software, what can you contribute to and improve? Can you make a project of your own available as open source or contribute to someone else's? If you're a beginner, you can just help track down bugs and possibly fix them, document code or translate something to another language. Familiarise yourself with GitHub, the number one open-source repository.

If you're an artist, open up your artistic process and share it with others. Share your work in progress, post your images to Instagram, pick a theme, play it out and engage people.

The expert interview hack

If you can get hold of someone who is revered in the field you're entering and interview them in print or as an audio/video recording and place it on a blog, podcast or YouTube channel, you've created something very valuable to others even though you may be a complete beginner.

A series of interviews is even more valuable. If you can find a really clear aim, theme or niche to your interview subjects, that can make your series all the more attractive for the right audience. For instance, a dozen up and coming architects under 40, 10 published cookbook authors or 20 people who treated their own arthritis by natural means.

You might be surprised by how many people would be willing to take part for free. If someone has just published a book, for instance, they will be keen to get as wide an audience as possible.

What's even more powerful is if the interview subject shares your interview with their followers – who are likely to be many times more than yours!

If your interview subject is very busy, an in-person interview is less likely. However, a video Skype call that you record might be possible. Audio is even easier. And if nothing else, offer to email three–five questions that they can type answers to and send back. Make it as easy for them as possible to take part.

All these examples represent an underlying guiding principle for life and work that is as simple as it is effective. In fact Scott Adams, creator of one of the world's most successful cartoon strips, *Dilbert*, sums it up in two words that make a pretty good moral code for the whole of your life:

Be useful.

There really isn't any excuse for thrashing around in your head not doing anything simply because you think you don't have a good enough idea yet. Get into action, be useful to others and something will emerge.

Take this approach and, while you might not be making money, you're out there in the world, giving value, connecting people, making contacts, helping others. And that's a great way to start getting known, test and build your skills and learn on the job. It's also far more powerful to make your entry into a field by *giving* rather than trying to get.

And, once you've found a way to be valuable, making money is never far away.

Today's task

- Do another 20-minute microblock on your project. Can you do something today that is useful or interesting to others, even if it's just in 20 minutes?

Your Global HQ

'One day offices will be a thing of the past.'
—Sir Richard Branson, founder of Virgin Group

Today let's take a little time to create the environment for running your project – this 30-day project that we're hoping will turn into something great, an income stream or even a lucrative business.

Every business needs a headquarters, so today you're going to create your own Global HQ. These days, a Global HQ can just be the kitchen table, a spare room or wherever you lay your laptop. If you want to, you can create a business you can run from a laptop anywhere in the world (as I have done).

Your Global HQ can just be the kitchen table or wherever you lay your laptop

---

Whatever space you have available right now, it pays dividends to set up your environment in a way that facilitates your inspiration, creativity and focus. But beware that this doesn't become a distraction from doing your actual project. Do your microblock for today first and then have some fun with the following.

If you have a spare desk or spare room or just one half of the kitchen table, spend some time today tidying it up and getting

97

it ready to use. Clear away any clutter – the more you can minimise distractions the better. I've seen some players even put up a 'Global HQ' sign on the door of their spare room!

If your Global HQ boils down to your laptop computer, make sure it's tuned up. Add any software, updates or upgrades you've been meaning to get. Clear the desktop of all the clutter and start a new folder for your project.

Make sure that you have all the tools you need, whether it's a good Internet connection, paints and brushes or a good-quality microphone for recording yourself. If there is anything you definitely need that you know is missing from your play kit, go place an order. Avoid the temptation, however, to splash a lot of money on equipment unnecessarily. Smart entrepreneurs can show how every expenditure for their business brings a return.

Want some inspiration? If you have a favourite quote or a photo, put it on the wall or on the wallpaper on your computer or phone. Who is your hero or inspiration for this project? If your hero is Richard Branson, Facebook COO Sheryl Sandberg, Peace One Day founder Jeremy Gilley or bestselling author Liz Gilbert, find a picture of them or their venture and stick it on your wall.

If you don't have a suitable space at home or if you know there'll be too many distractions, then make sure you find alternative inspiring places to play with your project. Which environments work for you? What helps you to focus? Is it the silence of a library or the buzz of a coffee shop?

I wrote the bulk of this book in cafés around the world including in London, Tuscany and Sydney and sitting on the beach in Bali and the Philippines. My favourite working environment is a combination of good coffee, a busy setting and my favourite electronic music played on quality headphones. If you like working to music, create a playlist to help you focus. (You can listen to my favourite energising tracks in my playlist on www.screwworkbreakfree.com.)

One important tool I recommend getting hold of today is a dedicated notebook for your Play Project – this is your Playbook. Keep it with you and use it to capture all your ideas and to play out your projects as they unfold. When you begin to take your own inspiration and creativity seriously, you engage a subtle but powerful process; you'll begin to find that solutions to problems appear at the most unexpected times, ideas for new products pop up and killer titles appear for products, blog posts and books. Record them all as they occur and you'll find that blog posts, presentations and marketing copy seem to start writing themselves. And when you treat every idea as worth capturing, this encourages your subconscious to come up with even more ideas.

The one best habit of great performers

Daniel Coyle, *The New York Times* bestselling author of *The Talent Code*, has spent a lot of time researching great innovators, artists and entrepreneurs from Leonardo da Vinci to Richard Branson to discover how they achieved their works of genius and as he explains on his blog:

Most of us instinctively look for Big Clues. Are they tightly disciplined, or do they work only when the spirit moves them? Are they from happy families, or tragic ones? Are they hermits or do they fly around in a social whirlwind?

And it usually turns out (surprise!) there's really not much of a pattern. Some top performers are super-disciplined, some famously not. Some are from happy families; some sad; some are hermits, some social. Judging by this, it would seem that top performers are pretty much like the rest of us (except, you know, better).

However, there's one small clue; one tiny, almost unnotice-able habit a striking number of top performers share.

> *They keep a pocket notebook.*
>
> *I'm not talking about a journal or a diary filled with reflections or dreams – this is a messy, working notebook that is with them all the time, like an appendage. (In da Vinci's case, the attachment was literal – he tied it to his belt.)*

So while you're setting up your environment and tools make sure you also get yourself a Playbook. Use something dedicated to the task; don't mix it with your shopping lists and other more mundane notes. You might like to buy something special to use, something beautiful that will inspire your creativity. But don't wait to find that elusive perfect Playbook – start today with whatever you have to hand. You can always transfer your notes later. If you prefer digital tools take a look at apps like Evernote, which can hold and organise all the ideas and notes you could ever come up with and keep them synchronised across all your devices.

Today's tasks

- Do today's microblock first and tick it off.
- Spend at least a few minutes on your Global HQ.
- Put your ticksheet from Day 2 on the wall if you haven't already done so.
- If you're working on a laptop, try some different places to work from, such as cafés, galleries or shared workspaces.
- Get yourself a Playbook, whether physical or digital.
- If you like, share a photo of your new Global HQ or your Playbook with everyone on Twitter or Instagram using the hashtag #screwworkbreakfree.

Player pointers

Got an idea for a new project? Create a bucket. As soon as I have an idea for a project, a book, a chapter or just a blog post, the first thing I do is start a 'bucket' – somewhere to throw all my ideas into as they come to me. For something small like a blog post the bucket could simply be a page in your Playbook. For a bigger project like a new product line, it could be a new Word document, Apple Notes page or Evernote entry. Then, whenever another thought comes to you, chuck it into this 'bucket'. Just make sure you capture it in one place. Later you can start to assemble your rough notes into the blog post or an outline of the new product – and you'll often find the job is half done already. For example, I wrote 20,000 words for this book in Apple Notes on my iPhone while walking around London, Tuscany and Sydney.

Don't believe the ridiculous myth that 'If it's important you'll remember it'. Why use something as precious as your brain to do something a piece of paper can do better? Keep your mind clear to think. Note down every idea as they occur. Don't let anything escape.

Workerbot thoughts to challenge

'I shouldn't write anything down unless I'm going to act on it.' Just because you take an idea seriously enough to write down doesn't mean you necessarily have to do it; that's why I call it a *Playbook*. It's somewhere you can play with ideas, play out your projects and experiment with new possibilities. Use the best of what you capture and leave the rest.

The Power of Playing in Public

'The secret: Do good work and share it with people.'
—Austin Kleon, artist and writer

Our workerbot training encourages us to only show the polished and perfected final results of a project. Today we are going to turn that idea on its head.

Dare to share your project as it unfolds and something important happens. You shift from an internal process of ruminating on ideas to an external one of realising ideas. Start to make a habit of sharing what you have to give. You may not yet think you have much to give the world, but trust me; if you follow the process in this book, you will surprise yourself with what you can create and the impact it can have on others.

The key to success is simple but not necessarily easy: it's to create and deliver value. Or to put it in everyday language, do good stuff and get it out there. This requires two separate acts of bravery: first, to engage in the creative process until you produce something valuable to others (you've already made a start on this simply by microblocking daily) and, secondly, to dare to share it.

Money comes from the second part. You don't get paid for being creative – you get paid for delivering what you create to others, for providing value. You can practise a song for hours but you don't get paid until you perform it or release it. You can develop your skills forever but you don't get paid till you use them to help someone. You might be the best writer in the world but you won't get paid till you finish your book and put it on sale. Until you've shared something, you're not done. The creative act is incomplete without an audience.

If you want to get paid to do something you love, it's going to take a while and there will be times when you lose your faith and wonder if you can ever make it. But I promise you this: if you keep creating and delivering stuff that other people value again and again, project after project, then financial return is *inevitable.*

If you keep doing stuff that people value again and again, then financial return is inevitable

---

Play in public

Matt Mullenweg, creator of WordPress, the system that powers 60 million websites, writes on his blog:

> You can never fully anticipate how an audience is going to react to something you've created until it's out there. That means every moment you're working on something without it being in the public it's actually dying, deprived of the oxygen of the real world.

Sharing the end results of your project is essential, but it is even more powerful to open up your process and share as you go along. Play in public! Write blog posts around your book topic and post them as soon as they're finished. Record a song or mix every week and post it to soundcloud.com. Place scenes from your low-budget thriller on YouTube and see how they go down.

Upload the best photos from every shoot to Instagram, Flickr or Facebook. Explore the focus of your interior-design business by collating examples of great design on Pinterest or Instagram. Offer your service early on and get feedback from your clients.

You'll see which blog topics get people commenting, which tweets get retweeted, which posts get shared and 'Liked' and which parts of your service or product people appreciate most – and it may not be ones you expect! This is all extremely valuable feedback. I chose some of the quotes in this book because when I tweeted them or shared them on Facebook they got a huge number of retweets and 'Likes', sometimes quite unexpectedly.

People will spot good things you weren't even aware of. They'll contribute new ideas, recognise themes and might even offer to collaborate or help share the word. Nothing can prepare you for the kind of lucky connections and opportunities that crop up when you play in public. This is where the magic happens.

Sharing valuable things throughout your project is the best form of marketing you can do – and ideal if you feel queasy about being salesy. Instead of saying, 'I'm brilliant, buy my stuff', you *demonstrate* how brilliant you are by sharing good stuff. This has the added benefit of engaging the power of reciprocity – the natural instinct built into us all that wants to return a favour.

As you do this, provide a way for people to follow you – your Twitter ID, LinkedIn profile, Facebook page or, possibly most powerful of all, subscription to your email list. Then you'll be building an audience as you go along – an audience who are very likely to be interested when you finally have something for sale.

If you make a regular habit of getting stuff out into the world – whether it's blog posts, events, performances, artworks or client projects – you'll get to a point where people start looking forward to your next output. They might even start chasing you for it, 'I didn't see your newsletter today; is something wrong?', 'Hurry up and write the next blog post!', 'When is your next event? Book me in now!' And once that happens, everything changes because it's no longer just you who gives a damn whether you finish or not. Some of your followers might become contributors or even collaborators. Or they could become raving fans and paying customers when you have something to sell.

Betty Herbert is the ultimate example of playing in public, with a subject that is normally very private:

How Betty Herbert played out The 52 Seductions in public and won a book deal

Like many couples, after ten years of marriage Betty Herbert and her husband had found that the passion had gone out of their sex life.

Unlike most couples she decided to take some drastic action to improve the situation: a year-long challenge to revive their love life and blog about it! She explained the story to me:

I got up in the morning with the idea fully formed and decided to write the blog: I would commit to spending the next year with me and Herbert taking it in turns each week to seduce each other in new and exciting ways.

I knew the title as well – The 52 Seductions. I started writing straight away and actually, although I edit a lot, the first blog post is more or less verbatim the first chapter of the book. I achieved a lot just in the first 30 days.

I hadn't even mentioned this to Herbert. I had written the first three blog posts before I got the guts to tell him! He was fine about it because I had been careful to be anonymous.

Betty later made the decision, after much consideration, to reveal that her real name is actually Katherine May.

I had already written a couple of novels under my real name but this time I wasn't even thinking about a book. I was glad to just be blogging, on a project I could really enjoy writing.

I also realised that if I blogged it other people would be watching so we can't just give up, they'd hold us accountable!

Although at times it was difficult managing relationships with readers who are cheering you on about having sex, even giving you ideas, I was spot on about the instinct that blogging it would help me to stick with it. No way would I have stuck with it if I hadn't have had all those people rooting for us and even telling us it had inspired them to rekindle their own sex lives.

Betty also tweeted about her blog and connected with other writers and social commentators on Twitter.

Twitter has been hugely important. You have to do the writing but Twitter is how people find you. It's how friends share information with each other. Things took off for me when some bigger figures on Twitter started to recommend me – that was very exciting.

Within a couple of months of starting the blog and engaging in conversations on Twitter, I was being chased by agents and to buy the TV rights just from the blog posts.

My strongest bit of advice to other writers is to blog to show your writing and your fantastic ideas, differentiate yourself from the crowd, give them your best work. No one's going to steal it. It's a massive myth that your stuff is going to get nicked if you put your best stuff out there. Actually it's the best way I know of avoiding the slush pile.

Betty's book *The 52 Seductions* received rave reviews and has now been translated into nine languages. Check it out on Amazon and follow Betty on Twitter at @52Betty. At the time of writing Betty is on another challenge – to walk the entire 630 miles of England's South West Coast Path before she turns 40 in 2017.

You might not be ready to be quite as public as Betty was, but here are some pointers to dip your toe in the water:

- If you're worried about being open, share somewhere like Facebook at first where only friends will see it. YouTube is famous for attracting some rather unhelpful comments so if you're particularly sensitive to feedback you can disable comments at first.
- If you don't want to post publicly yet, do at least share with a buddy or your most supportive friends.

If you're a perfectionist, you might be tempted to cook up your project in secret and go for a big reveal at the end. This is usually a bad idea. It makes for a much more solitary experience, it's easier to lose motivation and you miss out on all the connections, happy coincidences and audience building that happen when you play in public.

The courage to be seen

'Courage starts with showing up and letting ourselves be seen.'
—Brené Brown, University of Houston
research professor, author and speaker

Daring to share something of yourself – even if it's to just one person – can make us feel exposed. Even starting a Play Project can make us feel vulnerable because it means daring to admit that you care about something – whether it's your writing, your comedy or your business idea – enough to take action on it. But it gets easier. The more you risk being vulnerable, the more you realise you're OK, whatever anyone says. And most of what we fear might happen never does anyway.

When I took a stand-up comedy class and performed a few gigs, the first thing friends would say when I told them what I was doing was, 'But what about the hecklers?' In reality I wasn't heckled once and yet it was everyone's first concern. How many times do we stop ourselves doing something because we imagine the worst possible response?

The real reason people don't achieve the success they want in life is actually not laziness or lack of time. It's not even the fear of failure. It's the unwillingness to be vulnerable – to show up, put ourselves out there, let ourselves be seen and not be able to control what happens.

If you can learn to accept this feeling of vulnerability (and cope with the discomfort when things don't go quite right), you'll be developing your very own superpower and unimagined successes become possible. That's what the most successful people in the world make a habit of doing.

This isn't about being super-confident or being able to weather any amount of criticism, it's simply about practising putting yourself out there. The criticism you imagine is probably never going to happen and you can start with the smallest of steps, then grow your confidence over time.

The following line from social scientist and author Nicholas Lore's book *The Pathfinder* has been my guide for the last few years and it has served me well. Why not make it yours, too?

'If you are willing to experience fear, disappointment and embarrassment, you become an almost unstoppable force of nature.'

Today's tasks

- What can you share *right now*? Find ways to share what you're creating as you create it. Tweet about the things you're finding out; see how people react and which tweets they find most interesting. Write your book one blog post at a time. Share your best photos on Instagram or Facebook as you go along. Create a first version of your talk or workshop and try it out with a forgiving audience. If you want to run a restaurant, set up a taster session for friends.

How widely can you share? Even showing one person is a good start if you haven't done that before. Choose somebody who you think will be encouraging. Explain that it's a Play Project – you're not making any great claims for genius abilities or a killer business idea.

Player pointers

Share with the right intention. Often people new to playing in public will share things in order to 'get feedback'. What's really going on here is our workerbot conditioning to look to others for whether we are good enough. Sure, feedback can be useful further down the line (when asked of the right people) but when you're taking your very first steps, you don't need feedback, you need encouragement. Your early work – performing, making, coding, speaking – is about finding out what the experience is like for you and seeing what you can create. Don't mix that up with evaluating your talent. The chances are that you won't be great right at the beginning, but you can get there if you keep going. And for that you need encouragement. There's time later to ask for suggestions for improvement.

Show your face. Include a photograph and your name on your website or blog – it promotes trust. If revealing your identity could get you into trouble with your employer, use just your first name or perhaps a pen name. It's good to have an identity even when you can't use your real name.

How much is too much? Although relatively few people will see your early shares, realise that whatever you share could be read one day by anybody and everybody, so act accordingly. For instance, don't say something online about a person that you wouldn't want them to ever find out.

Workerbot thoughts to challenge

'What if someone steals my idea?' An idea in itself is not that valuable. It's how you execute it that matters. While someone could theoretically copy your idea, they can't copy all the thoughts in your head about how it should work and all your strengths you will put into making it happen. Besides, no one with any level of success is going to be interested in copying your idea until you've already made a lot of money out of it.

The exception to this is a domain name or title that you think has real value. If you have a fantastic idea for a domain, invest the $10 to buy it before you tell anyone. And if your book title is a stroke of brilliance, it's OK to share what the book is about but don't share the title until you are close to publication and have bought the domain name.

I've noticed over the years that the people who refuse to tell me anything about their idea (or ask me to sign a non-disclosure agreement before saying a word) rarely end up achieving anything.

The Play Cycle

'Accept that everything is a draft.'
—'The Cult of Done Manifesto' by Bre Pettis and Kio Stark

You've started your project but in all probability you're still not that sure whether it's the right one, whether it will work and make money or whether you're even going to enjoy it in the long run. That's OK. Uncertainty is a normal part of the process. But that doesn't mean you should charge on right to the end without any clue whether it's going to work.

When you understand what I call the Play Cycle, you'll be able to check your progress every step of the way and correct your course so that you don't waste time heading in the wrong direction.

The Play Cycle is how children naturally behave and learn, it's how people find their grand purpose in life and, contrary to the standard view, it's also how modern businesses are built. Once you understand it, you'll know that you no longer need to bite your project off in one chunk, you don't need a complete plan to make your whole project happen and you don't even need to be sure what you want to do. The Play Cycle allows you to launch a project straight away and fix things on the fly. It's ready, fire, aim.

The Play Cycle allows you to launch a project straight away and fix things on the fly

The Play Cycle is a simple three-step cycle: ACT, REFLECT, ADAPT and then repeat. Keep cycling round these three steps until your project is where you want it to be. In the startup world this is called *iteration* and is a fundamental part of twenty-first-century business strategy.

The Play Cycle may look simple but don't underestimate its power. This iterative process is at the heart of the scientific method that has given us our modern understanding of the world, it's how all medical innovations are created and it's similar to how all life on earth evolved.

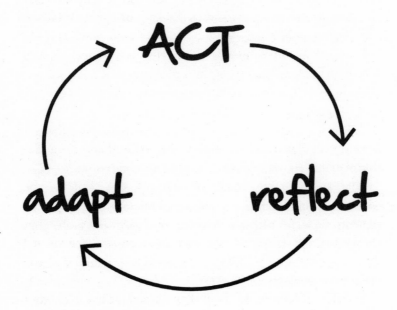

The Play Cycle

Here's how to use the Play Cycle to make your project a success:

Step 1: Act

Jump into action, create something and share it. You've already begun this process simply by microblocking every day. The key is to cut the crap and focus on the very heart of your project. Write a white paper that lays out your new process for managing projects. Make a video that illustrates the problem you want to address. Write an essay or blog post that captures the idea for your non-fiction book. Finish it and get it out there, because it's in action that the connection and learning happen.

MISTAKES TO AVOID

- Sitting around thinking rather than taking action. This is usually driven by workerbot thinking or a fear of failure. No matter how long you think and research, you'll never be able to guarantee everything is going to go smoothly. You have to be willing to play it out.

Step 2: Reflect

After you take action (and even while you're doing it), notice what happens – both the internal and external feedback.

Internal feedback is about how it felt. Which parts did you enjoy? Which parts didn't you enjoy? Is this an approach that suits you or is there a more in-flow way for you to work? Are you doing the work you were drawn to do or have you strayed off course into what you think you 'should' be doing? Are you saying what you wanted to say?

External feedback is about how others reacted to your project so far. Which bits did they value and which bits didn't they? Which of the ten posts on your blog got the biggest reactions and most comments? What gets misunderstood? What gets retweeted? Which product sells the quickest and easiest? Which song did your audience hum as they left the gig? Prepare to be surprised! I've written things I thought were profound and life changing which garnered nothing more than a collective 'meh', and I've put things out which I thought were nothing special and seen them go viral.

MISTAKES TO AVOID

- Ignoring the fact it's not working through fear or arrogance (same thing) and keep charging on regardless.
- Ignoring the fact that it really *is* working and drop the project out of apathy or fear. I've seen creative people hit on a winning idea that people are responding really warmly to – they have a potential smash hit on their hands – but they just ignore it and move on to something completely different.
- Realising it's not working and panicking, thinking this proves that your idea is a bad one and you should abandon it. Instead, move on to the next step of the Play Cycle – Adapt.

Step 3: Adapt

'Men occasionally stumble over the truth, but most of them pick themselves up and hurry off as if nothing ever happened.'
—Sir Winston Churchill, British Prime Minister
1940–45 and 1951–55

Taking into account all the feedback you received, adapt your project to make it even better. If everyone loves your novel's lead character but got confused by the plot, change it. If you launch your business and find everyone's most interested in something you thought of as a sideline, consider making it a central part. If the part you loved most about your blog was designing it or using your own photos in it or doing the techie stuff for it, consider whether this should be the focus of your next Play Project.

MISTAKES TO AVOID

- Giving up as soon as you hit a setback or negative response – obstacles are part of the game. If there were no obstacles, someone would have done it already. So adapt and keep playing.
- Taking others' feedback literally and do exactly what they ask for. Instead, take their feedback on board while staying

true to your personal vision. As Ford Motor Company founder Henry Ford reportedly said, 'If I had asked people what they wanted, they would have said faster horses.'

• Ignoring all feedback and hoping if you keep going in exactly the same way, something will magically change.

Rinse and repeat

Once you've completed Step 3 and adapted what you're doing, then it's time to iterate – to go round once again but with an improved version. Put your adapted approach into action, then reflect on what happens and adapt once more. Continue going through the cycle: ACT, REFLECT, ADAPT ... ACT, REFLECT, ADAPT ... until you've achieved success.

If you're willing to take action, try to create something useful or interesting to people, even if you're not sure it will work, and then adapt what you're doing according to feedback, your success really is guaranteed.

How following the Play Cycle turned a hobby into one of the most famous websites in the world

In 1995, 43-year-old Craig Newmark was working in IT at American brokerage firm Charles Schwab. In his spare time he started an email listing that he sent out to friends and their friends of arts and tech events going on in the San Francisco Bay Area.

It was a hobby; no grand plans, not even a website initially, just CCing the people who had expressed an interest on regular emails with a list of interesting events. The email list grew and then turned into a listings website. Craig's only aim was to be helpful, to be of value to people. He kept listening to what

---

people were saying, reflecting on it, adapting his approach accordingly and acting again.

The result of following the Play Cycle in this way was Craigslist, one of the most visited websites in the world. Here's Craig's own simple description of how he got there, as written on Quora.com:

– from beginning, did something simple and useful
– from beginning, began cycle:
  – asked for community feedback
  – did something about it
  – repeat, forever
– got lucky with simple site design, realizing I have no design skills (didn't waste time doing fancy stuff no one wanted)

By the end of 1997 craigslist.com was getting a million page views per month. It was no longer a hobby as Craig explains in another post on Quora:

in 1999, made craigslist into a real company for it to survive effectively. decided I didn't personally need to make lots of money. NOT altruistic, just knowing when enough is enough.
   updated software in latish 1999, ceased coding, committed to customer service work, but only as long as I live.
   made Jim Buckmaster CEO in 2000, since as a manager, I suck.
   Now doing customer service work, but personal major focus on public service and philanthropy at craigconnects.org

Despite Craig's humility, the remarkable global value he created with Craigslist resulted in a personal fortune estimated by *Forbes* in 2010 to be $400 million. Craig's formula is one we can all emulate: do something simple and useful, then keep increasing the value to people again and again by moving round the Play Cycle, acting, reflecting and adapting.

The Play Cycle is about experiential learning. This was your natural way of approaching everything before you got into school. When you were a baby and the urge took hold of you to stand up on your own legs and try to walk you didn't ruminate on it much. You didn't think, 'Will I be able to do this? What evidence do I have on my CV that I could be a walker? I've only ever been a crawler ... I'd better go and read up on walking before I start ... But there's really no point even learning because someone else will always be better at walking than me anyway.' Nope. You just stood up on your wobbly little legs, tried to take a step and then fell over. And what did you do next? You iterated. In fact, a baby typically takes a thousand hours of practice to learn to walk. That's the persistence you were born with and that you can draw on now.

Today's tasks

- Do today's microblock but notice the internal feedback you're getting as you do it. Is this enjoyable? Does it feel in flow? Just notice at this point; no need to make any big changes as it is still early days. Tomorrow we'll do a check-in process and see if you need to adapt what you're doing or how you're doing it.

Player pointers

The Play Cycle works at every level. At the end of your project you'll reflect on how it went and then adapt what you're doing before starting another project. Day by day, you can check how people are responding to what you're doing – what's valuable to them and what isn't – and continually adapt to make something they'll love even more. And moment by moment you can tune in to how you are feeling about what you're doing and adapt to have a better experience. If you notice yourself getting distracted working at home, you could go out to a café to work instead. If you notice that you particularly enjoy working with one kind of client, adapt your focus to find more of that kind.

The faster you move through the Play Cycle the faster you progress. Anything that shortens the cycle from taking action to getting feedback and adapting will make your journey faster. Famous architects are usually over 60 years old because it takes years to go through the cycle of getting commissioned, designing a building, having it constructed and then seeing how people respond before you can learn from it and design a better building next time. Contrast that to stand-up comics who find out how successful a new joke is within seconds. For that reason it's not unusual for the best stand-ups to become worldwide sensations in their 30s or even their 20s.

Remember this is just version 1.0. Get the first version done of your idea, website, book or whatever it might be and know that you can make it better and add more to it in the next cycle. In book writing, you might not even show anyone your first draft but you need to get the whole thing done before you can go back and start improving it. This is why some authors advocate 'fast drafting' to get the first draft done as quickly as possible – sometimes in as little as 30 days – so that you have something to build on.

Think about how you can get a first version out there as soon as possible. Author John Purkiss had already had one bestseller with *Brand You*. His new book *Change From Within* though was on a very different topic: meditation and spirituality. To test out his approach in the book he printed a hundred copies of a 'beta release' of his book and gave them away. This allowed him to get feedback on the ideas in his book and see which parts needed adding to, removing from or improving. And he also gave a handful of live talks to see which exercises from the book worked best. John even tested the title of the book; he created a Facebook page called *Change From Within*, which received a few 'Likes'. He then posted the same material on a new page called *The Art of Letting Go*. This received almost twice as many 'Likes', so he renamed the book accordingly.

Hold your idea lightly. Accept that when you follow the Play Cycle your idea often takes on a life of its own: your documentary idea turns into a comedy as you try to make it. Your humour blog turns into a political campaign or a philosophical exploration. Your business morphs under your very eyes. This is normal. The business you start is rarely the business you end up succeeding with. As long as you're staying true to your values that's OK. Accept that, as author Steven Pressfield says, 'Your idea is smarter than you.'

Workerbot thoughts to challenge

'I don't want to do something that fails.' If you approach your project in the step-by-step way I am recommending, you can avoid any expensive failures. But that doesn't mean things will always turn out the way you expect or want them to. It's your willingness to go round the Play Cycle and learn from it that separates you from the millions of people who refuse to start until they have a guarantee of success.

Week 1 Check-in:
Are You Having Fun Yet?

'How often I found where I should be going only by setting out for somewhere else.'

—R. Buckminster Fuller, architect, inventor and innovative thinker

We're seven days into your project and it's time to check in on how it's going. This simple check-in process will keep your project on track – even when you're not sure where it is you're heading. It's based on the Play Cycle of ACT, REFLECT, ADAPT you learned yesterday.

ACT you've already done as you played out your project for at least 20 minutes a day over the last 6 days. Now it's time to REFLECT and, if necessary, ADAPT before choosing what to ACT on again for the next week.

We'll be doing this check-in at the end of each week for the remainder of the 30 days. If you're working with a buddy or a group to help you keep motivated and accountable, meet up with them and go through the questions together.

REFLECT: How did this week go?

Write the answers to the questions below in your Playbook.

- Did you do your microblocks for at least six days this week? If not, what happened? Did you forget to put them in your diary as real appointments? Did you tell yourself there was no point only doing 20 minutes?

- Have you filled in your ticksheet as you went along? If you took a rest day did you log it with an 'R'?
- What can you pat yourself on the back for this week? Progress can seem slow at the start so it's important to acknowledge everything that went well, no matter how small, in order to stay motivated. If you did every micro-block, that's a success. If you found yourself really in flow while doing a particular task, that's an important realisation.
- What part of your project have you enjoyed the most? Which part the least?
- How is your approach working for you? The length of micro-block, the timing, how you're working on your project?
- Have you noticed anything else interesting about your project or how you've been approaching it? Perhaps you work better with the TV on than in silence. Or you have all your best ideas while ironing. Even if it seems to make no sense at the moment, write these discoveries down. As Isaac Asimov once said, 'The most exciting phrase to hear in science, the one that heralds new discoveries, is not "Eureka!" but "That's funny … ".'
- Have you received any external feedback yet about your project? It's early days so it's quite possible that you haven't but if you've had a good response already to something you've done or shared, make a note of it. We'll be paying more attention to external feedback in later check-ins.

Things not going well?

If it seems like things aren't going well, that's OK. Remember that in the early days, you're likely to be off-course more than you're on-course. Try to be forgiving of yourself when you're reflecting on your progress. As long as you move on to the next step and adapt what you're doing, it will be OK in the end.

*Remember that in the early days,
you're likely to be off-course more
than you're on-course*

Surprised how well it's going?

Congratulations! Stick at it and do more of what's working.

ADAPT: How can you use what you discovered?

What can you do differently next week to get even better results? Perhaps you need to be more realistic about what you can get done in a week? Or you might need to take your appointments with yourself more seriously. If you have a project buddy, ask them to hold you accountable.

If you've noticed you get better ideas talking to someone else rather than sitting on your own, arrange to meet with someone next week to talk over your project. If you're finding your project a hard slog, what changes can you make to make it more enjoyable or exciting?

Get ready to ACT again

I want you to get clear about what you're really committing to do between now and seven days' time. Not what you *hope* you'll do if there's time, if you don't get interrupted, if the cat doesn't attack your laptop again ... what you *will* do, come rain or shine. This is like a hard contract. It is non-negotiable. Scary, huh? Well, not necessarily. You see, creative people are often not the most disciplined people in the world. We don't have a strong sense of timing, we're not natural project managers. In fact, if we were, we might not be creative in the same way. It's our ability to forget time, lose ourselves, get distracted, ignore boundaries and see bizarre connections that no one else sees that makes us the creative geniuses that we are.

But ... that means we need to learn how to put structures in place that hold our creativity and channel it out into the world ... So that we can express ourselves, make our mark, share something only we can share, make some piece of the world a little better and receive all the more in return. Today is when you commit to the actions you're going to take between now and Day 14. This technique is at the heart of the Play Process – it keeps your project moving forward even if you've let it slip in the past.

You're going to make a written commitment to yourself about what you're going to do, or not do, in the week ahead. You're already committed to achieving your Play Project. Now you need to get to know yourself as a person who does what they say they will do, someone who trusts themselves to make their ideas happen and their dreams come true. And when you start to do that ... well, it really does transform your world.

Your commitments this week

In your Playbook, use the following prompts to make a list of actions that you're committing to take during this coming week.

- *'By the next check-in on Day 14 I will ... '* List the things you are absolutely committing to do. You're not committing to an *outcome* (which may be out of your hands) but to *doing* something. It can be as simple as 'I will write one blog post'.

- If you find it difficult to stick to your own commitments, try rewarding yourself. Is there a treat you can give yourself if you keep your promise? If so, write down what you'll treat yourself to if you've taken action on your project: *'My reward for taking action at least 20 minutes a day for 6 days this week will be ... '*
- If you respond better to stick than carrot you could set up a penalty for yourself if you don't do what you promised. Noel Langley is a successful trumpet player who has performed on countless hit records by other people but was finding it difficult to make the time to work on his own album. Aside from being busy, Noel realised he was also procrastinating – creating his own music felt a lot more personal than playing on an album by Radiohead or Adele. Noel decided to join The Screw Work 30-day Challenge and used the principles you're learning in this book to finally get started on his own album. And to make sure he followed through to completion, he made the commitment to his friends that he would deliver his own album by October the same year or take the forfeit of having to walk naked through Trafalgar Square playing his trumpet! Driven by the desire to avoid his forfeit, Noel met his commitment and his album, *Edentide*, was released to critical acclaim in 2014 and hit the number one spot in the iTunes Jazz chart.
- *'I also want to ... '* List the things you'd like to do but can't absolutely guarantee you'll manage – I'm not holding you to these!

Open your diary and check you can really do what you've promised. If you know you may need to do something else on one day of the week, reduce your commitment. It is better to promise less and meet your promise than to promise more and be disappointed at the end of the week, which reinforces a sense of powerlessness over your life. Adopting this simple habit will transform your productivity and it's also great for your self-esteem.

Make a commitment to others – share it!

Commitments are far more powerful when you make them to others and not just to yourself. So if you're working with a buddy or group, tell them what you've committed to for the next seven days. Or share your commitments with your friends on Facebook.

Assuming it won't get you into trouble with your employer, why not also share it publicly with others following this book? Post your top commitments to Twitter or Instagram with the hashtag #screwworkbreakfree and see what others are committing to. You can read more about this on screwworkbreakfree.com.

Player pointers

Committing is not about making yourself feel bad. Far from it. In fact it's much better to promise to do one smaller thing that you know you will definitely do than to give yourself a big, long list of actions that sets you up for failure. If it looks like you've committed to do too much, move some of your tasks from the '*I will do* … ' category into '*I also want to* … '

If things haven't gone as well as you'd like this week, don't give yourself a hard time. This is probably a very unfamiliar process for you. Think of it like having the training wheels on. You might have set off with wildly unrealistic expectations. As long as you keep microblocking and keep doing the check-ins you *will* make real progress.

On the website

Go to screwworkbreakfree.com, where you can hear me interview Noel Langley about his creative process to record his first album.

Getting Deeper Into Your Project

Now you're up and running, this week will take you deeper into the entrepreneurial mindset and strategies that lead to success. And we look at how to focus your project to make it ten times faster to take off.

DAY 8

Curate, Copy and Steal

'I invented nothing new. I simply assembled the discoveries of other men behind whom were centuries of work.'

—Henry Ford, founder of the Ford Motor Company and pioneer of mass production

You might be worrying at this early stage of your project that it looks too similar to other people's work, but that's OK. When we're starting out with something new, we usually start by emulating the people who inspired us to get into the field. Stephen King started writing as a child by copying the comics he loved word for word – until one day his mother suggested he write his own story.

The path to true originality has humble beginnings. We are first a consumer, then curator, then copier and finally a creator. Here's how it might look for a musician: you start as a listener, consuming as much music as you can. Gradually you narrow your focus to one or more styles. You start to build a collection, create playlists and share these with other people who come to appreciate your role as a curator, introducing them to new artists and songs. Then you take up an instrument and learn how to play your favourite songs. Over time you start to write your own, copying the style of artists you love. Slowly, without planning it, your own style emerges: something different and uniquely you. You have become a creator.

The path to true originality has humble beginnings. We are first a consumer, then curator, then copier and finally a creator.

The same process occurs in all creative endeavours, including starting your business. You may start with something that is similar to others but, as you play it out, you will discover your own unique vision and spin on it. You might find you can provide a more beautiful product, a simpler app, truly caring customer service or you find your business fits a particular niche of people much better than the current leaders.

Become a curator

Your project doesn't need to create something completely new to be of value. The act of curation – of selecting others' content, arranging it and sharing it with others – is a creative and valuable act in itself. A DJ on a radio show selects and shares records according to the theme of the show. A TV channel curates programmes. Much of the value of a business conference is in curating the roster of speakers and the list of attendees to network with.

Curating is a great way to start out in a field. Choose a topic you are excited about and consume as much as possible of the best content, news and ideas. Then start compiling the stuff that is most interesting to you. Share what you find on a blog. Or follow the leaders in your field on Twitter and turn that into a Twitter list that others can follow too. You can then turn their tweets into a daily online newspaper for others to subscribe to, using paper. li. Or find your favourite interior-design images for the particular kind of design you love and compile them on Pinterest for others to follow. Create a channel on YouTube and compile your favourite videos in your topic, whether it's rising stars of stand-up comedy or the best videos on business innovation – and don't forget to encourage viewers to subscribe to your channel. The more clearly you can niche your focus, the easier it'll be for people to decide to follow you (more on that in Day 13).

Later you might start to include your reviews or comments on why you think a particular person or business is important to this field. Even better, you could start to interview some of the most interesting people in your field and share them on a blog, podcast or YouTube series. Then you're starting to create original content of your own. (Read the story of the very successful curator, Wolfgang Wild, on Day 10.)

Everything is a remix

There is nothing new under the sun (including that phrase which is taken from the Old Testament and is therefore over 2,000 years old). In the superb online documentary series *Everything Is A Remix*, New York filmmaker Kirby Ferguson makes the compelling argument that 'everything we make is a remix of existing creations, our lives and the lives of others'. He shows that the original *Star Wars* movies, for instance, borrow from *The Good, the Bad and the Ugly*, *The Dam Busters* and other war movies, films by Japanese director Akira Kurosawa and *Flash Gordon* serials from the 1930s.

Even Shakespeare is known to have borrowed from well-known historical and oral legends and, sometimes more directly, other writers' works. Can you guess which famous romantic play of his was inspired by a 1562 narrative poem called *The Tragical History of Romeus and Juliet*?

Cormac McCarthy, author of *The Road* and *No Country for Old Men*, was quoted in *The New York Times* in 1992 as saying, 'The ugly fact is books are made out of books ... The novel depends for its life on the novels that have been written.'

New scientific discoveries also depend on what has been discovered before. Isaac Newton said that 'we stand on the shoulders of giants' (which was actually an adaptation of something written by French philosopher, Bernard de Chartres).

Similarly, Henry Ford didn't invent mass production, the assembly line or the automobile, but he combined and developed all these elements to create the first mass-market car.

So it's time to end the myth that creativity is a magic act, pulling something out of nothing. There are no completely original ideas. The genius, if required at all, is in how to combine, translate or evolve what has gone before.

Keep learning, playing out your idea and curating interesting stuff, filtering it through your own experience. See what you can mix together and what you can add to it from your own life and you'll come up with something new.

Steal like an artist

Now you know that you are likely to start out emulating other people and businesses you respect, how do you avoid straight-up plagiarism?

Here are some guidelines. Steal patterns but not content; copy the *structure* of your favourite book but not the words. Steal the business model but not the brand. Copy the *feel* of your favourite café but not the design or the name.

Take from multiple sources, choosing only those that resonate with you. As the saying goes, 'To steal ideas from one person is plagiarism; to steal from many is research.' Combine them together according to your taste, and give it your own particular spin to produce something new.

If your project is to become a public speaker, author or artist, remember there is no brand-new message to give, but there is your unique way to give it. And as French writer André Gide said, 'Everything that needs to be said has already been said. But since no one was listening, everything must be said again.'

When you want to use a chunk of someone's work unaltered, quote them. When something is heavily influenced or inspired by someone else, credit them. These few paragraphs, for instance, are informed and influenced by Austin Kleon's excellent book *Steal Like An Artist*.

If you want to look like a true genius, lift the styles and ideas of a completely different field. Vidal Sassoon took much influence from modern European architecture in creating his legendary geometric haircuts of the 1960s, saying, 'For me the working of hair is architecture with a human element.' I can't imagine his greatest influence, Bauhaus architect Mies van der Rohe, had any complaints of plagiarism by Sassoon.

You can use the same principle to come up with innovative business ideas – translate someone else's successful business idea into a different field. Airbnb took the model of the hotel-booking site and applied it to the home rental market, adding ratings in the style of eBay and professional photography of the kind normally taken by estate agents. The result is a business now valued at over $25 billion.

Of course, if you deliberately steal someone's content or brand wholesale and without attribution, you will not only risk breaking copyright law but you'll also alienate the person you most respect. You'll often be better off approaching the person or business you revere and trying to partner with them instead. Offer to assist them, collaborate with them or promote their work on commission. You'll often make more money that way too.

Today's tasks

- Find and follow the best sources for your topic whether it's by email, Twitter, LinkedIn, YouTube or other channel.
- If you have already found some favourite posts on your topic, share them with others. Retweet the best links you find on Twitter or write a list of 'Ten people to follow in the world of [your topic]' and share it with others.

Workerbot thoughts to challenge

'**I'm scared I'm going to break copyright laws.**' It's common as a beginner to be overly cautious about borrowing from others, even to the point of not wanting to quote someone on your blog. In reality, it's absolutely fine to name someone else's work or link to it. And when quoting part of it, copyright law allows for 'fair use'. This is a vague term but many writers work on the basis that, if they quote up to 300 words and attribute it correctly, permission is not needed.

The True Foundation for Success: VALUE

'A business is simply an idea to make other people's lives better.'

—Sir Richard Branson

I f you want to create something massively successful you probably expect to put a lot of attention from the start on how it's going to make money. So you may be surprised to find that's not the focus of many of the world's most successful organisations.

Google, Facebook, Virgin and Apple have all publicly declared their focus on creating value rather than monetisation. The brilliant Sir Jony Ive, Chief Design Officer of Apple, explained it in the following way in 2012 at the British Embassy's Creative Summit:

> We are really pleased with our revenues but our goal isn't to make money. It sounds a little flippant, but it's the truth. Our goal and what makes us excited is to make great products. If we are successful people will like them and if we are operationally competent, we will make money.

Jony explained how, in the 90s, after Steve Jobs had been forced out, Apple was very close to bankruptcy. When Steve returned to the company in 1997 to save it, his focus was not on making money but on making better products.

This is how Jobs himself described the shift he made when he came back and took over from former CEO, John Sculley:

> My passion has been to build an enduring company where people were motivated to make great products. The products, not the profits, were the motivation. Sculley flipped these priorities to where the goal was to make money. It's a subtle difference, but it ends up meaning everything.

Steve's new focus on creating a small number of very valuable products directly led to Apple becoming the most valuable company in the world.

Perhaps your idea is a little more humble than those of Apple. No matter the scale of your idea, creating value is still the key to making a living out of it. While most people stress about how they're going to make money, smart people concern themselves with how to create something of real value. Because once you've done that, making money is relatively straightforward.

While most stress about how they're going to make money, smart people concern themselves with how to create something of real value

---

The opposite extreme, chasing the money even when it's against your best judgement, rarely turns out well. Award-winning author and screenwriter Neil Gaiman said in his University of the Arts commencement address, 'It's true that nothing I did where the only reason for doing it was the money was ever worth it except as bitter experience. Usually I didn't wind up getting the money either.'

Brian Eno, renowned producer of bands such as Coldplay and U2 and one of the most respected innovators in music, puts it even more strongly, saying, 'If all I'd ever wanted to do was make money, I'd probably be really poor by now.'

How do you ensure your project has value to others?

We typically have a poor understanding of value because the bulk of the public conversation about business is about pricing, revenue and profit – in other words, money. In addition, as an employee, the value we create is somewhat detached from the money we make; just because you do something brilliant at work today doesn't mean your paycheque will be any bigger at the end of the month.

The other reason value is difficult to understand is that we see what we are creating from our own perspective. But value is about seeing what other people want, from their perspective. Your customers, clients or audience are always tuned into what's been called WIIFM, or 'What's In It For Me?', so you need to get onto their wavelength in order to create something of value. You can create the best-quality product in the world but, if your target market never wanted it in the first place, it's of no value to them and you'll still make no sales.

Here's how to focus your project to ensure that it's valuable to people. No matter how logical people may think they are about making decisions such as a purchase, it has been proven in psychological experiments that all decisions are really emotionally driven. The emotion – desire, for instance – comes first. Then we construct logical reasons afterwards (often subconsciously) for why it was the right decision to buy. So we need to tune into the emotions of the people we think will want our stuff. Look for something people feel strongly about if you want to create something that will be really valuable for them.

Your idea will be valuable and therefore successful if your target market either:

- Has a clear desire to have something they don't have right now and you can provide it – they are craving a holiday or they want something beautiful to hang in their newly decorated living room. In psychology this is known as 'towards' motivation.

Or ...

- Feels bad about the situation they're in right now, so they're motivated to do something to alleviate these negative feelings – they feel embarrassed about being unfit, they feel fed up with being single or they're worried about their finances in retirement. This is known as 'away from' motivation.

The stronger the customers' emotion, the more value your good solution will have. Note that it is usually easier to market to the 'away from' motivation than the 'towards' – i.e. to solve a pain or frustration rather than simply fulfil a desire. This is because our brains are wired to prioritise avoiding pain, discomfort and risk before exploring new opportunities. I guess that's the result of natural selection in early man – favouring those of us who got out of the way of a sabre-tooth tiger before we stopped to pick up a juicy mango.

Remember that even if people *should* value something (for instance, because it will improve their health, have long-term business benefits or contribute to making the world a better place), if they currently do not have any strong feelings about it you will not be able to sell it to them. Do not try and convert people who have no desire to change a situation; it's exhausting. Instead, connect what you offer with the things they already have awareness of and concern for.

Sometimes that means you have to, 'sell what they *want*, deliver what they *need*'. For instance you might be passionate about raising staff morale within companies. But the company may be more concerned with underperformance and high staff turnover (typical symptoms of low morale). So your conversation starts there – solving the problems of performance and retention. Part of your solution, of course, will be to address the poor staff morale behind the problem.

So how do you find out what people really want?

Sometimes you have to sell what they want *and deliver what they* need

---

Go to the coalface

The best information you can get is out in the real world, interacting with your market, learning more about them, working with them and marketing and selling to them. To start learning what your target market or audience really value, seek out any situation that gets you in direct contact with them. There's nothing as revealing as being in a room with the people you want to become your customers, clients or fans.

How do you make that happen? Organise a networking or social event to get people in the room with you; arrange appointments to see a handful of people individually to ask them what their challenges and needs are. Email key people in companies to ask to meet them and ask what their number one concern is right now.

The closer you can get to your market the better because then, instead of guessing, you can find out directly what it is they need and want. What are their desires in this area? What are they excited about? What are their challenges and frustrations? Where are the current solutions still leaving people unsatisfied? If you want real answers ask the experts – your target clients and customers.

The same goes for art and performance. When you've got something you think is good share it. Take your best photos to an exhibition and see which pieces get the most interest. If you're a stand-up comedian and you've got five minutes of good material, go try it out at a friendly open-mic night. You'll learn very quickly which bits were valued by your audience!

'Help! I have no idea how to create something of value'

At this early stage you might have no idea how to create something of value or even know who your target market is, you just have a desire to do something with your passions and creative abilities. That's fine!

Just put your skill, knowledge and effort into doing something good, keep trying to be useful or interesting to others, offering what you think might meet people's wants and needs and you will eventually hit the value target. How will you know when you do? People will tell you.

They'll click on your links, comment on your blog, ask you questions, argue with you, show up at your events, ask when you're going to write another post, ask you if you're for hire, ask you what other products or services or pieces you can provide and they'll also start to share your work with others spontaneously. When that happens, monetisation can be as simple as slapping a price on it.

Tomorrow we'll look at how VALUE is the central element of the five-element Playcheque Formula for a money-making idea you love.

Today's tasks

- Think about how you can maximise your time creating things that are interesting or useful to others – i.e. creating value.

- And along the way consider these questions:
  - Who would like what I'm offering?
  - What can I offer that might be of particular interest to them?

  If you don't know the answers to these questions at this point, that's OK. Just keep them in the back of your mind as you progress your project. And if you get the chance to interact closely with your target market, take it and learn what you can about their interests, desires and frustrations.

Player pointers

Creating value takes time and effort. There are no get-rich-quick schemes. If there were a way to create something valuable with no effort, everybody would rush to do it and then the value in it would collapse. This is why it's important to choose an idea that both energises you (so that you can stick at it) and that uses some of your skills and natural talents (to give you a competitive advantage). More on this tomorrow.

Workerbot thoughts to challenge

'**I can't go meet anyone or share anything until I have business cards and my website finished.**' This is rarely true. If nothing else, you can always create your profile on LinkedIn to share with others or simply email people with details of what you do. Leave aside the trappings of business and instead focus on creating value and finding out more about your target market. Both of those can usually be done without waiting for the perfect website and business cards.

'**I asked my friends/colleagues/mum about my idea and they said it was great.**' Asking people's opinion on your idea without actually taking action is a very unreliable way to gather information. The test is whether they're willing to invest something

– time, attention or money. And to prove that you'll need to have something tangible to offer them.

'I need more traffic to my website.' Until you've got something people value there is no point trying to get tons of traffic to your site. And you can usually test whether you've created something of value by personally talking to a small number of people. Once you've done that we'll learn about how to bring more people to your website in Week 4.

DAY 10

The Playcheque Formula: The Five Ingredients of a Money-making Idea You Love

'I haven't "worked" since 1962.'
—Tom Jones, singer

Today, we're going to look deeper into what makes up a business idea that is successful in every way – that's one that not only makes money but that you enjoy doing; something that suits you so well it feels more like play than work. I've discovered over the last ten years of helping people with this that there are five essential elements you need in place. As soon as you have all five elements in place, you switch on a stream of income. This is the Playcheque Formula.

What does success mean to you? To write a bestselling book? To find work you love and make a good living from it? To make your mark on the world? To change things for the better? To create a booming business and get rich? Whatever it is for you, the Playcheque Formula is your key to unlocking it.

What we're talking about here is authentic success: not just making a living, but making a life that has meaning for you. So, let's take a look at the five elements and how they fit together.

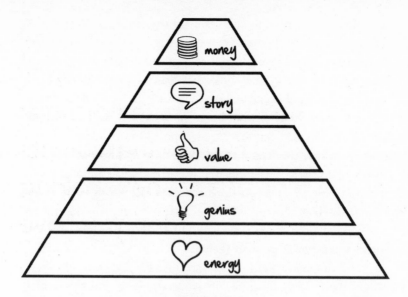

The Playcheque Formula

1. ENERGY: Do something you are drawn to and enjoy

The first element of the Playcheque Formula is to find something you like, that excites you or that gives you energy. To create something successful, go where the energy is. This is your starting point.

Sure, you can try and force yourself to do something because it's lucrative, but it will be a hard slog all the way. And when you hit the inevitable setbacks you'll be tempted to give up. Instead, find a way to build on those things you do *anyway*. Then you're building a life around the things that *give* you energy rather than drain it, the things you think about and engage in when you're not even trying. That means you do more of it and so have a competitive advantage.

Towards the end of my career as a consultant in tech strategy to broadcasters I knew the spark had left me when I could no longer face keeping up to date with the latest industry news. I had boiled down my minimum investment to reading a single page – the tech page – of the weekly trade paper, *Broadcast*. And when I could no longer bring myself to read even that it was clearly time to leave. Today, the books and articles I read for my business fascinate and excite me. And what I read for work is almost indistinguishable from what I read for pleasure. As a result I am very well informed and that's a huge boost to my business.

Remember, though, that the only way to find out if something energises you is to go try it. Sitting and thinking about it won't help. When you do discover which things you enjoy doing, you'll often realise they're part of a long-running theme and you've been doing them in some form your whole life. So guess what, you're good at them!

Of course, you need more than just ENERGY if you want to get paid. The advice to 'do what you love and the money will follow' is grossly incomplete. You need the other four elements too.

2. GENIUS: Use what you've got

For your project to be a success and make you money, you'll need to put what's special about you into it. Sadly our workerbot training has convinced most of us that we are distinctly average and have nothing very special to offer. But in reality, even if we're no Einstein or Da Vinci, we all have spots of genius.

Put simply, GENIUS is all those activities you find easy that others don't. It's all the skills and knowledge that you've developed over the years and it's also your natural talents that don't appear on any CV or résumé. You might have a genius for coming up with ideas (even if you're not so good at following through on them), or for inspiring a team, for visual design, for taming technology, for bringing order to chaos or for explaining complex concepts in simple terms.

GENIUS also includes any other assets you possess that others don't – your contacts, industry knowledge or life experience.

If you're struggling with identifying yours, don't worry because we'll explore this more tomorrow.

3. VALUE: Create something that people like

The key to getting paid is to create something other people value – something they find interesting, enjoyable or useful. As billionaire investor Warren Buffett is fond of saying, 'Price is what you pay; value is what you get.'

Just focusing on doing what you love is not enough. I love watching *The Simpsons* but no one's about to start paying me for it. But if I can take what it is that I love so much about *The Simpsons* (the humour and the frank social commentary) and use some of my GENIUS to create something of VALUE to others, then I can make some money. So, for instance, I could use my writing to create a humorous book with some of the same style of social commentary I love in *The Simpsons*.

We covered VALUE yesterday. Remember that you'll know when you've succeeded in creating something of real value because it will take on a life of its own; your blog posts get shared, your tweets get retweeted and you get word of mouth referrals.

4. STORY: Communicate the value you provide

Even when you've proved that you can provide something people really value, you'll have a hard time making money unless you can communicate that value to the wider world.

That's where STORY comes in. It can be as simple as changing the title of your product to make it more memorable or make it clearer what it is and who it's for. It's also describing what you do on your website in the most compelling way. Sometimes it's telling your personal story (when it's relevant) to explain the background and purpose to your business, blog or product.

If you find describing what you do or trying to sell yourself difficult, you can simply tell the story of a client or customer who got a huge amount of value.

A clearer focus and a small tweak in name can be all that's needed to make your project ten times more interesting for others to participate in. We'll look more closely at this in the final week.

5. MONEY: Find a way to make money from your creation

The final element is about finding a way to get some return from the value you've created. As long as you have created something of real VALUE to others and can communicate it, there will pretty much always be a way to monetise it. This element is about finding the best package, price and channel because some will reap much larger rewards than others.

For instance, content that would be difficult to charge for on a website might well make money if delivered as an app on mobile devices. Or selling a course for $20 on the online learning marketplace Udemy might make you more money than selling it for $200 on your own website because low-price courses make so many more sales.

There are so many ways to monetise what you do now that the MONEY element is just as creative as all the others. If you've developed a great way for people to manage email inbox overwhelm, you can package that as one-to-one teaching with individuals, group workshops in organisations, a self-published book, an online course or an app. The choice is yours!

The financial return from your project might be indirect. You might write a book, for instance, to boost your status as a public speaker or consultant or to get you on TV. Even though the book itself makes relatively little income from book royalties, you could win a lot more speaking gigs or consultancy work as a result of your new positioning as an expert.

We'll dive deeper into the MONEY element and how to play the money game on Day 24.

Putting it all together

The Playcheque Formula is represented as a pyramid because each element serves as the foundation for the one above. If we get ENERGY from doing something, we're likely to do more of it and therefore develop our GENIUS in it (and, in addition, the things we are drawn to doing are often the things we already have a natural talent for). And when we employ our GENIUS it becomes much easier to create VALUE. Once we have something of value, we can create a STORY to tell. And when people understand the value we're providing, there will be a way to make MONEY, even if it's indirectly.

The only way to unlock all five elements is to play it out. Do *not* put your project on hold while you sit and think about it! Take your best shot at doing something you enjoy in your project, try to use some of your best assets and see if you can create something people appreciate. Use the Play Cycle from Day 6 to keep adjusting your course until you prove you have something people really value. Then tell your story and choose a way to get paid.

As soon as all five elements of the Playcheque Formula are in place, income and opportunities start to flow to you

---

It's a little like clicking all the tumblers in a lock into place. As soon as all the elements are in place, suddenly the door is open and income and opportunities start to flow to you – as Wolfgang Wild found out with his idea for Retronaut.

How Wolfgang Wild unlocked the Playcheque Formula and turned an impossible dream into his own global brand

Eight years ago Wolfgang Wild had more ideas than he knew what to do with. He met me for some mentorship sessions to decide which one he should pursue. One of them was about bringing photographs of the past alive and was based on a seemingly impossible dream.

Ever since I was a small boy I've wanted to go back in time. But it took me 20 years to admit to myself that this was my dream.

I'd started to collect old photos of a particular kind – rather than looking old, they look like a different version of now. For example, most of us imagine the past in black and white but the earliest colour photos are from the 1870s. When we see them, we get a kind of time-travelly buzz: they don't look like now but they also don't look like something historical.

The idea based around these kind of photos seemed to have the most potential to me and so Wolfgang started to play out the idea and see where he could take it. It was fortunate timing:

I'd just been fired from my job and my wife told me 'You're never going to hold down a proper job so you might as well do something of your own'

His initial Play Project couldn't have been more unassuming:

I was in a café showing a friend some of my historical photos and he loved them so much he said, 'You should start a blog'. I didn't know anything about blogging at that time so I googled how to do it.

I chose the name Retronaut to represent the feeling of travelling through time. A friend helped me install WordPress and I started the Retronaut site in January 2010. For three weeks it was mostly my mother and I looking at it. I was getting about 300 hits a day. Then one day a post on the blog with colour photos of Piccadilly Circus in 1949 went viral.

I logged in to check my stats and saw I had 30,000 hits in one day. When I saw the number I didn't immediately understand what it meant. I phoned up my friend who was helping me with the blog and asked, 'Is this significant?'

Wolfgang has posted every day on the site ever since and the impact has been remarkable. The site climbed to 200,000 hits a day and attracted praise from *The Guardian, The Daily Mail, The Financial Times* and many others.

Retronaut now has 250,000 Facebook followers, 110,000 on Twitter and *The Times* declared Wolfgang one of the top 50 people to follow on Twitter. *National Geographic* published his first book in 2014 and he has three more books planned this year. Now he's secured an exclusive licensing deal with Mashable.com (where it is among the most shared content on the site) and is planning an online TV series for Retronaut.

What Wolfgang's story shows is the power of unlocking the Playcheque Formula. He chose something that really excited him (ENERGY) and that used his talent for visual arts and his lifelong indulgence in a particular kind of historical photo (GENIUS). His blog was so interesting to people it spontaneously spread (VALUE).

He was also smart in choosing a very specific and narrow focus for his blog; instead of calling it historical photographs (which sounds rather dull to most people!), he focused on particular images that give that disorienting time-travel feel and used the term Retronaut to describe it (STORY).

Once he had the first four elements in place, the MONEY element came in numerous forms: licensing deals, book deals, speaking and international exhibitions – the most recent of which, 'Retronaut's New York', was right on Fifth Avenue.

Read more about Retronaut at www.retronaut.com. Watch my interview with Wolfgang on screwworkbreakfree.com.

Today's task

- As you do your microblock today, consider how many of the Playcheque Formula elements your project is hitting. Take my online assessment to help you at screwworkbreakfree.com.

Discover Your Inner Genius

*'Everyone is a genius. But if you judge a fish
on its ability to climb a tree, it will live its whole
life believing that it is stupid.'*

—Albert Einstein, theoretical physicist

Today's all about playing to your strengths, because when you focus on what you're great at you can create something really valuable for others and, as we saw on Day 9, VALUE is the building block of a successful business.

So today we're going to uncover your inner genius. Yes, I know the G-word is a little contentious. But did you know that until the seventeenth century, 'genius' simply meant an innate ability, inclination or disposition? It was only later that the word came to mean something exceptional, excluded from the experience of the ordinary mortal.

When we think of genius today, we think of Leonardo da Vinci, Albert Einstein, Marie Curie or Jane Austen. This is a tough benchmark to measure ourselves against.

The education system doesn't help with its narrow definition of talent. Anything that wasn't deemed useful in an academic setting (or in a conventional corporate job) pretty much gets ignored as a talent – making people laugh, charming others into seeing your way, negotiating, inspiring people, imagining new possibilities, being creative, being good with your hands. This is why inventor and innovative thinker Buckminster Fuller said that, 'Everyone is born a genius, but the process of living de-geniuses them.'

And once you get into the world of work you find that too often companies downplay the uniqueness of employees' talents in order to maintain the belief that we are easily exchangeable. It's no wonder so many of us have a hard time thinking of ourselves as talented, let alone a genius.

Warren Buffett is the world's most successful investor with a net worth of $67 billion and has gifted over $37 billion to charity. He's known for ignoring trends to try to make a quick buck and, instead, investing in companies based on their real value, holding their shares over the long term. And he steers clear of any company he doesn't easily understand. Many consider Buffett a genius but he has a very interesting take on his own talents as he explained to *Forbes* in 2010:

> There's a whole bunch of things I don't know a thing about. I just stay away from those. I stay within what I call my circle of competence. [IBM founder] Tom Watson said it best. He said, 'I'm no genius, but I'm smart in spots, and I stay around those spots.'

Buffett built a multibillion-dollar fortune on his smart spots, his spots of genius. What can you do with yours?

Even if you are not Einstein or Da Vinci, we all have 'spots of genius'

Give yourself an unfair advantage

Finding and using your spots of genius is one of the most important things you could ever do, because these spots are where you can create the greatest value, have the greatest impact and reap the greatest rewards.

Finding your genius spots can be challenging though. We often miss them or underestimate their importance for the very same reason they are valuable: they are easy for us. In psychology this is called 'unconscious competence' – you're so practised at something it has become second nature.

We underappreciate our own skills and talents for the same reason they are valuable: these things are easy for us

---

There are two kinds of genius spots we're looking for, both valuable in their own way. Firstly, there are the practical skills and knowledge we've built over several years in our professional career (or sometimes in our personal lives). We'll look at those in a moment but the second type of genius spot is more easily missed. These are the skills and talents that are a core part of who you are because you've been doing them in some form all your life.

To find these natural strengths, we have to broaden our scope way beyond the narrow range of skills and talents that appear on a CV or résumé: connecting with new people, observing the natural world, seeing the patterns behind a situation, understanding technology, explaining complex concepts, getting the best price on everything, throwing a great party. Often these will be things you enjoy doing and you've been doing in some form since childhood.

Take a moment now to think of five natural strengths or talents and write them down. You can include personality traits in your favour. Don't just pick the socially accepted ones – include things like 'stubbornness' and 'incredibly good taste'. Also include activities or topics you've been fascinated by and immersed in for years.

Do something for long enough and it forms structures in your brain. That means your brain is literally wired differently; you see things others can't see and find meaning that others can't identify. Your way of seeing the world is unique but to you it's just 'seeing'. What could be more ordinary? What could be special about that? And yet you're one in seven billion. Your unique experience is a special lens you can't remove; you've never seen the world without it. If you can put these natural strengths to good use in your project you give yourself an unfair advantage.

> *Use your spots of genius to give*
> *yourself an unfair advantage*

Put your skills and knowledge to good use

Aside from your natural talents, the more you can use skills and knowledge you've developed from your previous career (or from many years of personal experience), the faster you'll be able to create value.

If you don't enjoy your current work you might be tempted to wipe the slate clean and invent a new career that uses nothing from your old career. If you do that you will have a long road ahead of you before you create something of real value (and therefore be able to make money from it). Generally, the more skills and knowledge you can carry into your new project the shorter the time until you can get paid for it.

Just because you're not enjoying your current job doesn't mean you should throw away the skills you've spent years developing – particularly if you would enjoy using them in the right situation. If you're sick of software development in a bank but you still love coding, use it in a different environment – create an app, teach coding to kids or simply use your general tech skills in something that really excites you. If you hate your sales job but you know you would still enjoy using your skills in communication, relationship building and persuasion, if it was for something you really cared about, take advantage of them in your project.

How Rik Spruyt used his genius to launch a global business network in 30 days

Rik Spruyt had a good job in international logistics based in Beijing but he had always wanted to start something of his own. Having lived and worked in China for the past six years and Africa for seven before that, he was particularly interested in the burgeoning trade between Africa and Asia – currently $300 billion a year.

So he joined my mentorship programme and started work on a membership network to connect logistics companies in Africa with those in the rest of the world, particularly Asia and Europe. He created a website on WordPress and reached out to his personal network to invite them to join for an introductory annual membership fee of $2000. Within 30 days he had a membership website set up and his first paying member. CrossTrades was born.

Given Rik's good standing in the industry, he continued to pull in major players across the world. And while in the early days there wouldn't be that many others for people to connect with, Rik promised personal attention to these 'charter members' to help them find contacts and do more business.

Before long CrossTrades had 50 members. One year later the membership is on track to reach 120 members and Rik recently held the first global CrossTrades conference in Johannesburg. The results have been remarkable, with members winning multi-million-dollar contracts through the network. Now Rik has attracted investment in CrossTrades from inside the network and a commission deal on future business development.

Check out Rik's business at www.crosstrades.net.

What if my project is something completely new for me?

Hopefully you've chosen a project that at least suits your natural personality traits and strengths. If it's also something that can use skills and knowledge you've built up over many years (even if in a different field or environment) then you're in for a relatively short game. But if your project doesn't use any of your hard-earned skills and experience, realise it will be a much longer game.

Do you want to play a short game or a long game? The choice is yours; just make it consciously and be honest with yourself. If you choose to build your project around an emerging talent, you'll be in for a longer game because you will need to invest the time to get good at it. But you won't be starting from scratch if you're able to use some of your natural strengths. I've never taken any formal writing courses but when it came to writing my first book it really helped that I'd been a lifelong voracious reader of non-fiction.

Having knowledge or skills that are rare can be a real benefit. If you make a great cup of tea, that's something a lot of people can do. It's not much of an advantage in creating a teashop or an innovative new tea brand. But if you have an encyclopaedic knowledge of tea and its history, or you have connections with importers, or perhaps a knack for finding underpriced commercial property, or creating a unique and desirable experience for visitors or creating successful brand identities then you might have a head-start.

Whatever your abilities are you can and should grow them even further – in fact that's such an essential part of entrepreneurship we focus the day on it tomorrow.

Today's tasks: find your genius

- In your Playbook, without over-thinking it, write down the following:
  - Five skills, talents or areas of expertise that you know you have.

- Five things you find easy. Maybe you find it strange others can't do the same. Clue: they're usually things you enjoy doing.
- Five things other people tell you you're good at, even if you think it's nothing special (include anything you've heard others say, not just professional skills).
- Five things you could easily teach other people, even if it's just the basics. Don't get hung up on the conventional image of a teacher: it could be to an audience of a hundred or one to one with a friend; it could be on a blog or in a YouTube video.
- Five things you have a deep experiential understanding of. Some might be from work, some might be from your personal life, even your childhood.
- Any unusual skills or traits you developed as a result of challenges in your life. Some of the people we consider to be unusually talented developed their unique traits as a way of coping with difficult childhood experiences – loss, disability, bullying, neglect or abuse. Numerous successful comedians have reported developing their talents as a way to avoid getting bullied at school. People who felt ignored as a child sometimes develop incredible charisma or performing skills in order to get attention. Others buried themselves in reading and study as a way to escape a painful situation at home. These traits can bring their problems but they can also bring great talents and, if managed well, great success.
- Now, read through everything you've written and look for any themes. Out of all of them, write down five of your key genius spots, whether it's skills, knowledge, talents, traits or other assets. How could you make use of these in your project? If you're great with people, use that in your project. If you're a research nut, try to make your project benefit from that. If your favourite part of a project is coming up with the initial idea, see if you can turn your project into an opportunity to use your passion for idea generation. If you

love being the centre of attention, see if there's a way your project can give you a chance to perform or present – get up on stage, appear on a radio show, change your blog into a video blog. Start to give yourself an unfair advantage.

Player pointers

You may feel that none of your spots of genius is particularly valuable. But what if you combine them?

The power of combining multiple skills

Creator of the *Dilbert* cartoon strip, Scott Adams, wrote in his excellent book *How to Fail at Almost Everything and Still Win Big*:

I'm a perfect example of the power of leveraging multiple mediocre skills. I'm a rich and famous cartoonist who doesn't draw well. At social gatherings I'm usually not the funniest person in the room. My writing skills are good, not great.

But Scott discovered that

When I combined my meager business skills with my bad art skills and my fairly ordinary writing talent, the mixture was powerful. With each new skill, my odds of success increased substantially.

Dilbert now appears online and in 2,000 newspapers worldwide; 20 million *Dilbert* books and calendars are in print.

Can you combine several of your genius spots into your project to boost your odds of success?

Workerbot thoughts to challenge

'**What if I find out I don't have the talent?**' Ah, that old one. This fear is big enough for many people that they never actually start doing the thing they really want to do, just in case their worst fears that they are talentless nobodies after all are confirmed. But science is casting a new light on talent and it turns out not to be as cut and dried as we thought. Much of what we think of as innate genius is in fact learned. We'll find out all about that tomorrow.

How to Become a Lean Mean Learning Machine

'Be so good they can't ignore you.'

—Steve Martin, Emmy Award-winning comedian,
actor and author

Yesterday you discovered some of your spots of genius and the importance of making use of them. Today we're going to look at how to grow your genius even further. The willingness to learn is at the heart of entrepreneurship. Let's find out how to approach it.

To start with let's talk about talent and what it really is. When we think of remarkable innate talent, Mozart is someone who often comes to mind. Surely here was a person gifted with a level of genius most of us were not lucky enough to achieve. But look a little closer at Mozart's story and it's not so simple, as Michael Howe explains in his book *Genius Explained*.

Wolfgang Mozart's father, Leopold, was an experienced musician and started teaching Wolfgang on a schedule of three hours of practice every day from the age of just three years old. By age six the young Wolfgang had already logged an astounding three thousand five hundred hours – three times more than anyone else in his peer group. So how much was Mozart's talent a product of genes and how much simply of practice?

Everywhere we look at examples of great talent we see similar levels of practice. Picasso created approximately 50,000 artworks in his lifetime. That's almost two per day every day of his life. So was he born a genius or is it, as Ray Bradbury said, that, 'Quantity produces quality'?

Recent research shows that genes do play their part in our abilities but probably a smaller and more complex one than was once thought. It's time to abandon this idea that the lucky few are born talented and the rest of us are doomed to mediocrity.

It's time to abandon this idea
that the lucky few are born
talented and the rest of us are
doomed to mediocrity

While growing up, whatever you enjoyed doing you did a lot of. And when you do something a lot you get good at it. Know that whatever your spots of genius are now, you can grow them with practice. Here's how.

First, check your mindset

Professor Carol Dweck of Stanford University spent 20 years researching success traits and discovered that people fell into one of two distinct mindsets about their own talents: fixed or growth. And she found that the mindset you adhere to has a huge impact on your ability to reach your goals. As Dweck writes on her own website mindsetonline.com:

> In a fixed mindset, people believe their basic qualities, like their intelligence or talent, are simply fixed traits.

They spend their time documenting their intelligence or talent instead of developing them. They also believe that talent alone creates success—without effort. They're wrong.

In a growth mindset, people believe that their most basic abilities can be developed through dedication and hard work—brains and talent are just the starting point. This view creates a love of learning and a resilience that is essential for great accomplishment. Virtually all great people have had these qualities.

A surprising result of Dweck's research is that, even if you have been gifted some particularly valuable talents, a fixed mindset will still hold you back from success. That's because people with a fixed mindset are focused on proving their worth and avoiding situations where they could fail or look incompetent. People with a growth mindset on the other hand seek out experiences that will stretch them and help them to learn. You can see why the latter correlates with success.

So for the duration of your project, try to notice whether you're operating from a fixed mindset or a growth mindset. When you find yourself worrying about limitations in your abilities remind yourself that you can learn almost anything you need to.

> 'Don't ask kids what they want to be *when they grow up but* what problems do they want to solve. *This changes the conversation from who do I want to work for, to what do I need to learn to be able to do that.*'
>
> —Jaime Casap, Google's Chief Education Evangelist

Now you know that your skills and talents are not fixed but can be grown, a whole world of opportunity opens to you. What would you like to get good at? And once you've identified something to learn, how do you go about it?

Well, firstly, there are two distinct modes of learning that are both useful in entrepreneurship: theoretical knowledge and real-world experience.

Boost your knowledge

'Anyone can become an expert at anything in six months, whether it is hydrodynamics for boats or cyclonic systems for vacuum cleaners.'

—Sir James Dyson, founder of Dyson

It's never been easier to gain knowledge than it is today. So much information and instruction is available for free on the web. But don't underestimate the value of books – their long-form narrative allows you to soak yourself in a writer's argument in a way discrete blog posts and other tidbits do not. And books still offer the best value to price ratio of almost any product you can buy. If you read the five best books on a topic, you will have a level of knowledge that exceeds that of many beginners in the field and even some who have been working in it for a while.

Think of someone famous who has achieved what you want to achieve and the chances are someone has already written a book on how they did it. I had a client once who was interested in opening an innovative chain of cafés and had even considered selling her home to finance it. She had a lot of questions and concerns about how to run a café. I asked her if she had read any of the books detailing how coffee chains like Starbucks, Coffee Nation and Coffee Republic got started. 'No' she said.

That's kind of crazy, when you think that someone has successfully been through the whole process you are considering, made their mistakes and then made it work, and you can find out how they did it all for the price of a couple of lattes. 'Success leaves clues', as author and entrepreneur Jim Rohn said. They're there waiting for you to read them.

Experience is the greatest teacher

'Genius is experience.'
—Henry Ford

Intellectual knowledge will only take you so far on the entrepreneurship trail. There is another important component to your genius.

When you not only read about a topic but actually live it and breathe it in practice you gain something incredibly valuable – experiential understanding. This is a deep understanding that feels like it has seeped into your very bones. You'll know this feeling already, somewhere in your life. It's the experience of having driven through an area so much that you know when to ignore the directions of your Sat Nav. It's the hunch you get as an experienced cook to deviate from a recipe. And it's the gut feeling to avoid getting into a business relationship with someone even though you can't quite explain why. This deep knowing comes from *doing* something again and again, from practice and experience, not just reading about it.

You can read the best sales books in the world (and that's a great idea if you're going to be selling your own products or services) but until you actually practise selling to people, you won't truly understand it. So whenever you have an opportunity to gain real-world experience that will be helpful to your project, take it. Be willing to experiment and learn – make your life a laboratory.

The more you can use your experiential understanding in your project, the better. Remember though that this kind of deep knowing doesn't always communicate as a clear verbal message but as a gut reaction or even a physical symptom. George Soros is the one of the world's most respected investors. He started as a penniless immigrant to the US, now has a personal worth of over $24 billion and has given away more than $11 billion. And yet he has admitted to relying on what he calls 'animal instincts' and using the onset of back pain as 'a signal that there was something wrong in my portfolio'.

Many of the greatest minds of all time have stated the importance of experience. Leonardo da Vinci considered it so important that he sometimes signed his sketchbooks full of inventions, 'Discepolo dell'esperienza' – Disciple of Experience.

Steve Jobs considered experience to be the fuel for creativity and the broader the experience the better. For him that included learning calligraphy, travelling through India on a spiritual quest and working in an apple orchard (which some say inspired the company name).

He said in a 1995 interview with *Wired* magazine,

Creativity is just connecting things. When you ask creative people how they did something, they feel a little guilty because they didn't really do it, they just saw something. It seemed obvious to them after a while. That's because they were able to connect experiences they've had and synthesise new things. And the reason they were able to do that was that they've had more experiences or they have thought more about their experiences than other people.

Of course throwing yourself into new experiences is not always comfortable. For one thing, you have to be willing to do something you're not great at yet. This is a daily experience for children but as adults we're not very good at being not very good at things. Dare to be mediocre! It's the only way to mastery. Keep practising and what was once uncomfortable will eventually become second nature. Legendary science fiction writer Ray Bradbury had a great piece of advice for writers that could translate to just about any field: 'Write a short story every week. It's not possible to write 52 bad short stories in a row.'

Dare to be mediocre!
It's the only way to mastery.

The fine art of blagging

'It's a terrible thing, I think, in life to wait until you're ready. I have this feeling now that actually no one is ever ready to do anything. There is almost no such thing as ready. There is only now. And you may as well do it now.'

—Hugh Laurie, award-winning actor and comedian

You'll gain the greatest skills and knowledge on real-world projects – providing a service or delivering a product or some other result that you've promised to someone. Of course, the person or organisation you've made this commitment to probably expects you to already have the skills and knowledge you need!

If you turn down every opportunity that you don't have all the skills, knowledge, confidence or other resources for, you won't ever progress. The solution is to engage in the fine art of blagging – taking on a project you don't feel entirely ready to be doing.

Richard Branson on learning on the go

Richard Branson is a fan of blagging. In fact it's been a central part of his success. In a blog post on virgin.com titled 'Learning on the go' he describes his experience of starting *Student Magazine* in the 1960s:

When opportunity knocks, always say yes. You never know where it might lead you. It might lead to starting a business, or a new career. It will almost certainly lead to adventure ...

I started Student Magazine to protest against the [Vietnam] war and raise awareness about other causes I believed in. While I had no idea how to run a magazine, I just started it and learnt how to do it along the way. It's a principle I've followed ever since: if you don't know how to do something, say yes and learn how to do it later.

This philosophy of taking opportunities wherever they come up extended to how he got interviews for the magazine from leading thinkers of the time.

When I was 17, I came across the thought-provoking books of James Baldwin and was determined to secure an interview with him for my new magazine … He was a hard man to find, but I learned he was going to be staying in a London hotel one day and raced over as quickly as I could.

I managed to blag my way past reception and learn which room he was in. I knocked on the door and was soon face to face with a man who clearly did not want to be disturbed – especially by a teenager holding a prehistoric recording device bigger than his chest.

After explaining to James who I was and how interested I was in his work, he kindly submitted to a 10 minute interview.

Despite his inexperience, the lack of time and even discovering the battery in his recorder was flat, Richard managed to achieve a fascinating and powerful article for the magazine. That's why his advice is, ' … if you get an opportunity you should grasp it with both hands – then learn how to do it as you go along.'

Blagging is not about telling irresponsible lies. Obviously you shouldn't say you can fly a plane or treat someone's back pain if you are not fully qualified. What we're talking about is making promises you know you may not be able to fulfil right now but then running as fast as you can to meet your commitment by the time it's due.

And if that means you need to reach out to ask advice from an expert or hire someone who is more experienced that's OK too.

Once you get used to blagging you realise that everyone around you is doing it to a greater or lesser extent. That's why Academy Award-winning screenwriter William Goldman famously said about Hollywood: 'Nobody knows anything ... Not one person in the entire motion picture field knows for a certainty what's going to work. Every time out it's a guess and, if you're lucky, an educated one.'

Many a time in my varied career I have been surrounded by the greatest experts in that particular field and still thought that in reality, 'Nobody knows anything.' At least to some extent, we're all blagging it.

Today's tasks

- Learn something new. What could you dive into learning in just 20 minutes that will aid the rest of your project? One good article or instructional video can have a big impact.
- Build your reading list. Which books will you read on your chosen subject? Follow your energy when choosing your reading material. Don't choose a list of dry texts to slog through. What are you excited to read next? What would make the biggest difference to your project to learn? Which Twitter profiles and newsfeeds would you like to subscribe to to keep up to date? See what others are reading by searching for #screwworkbreakfree on Twitter and Instagram and post your own reading list if you like.
- Schedule it. When will you schedule your learning time? How about starting your day by reading something that you're fascinated by? Or sacrificing a little TV-watching time to read a book, even if it's just 30 minutes every evening?

Player pointers

When choosing projects in future, remember to consider what opportunity they offer for learning new skills. I volunteered to edit a medical charity newsletter some years ago because I felt passionate about the cause. The role helped me improve my writing but what I didn't expect was that it would force me to become an expert in using Microsoft Word (which was the only application I had available to prepare it on at the time). That deep expertise (hard won while swearing at the idiosyncrasies of Microsoft's software late at night after my day job) has stood me in good stead ever since, having given me a better knowledge of Word than 90 per cent of the people using it. Subsequent projects have taught me video making, audio production, copywriting, event marketing and hosting and many other valuable skills.

What skill, if you learned or improved it, would double the value of your other strengths – perhaps writing, speaking, marketing or even learning a relevant language? If a project gives you the chance to do so, it's well worth considering doing.

Workerbot thoughts to challenge

'But I'm just a beginner!' – the problem with comparing to others. Imagine a vertical line representing an axis of expertise. At the top are the world experts. At the bottom are the people who haven't learned anything yet about this topic. You are positioned somewhere on this line.

We tend to undervalue just how much we know or how great our talents are because we spend all our time looking up at the icons of our field. They are the ones we are inspired by and want to learn from. They're so much further ahead. They seem to possess an entirely different level of ability.

But if we only compare ourselves against those at the top we will inevitably end up feeling somewhat inadequate. Instead, take a moment every so often to look down and see how far you've climbed and how much you now know relative to the complete beginners below you. You might be surprised.

Remember also that you will improve as you play out your project. When Michelangelo was first asked to paint the ceiling of the Sistine Chapel, he refused, saying that he was a sculptor not a painter. The pope however persuaded him to take on the project. The result is one of the most famous works of art of all time. Over the course of four years Michelangelo's style evolved; the work at the rear of the chapel which he painted first is quite different to the work he did towards the end, at the front of the chapel. His final paintings have a stronger and simpler style and include his most powerful and most renowned – *The Creation of Adam*, where God's hand reaches out to touch Adam's. Everyone improves with practice!

Superniching: The Shortcut to Instant Brilliance

'I cannot give you the formula for success, but I can give you the formula for failure – which is, "Try to please everybody."'

—Herbert Bayard Swope, Pulitzer Prize-winning reporter and newspaper editor

When you're starting a new venture you'll usually find yourself up against others who are more established and have a higher profile and more experience. How can you compete? How do you even get noticed?

The solution is to narrow your focus. Stop trying to be all things to all people. Instead, superniche. Look for something you can get laser-focused on – a specific group of people you can best help, a particular thing you do well or a specific job your software or product is ideal for. Then you can put all your promotional energies into just this very narrow area.

This doesn't mean you're committing yourself to this focus forever. It's simply a way to get traction. You can, if you choose, expand what you offer later, once you've got something off the ground.

Superniching has three immediate advantages. Firstly, if you focus on an area you have particular expertise or experience in, i.e. one of your genius spots, you go from being a beginner in a very broad field to being an expert in a very specific area.

Focus on an area you have particular expertise or experience in and you go from being a beginner in a broad field to being an expert in a very specific area

Secondly, you make it much easier to understand who and what your product or service is for and, thirdly, you might find you make your project newsworthy as Saskia Nelson did.

Saskia finds her perfect match

When Saskia Nelson quit her job as a programme director in a charity at the beginning of 2013, she had no clear plan what she was going to do next. She just knew she wanted to do something with her love of photography.

It was important to me that my business be authentic and true to who I am, so finding something that aligned with my life experiences, my passions and talents was critical. I read Screw Work Let's Play and remember a section recommending paying attention to what you read, what you're drawn to, how you choose to spend your time etc. and when I looked back over my life I realised I had a lot of knowledge and experience from many years of online dating before I met my boyfriend on the Guardian Soulmates dating site. So when everyone kept asking me if I was going to be a wedding photographer,

I knew straight away that made no sense as it had no bearing on who I am as a person but it made me realise that becoming a dating photographer would be a great fit.

Saskia joined The Screw Work 30-day Challenge to get some extra support and launched the UK's first dedicated dating photography business, Hey Saturday, in just 30 days.

I was amazed at how bad – and how inaccurate – some people's profile pictures were. I wanted to help people create a set of photos that are of professional quality but look as though they were taken while the person was out with their friends living their life as usual.'

Within 30 days I had chosen a business name, found a designer to help create my brand and, most importantly, started doing free photography sessions with friends to test out the idea. Then someone in the 30-day Challenge referred me my first paying client. It was my first Playcheque!

Saskia continued building her business while working through her notice from her job, often in 20-minute micro-blocks after work. The business quickly started to take off. Saskia won 'Best New Dating Individual' in the 2014 UK Dating Awards and the innovative focus of the business soon attracted articles in *The Daily Mail, The Evening Standard* and *The Independent.*

The benefit of superniching her business was undeniable:

Finding a very specific niche was the most important thing I did for my business. The fact that it was a niche that was still unexplored, that was brand-spanking new, was even better. I own my niche – for now – and I intend to stay the industry leader in the field of dating photography (despite others coming along and launching similar businesses this last year).

Saskia now has five other photographers working for her in London, Brighton and Edinburgh and is planning to double that over the next twelve months, with a presence in other UK cities.

She is regularly asked to write for The Huffington Post, Match.com, eHarmony, Guardian Soulmates, Lovestruck, and Love and Friends and has been featured in UK and US podcasts as the leading expert in dating photography.

Find out more about Hey Saturday at www.heysaturday.co.

As Saskia discovered, when you stop trying to be all things to all people, you have a greater chance of being the best at what you do. Business guru Seth Godin says: 'You need to be the best in the world at what you're doing.' The number one in any field gets far more attention and more business than the next several competitors put together. In the world of online retail for example, Amazon makes more than all the other retailers in the top ten put together.

To be best in the world sounds like a very challenging goal, but don't panic. For me, the best dentist in the world is a local one I can trust who is good with nervous patients (for example, me) and matches my preferred budget. It does not mean the most technically able dentist on the planet.

How to superniche

So how do you go about superniching? Use the Playcheque Formula as your guide; choose a niche you have ENERGY for and that uses one or more of your spots of GENIUS. And in order to ensure you can create something that has VALUE to others, make sure it's a niche where there is demand – even better if it's something where demand is set to grow over time.

There are two approaches to superniching: narrowing your market (i.e. the types of people/organisations you are trying to appeal to) or narrowing what you offer. You can use either one or a combination of both.

Superniching your market

'Increasingly, the mass market is turning into a mass of niches.'

—Chris Anderson, author of *The Long Tail*

You can superniche your market by focusing on a particular subset of people. That might be *geographic* (for example, people near you). It might be a particular *demographic* (a specific age, gender or race etc.), a *firmographic* (a company of particular size or in a particular industry) or a *psychographic* (a particular personality or set of values, for example, people who are early adopters of new technology).

For instance, if you're particularly excited about helping women entrepreneurs, consider niching to that market. Or if you start a blog and find it is mostly read by men, embrace it and use it. If you want to help companies recruit in a smarter way and you have a background in medicine, consider using it your advantage and specialise in medical and pharmaceutical companies where your former career is then a competitive advantage.

When we look at powerful global businesses, we often forget that they started with a narrow focus on what they did and/or who they did it for. When Apple were up against the mighty Microsoft who dominated the PC industry in the 1980s, they didn't do what other competitors did – produce a similar operating system for general office use. Instead, they focused on a niche – designers and other creative users. That meant the aesthetics of both the software and the hardware mattered and they had to create apps that were best in class for creative tasks like publishing and video editing. Once they'd dominated the niche of the creative professional, they expanded from there.

> *'You can either build something a large number of people want a small amount, or something a small number of people want a large amount. Choose the latter ... nearly all good startup ideas are of that type.'*
>
> —Paul Graham, co-founder of startup accelerator Y Combinator

Many other giants today took a similar approach to get off the ground. Spotify founder, Daniel Ek, has said 'We chose a narrow market to begin with that we knew how to serve well – Sweden. Had we started with the US there's no way we would still be around.' PayPal focused their efforts initially on eBay PowerSellers (a target market of just 20,000 people who sold the most on the site). Facebook started with just Harvard students, then other US colleges and only later opened it to the general public. Facebook couldn't have succeeded any other way; if it had tried it would have got lost in the noise of all the other social networks of the time.

Peter Thiel, co-founder of PayPal and a guy smart enough to make the first external investment in Facebook, says that all startups should, 'Dominate a small niche and scale up from there, toward your ambitious long-term vision.' In fact it's excellent advice for pretty much any kind of business, as Saskia's story demonstrates.

Superniching what you offer

> *'Innovation is not about saying yes to everything. It's about saying NO to all but the most crucial features.'*
>
> —Steve Jobs

Narrowing the focus of what you do can also be helpful. It's better for your service, product or software to be brilliant at one particular thing people really want than to be vaguely useful for a whole range of things.

If you work with people individually, in groups or in corporations, and you know you can help people with many different needs, it's good to ask yourself what is the one thing you're brilliant at. What's your very favourite thing to help people with? If you've been doing this kind of work already, what do most people seem to keep coming back to you for? What do they refer friends and colleagues to you for? Whatever the answer is for you, it could be the basis of a great niche.

If your software, service or product can be used for lots of different things, what's the *killer use case*? 'Use case' is a term from software design but it's a handy one for all of us, offering something that can be used in a number of different ways. A use case is one particular job a user employs your software to do. The killer use case for Facebook in its Harvard days was apparently being able to check the relationship status of your classmates and flirt with them online! A later killer use case for Facebook was the sharing of photos with friends and family.

When a client tells me they've created an app that can be used in many interesting ways my question is always, 'What's the killer use case? What's the job I can use your app to do better than anything else?' This might be something very small, a real superniche of functionality. For instance, I subscribed to an app called TripIt which compiles your travel plans. But I paid for the Pro version for one simple thing: the automatic addition of flight and hotel bookings to my calendar – thus avoiding the danger of missing a flight simply because I made an error putting the times in my calendar.

What's the killer use case for what *you* provide, whether it's software or a service or some other product?

Evan Williams, co-founder of Twitter, warns against the danger of trying to be too many things to too many people in his

Ten Rules for Web Startups on his blog, evhead.com – and it's excellent advice even if your idea is nothing to do with the web:

> Be Narrow: Focus on the smallest possible problem you could solve that would potentially be useful. Most companies start out trying to do too many things, which makes life difficult and turns you into a me-too. Focusing on a small niche has so many advantages: With much less work, you can be the best at what you do. Small things, like a microscopic world, almost always turn out to be bigger than you think when you zoom in. You can much more easily position and market yourself when more focused. And when it comes to partnering, or being acquired, there's less chance for conflict. This is all so logical and, yet, there's a resistance to focusing. I think it comes from a fear of being trivial. Just remember: If you get to be #1 in your category, but your category is too small, then you can broaden your scope—and you can do so with leverage.

Today's task

- Think about what your superniche could be. Is it a particular market you want to work with or a narrow focus for what you'll provide? How can you niche around what interests you and what you're good at while providing something people want?

Player pointers

This isn't niching for the sake of it. The point is to give yourself an advantage and to avoid competing with larger players with the same broad scope. So make sure you niche on something you have a particular strength in (your spots of genius), that you're interested in and for which there is a demand.

No idea what your niche should be? If you haven't done this kind of work before, the chances are you won't have a clear idea of a niche yet. That's OK. If you're working with clients, groups or organisations, go win your first few pieces of work and see what emerges – what you enjoy most, are best at and which people want. If you're creating an app or product, your approach should be to explore what the smallest most useful thing is that you could create and focus on creating that to start with, then see how people respond.

Not sure about committing to your niche yet? You don't immediately need to change the focus, brand and name of everything you're doing. You can test out a niche first by running a promotion around it. That means running a marketing campaign around a particular topic or market to try to sell a niched offer and seeing how good a response you get. You'll learn how to run a promotion on Day 29.

Workerbot thoughts to challenge

'I don't want to niche because I can't afford to turn people down.' You might fear you'll end up with fewer clients or customers if you specialise but the opposite is more likely. People like specialists. And we'd rather use a service or product that is designed to solve our exact problem than a generalised solution that is a poorer fit. That's why marketing guru and author Al Ries says, 'The power of a brand is inversely proportional to its scope.'

'I don't know what my niche is so I won't do anything just yet.' Nope, that's not going to wash. If you don't know your niche, get out there, do stuff and be useful until you start to notice themes emerging. As always, play it out'don't think it out.

'I'll be bored if all I do is this one small thing.' Firstly, there is always a lot more complexity and variety in any small niche than it might look on the outside. Secondly, this is just to get you started. If it goes well then you can consider expanding your focus. Remember Amazon started as an online bookshop but they didn't stop there. Now they sell anything, they rent web servers to other startups, deliver packages by flying drone and their founder Jeff Bezos has started a space travel company on the side. Not bad for a bookshop.

Week 2 Check-in: How's It Going, Genius?

'It's not that I'm so smart. But I stay with the questions much longer.'

—Albert Einstein, theoretical physicist

So, how has this week gone? It's time to check in and review using the Play Cycle from Day 6. Look at the questions below and make notes in your Playbook.

REFLECT: What happened and what have you learned?

- On how many days did you do a microblock of at least 20 minutes on your project? Remember the aim is to do a minimum of a 20-minute microblock 6 days a week – and tick them all off on the ticksheet.
- In your first check-in a week ago you wrote a list of tasks you were committing to doing. How many did you complete? If you did all of them and you promised yourself a reward, today's the day to take it!
- If you didn't do all your tasks or didn't do six microblocks of time on your project, what happened? No need to beat yourself up here – it really doesn't help! Just be curious. Did you forget? Did you put it off because you thought there's no point starting unless you do more than 20 minutes? Was there a moment when you consciously

decided to skip your microblock? If so, what did you do
with the 20 minutes instead?

- What are the most interesting things you've learned over
  the week, whether it's from working on your project, the
  last seven days' lessons, or your reading list from Day 12?
- How much has your project been hitting the ENERGY,
  GENIUS and VALUE elements from the Playcheque
  Formula this week? How much does this project excite you
  (ENERGY)? How much does it use your spots of GENIUS?
  As you play in public, how much have people shown an
  interest in the things you're sharing and doing (VALUE)?

ADAPT: How can you use what you've discovered?

- If you didn't do all your microblocks, what can you do differently to ensure you do them all this week? Put them in your
  diary with a reminder? Make a commitment to someone
  else? Do them first thing before anything can get in the way?
- If you're having problems keeping your commitments to
  yourself, make them to someone else instead. If you're not
  very self-disciplined, stop imagining that you're suddenly
  going to change. Instead, ask someone to hold you accountable. When you've written your list of commitments for this
  week send them to your new accountability partner and ask
  them to check in seven days whether you did them. You
  could even build in a reward for completion and/or punishment for failure if you like!
- How can you use what you learned last week over the next
  seven days to improve your project and/or the way you work?
- Fine tune your project: Given what you've learned about
  ENERGY, GENIUS and VALUE and the benefits of superniching, how can you tune your project to focus on the things
  you enjoy, are good at and that people appreciate? Keep iterating to increase these elements and you can't help but succeed.

ACT again: what will you do next week?

It's time to set your commitments for your third week on your project. Open your Playbook and write the following:

- *'By the next check-in on Day 21 I will ... '* and then list the things you are absolutely committed to doing.
- *'I also want to ... '* List the things you'd like to do but can't guarantee you'll manage. It's good to be clear which things are definite commitments and which are not.
- Check your diary to make sure that you can do what you've promised yourself and write in the time for your microblocks.
- Share your commitments with others if you can – declare them on Facebook to your friends or post your top commitments to Twitter or Instagram with the hashtag #screwworkbreakfree (and take a look to see what others are committing to).

If you find you've hit a bit of a slump, tomorrow we'll get you back on track. Meanwhile, take some inspiration from the story below about what happens when it all goes right ...

DJ and club promoter Sean Rowley on noticing when you have a hit on your hands

There are sure to be plenty of setbacks along the way on your entrepreneurial journey but it's also important to recognise when you might have just hit the jackpot. DJ Sean Rowley was presenting live on BBC Radio when he accidentally discovered a hit concept that he then turned into a brand, a successful club night and a series of compilation albums.

I'd just started hosting my own radio show on BBC Radio London on a Tuesday evening. And it was a joy to be able to play whatever I wanted to and not be restricted by a playlist. But not long into it the head of the radio station called me into a meeting and told me, 'You're just a bit too out there with your music choices. You need to play some more familiar choices.' I remember leaving the meeting disappointed and thinking, 'This isn't me, I don't want to be Tony Blackburn playing mainstream music.'

But I went away and thought about it and realised there was all this old pop music, like David Cassidy, 10CC, Queen and ELO, that I'd bought as a child that I still loved. And a phrase from a friend of mine popped into my head from when we'd been listening to an old song by Wings; he'd described the track as 'a bit of a guilty pleasure'. And I thought that's what these old, supposedly unfashionable records are – guilty pleasures.

So I went on the air next week and said, 'I'm going to do something a little bit different now; I'm going to play a record that I would call a guilty pleasure,' and I played an old record from the 70s by ELO. And the switchboard just lit up. I thought, 'Oh no, they're all calling to complain. What was I thinking? What am I doing playing this cheesy old stuff?!'

But in fact it was the exact opposite. They were calling to say, 'I love this record! And what about this one as well ... ' Everyone wanted to confess to their guilty pleasures – records they loved but had been too ashamed to admit it because the music was no longer deemed to be cool. My producer said, 'I've never seen anything like this!'

So we went from playing one or two guilty pleasure records each week to eventually doing a full two-hour guilty pleasures show. Later I started to play these records at a festival and the reaction was incredible. I knew I was on to something.

Sean could have seen the response from his radio listeners as curious and not very important. I see many beginning entrepreneurs make exactly this mistake, writing off an unusually good response to something they do as no big deal. Then they go back to what they were doing before as if nothing had happened. Luckily Sean pays attention and he recognised the response he was getting as meaning he'd accidentally hit on something with huge VALUE to people. So he took the guilty pleasures concept and ran with it. He created a Guilty Pleasures club night that has been running for a decade with up to 1,800 attendees, released two compilation albums and helped create a spin-off TV show.

So when, one day, a post on your blog gets a much bigger reaction than usual or everyone wants to hire you to do something you never considered to be very important, pay attention.

Read more about Sean Rowley and Guilty Pleasures at www. guiltypleasures.co.uk.

Watch my interview with Sean in his record library at home at www.screwworkbreakfree.com.

WEEK 3

Dissolving Obstacles

If you're getting stuck on your project, this week will sort you out as we dive into the internal and external obstacles that get in the way of success and learn how to dissolve them.

The Mid-Project Slump: What to Do When You Don't Feel Like Doing Anything

'You'll come down from the Lurch/with an unpleasant bump./And the chances are, then, that you'll be in a Slump./ And when you're in a Slump,/you're not in for much fun./ Un-slumping yourself is not easily done.'

—Dr Seuss, *Oh, the Places You'll Go*

So, here we are at the halfway point in your project. It's at this point you might find things start to unravel a little. So if you're finding yourself flagging, losing motivation, procrastinating or hitting the doldrums, rest assured this is not unusual; you're just in the mid-project slump.

If you're finding yourself flagging, losing motivation, or procrastinating, rest assured this is not unusual; you're just in the mid-project slump

---

The going gets tough about halfway through. At the beginning it's all excitement and possibility and at the end you have the finish line in sight and the pressure of a deadline. But the middle ... the middle is trickier. As Harvard Business School professor Rosabeth Moss Kanter says, 'Everything feels like a failure in the middle.'

In the classic three-act structure of a play or movie, we're now into Act Two where the hero (that's you!) is forced to battle all manner of setbacks. People struggle with this halfway point in different forms. It challenges our commitment, our stamina, our fear of the unknown and our ability to keep ourselves motivated. And it brings out our *Top Dog*. 'Top Dog' is Gestalt psychology's name for that critical inner voice that says 'This will never work' or 'You messed *that* up!' or 'Who are you to think you can pull this off?' and it loves to strike when you're feeling most vulnerable.

When you've hit this point in the past, you may have given up and walked away because you didn't know what else to do. Let's make this time different. You're a player now. Players learn how to *deal* with this mid-project slump. Learning what to do to get yourself out of it will be one of the best discoveries you can make.

Every creator, inventor and entrepreneur has at some point faced these moments of doubt, setback and far worse. Thomas Edison said about inventing, 'The first step is an intuition – and comes with a burst – *then* difficulties arise.' In the early days of Elon Musk's space-rocket company, SpaceX, so many of their rockets blew up during testing that, instead of calling them explosions, Elon and the team coined the tongue-in-cheek acronym RUD, meaning 'Rapid Unscheduled Disassembly'. The company eventually solved their problems and went on to conduct 25 successful launches and win contracts with NASA and other organisations around the world worth over $10 billion.

Richard Branson may look like an entrepreneur without a care in the world but he too has had his trials by fire. During the 1980s, in the midst of launching his airline and running his record label and stores, Richard Branson came home to a nasty surprise.

From triumph to crisis

Richard Branson describes in *Losing My Virginity* the moment in 1984 when he returned from the triumphant inaugural flight of Virgin Atlantic to find his bank manager sitting on his doorstep …

As we pulled up at my house I saw a rather uncomfortable-looking man was sitting on the steps. At first I thought he was a journalist, but then I realised that it was Christopher Rashbrook, my account manager at Coutts. I invited him in, and he sat down in the sitting room. I was exhausted and he was fidgety. I was rather slow to understand what he was saying. But then I suddenly heard him say that Coutts were unable to extend Virgin's overdraft as requested and would therefore regrettably bounce any cheques that took our overdraft over £3 million. I rarely lose my temper – in fact I can count the times I have lost my temper on the fingers of one hand – but as I looked across at this man in his blue pinstripe suit with his neat little black leather briefcase I felt my blood boil. He was standing there in his highly polished black Oxford brogues and calmly telling me that he was going to put the whole of Virgin out of business. I thought of the numerous times since March when I and the Virgin Atlantic staff had worked through the night to solve a problem; I thought about how proud the new cabin crew were to be flying with a startup airline; and I thought about the protracted negotiation we had fought with Boeing. If this bank manager bounced our cheques, then Virgin would be out of business within days: nobody would supply an airline with anything such as fuel or food or maintenance if word went about that the cheques were bouncing. And no passengers would fly with us. 'Excuse me,' I said as he was still making excuses. 'You are not welcome in my house. Please get out.' I took him by the arm, led him to the front door and pushed him outside. I shut the door in his bewildered face, walked back into the sitting room and collapsed on a sofa in tears of exhaustion, frustration and worry. Then I had a shower upstairs and called Ken [Berry, Virgin executive]: 'We've got to get as much money in from overseas as possible today. And then we've got to find new bankers.'

Richard and his team rushed into action to pull in enough money from his record business that week to keep them just below the £3 million overdraft limit. That meant Coutts had no reason to bounce their cheques, and so the entire Virgin group was saved from ruin.

Creating anything – whether it's a business, a book, a service, an app or a TV show – is challenging. At some point you're going to hit a setback or simply come up against your own doubts and demons. This is exactly why most people don't even try. They're happy to spend their days working unfulfilling jobs, watching TV and scrolling through Facebook.

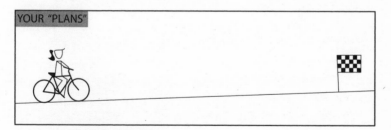

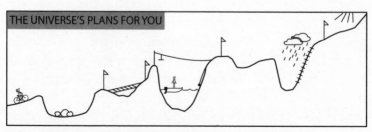

Cartoon from www.thedoghousediaries.com used with permission

What you're facing is a test; not a test of whether your idea works or whether you've chosen the right thing. This is a test of your *mettle*. You're in the midst of one of the most worthwhile challenges life has to offer. Not whether you can make money or get your marketing right or choose the right target audience – or even whether you'll have to give up, slink away and go back to your day job.

This is much much bigger than that.

This is about you deciding to find out what you're made of, what lies dormant inside you. It's about finding out who you are, what you can create that only *you* can create and what impact you can have on the world.

This is an adventure in finding life's meaning – an adventure every bit as great as finding your life partner or raising children. What can you give to the world? What are you willing to go up against in order to give it? Can you stare down embarrassment, failure and the risk of loss to get there?

Because if you can, you've made yourself into an entrepreneur – the kind of entrepreneur who goes on to have a life that other people look at and say, 'Wow, I wish I was lucky enough to have a life like yours.' And when that happens you are fully allowed to laugh out loud at them – because you know it has very little to do with luck and a very large amount to do with bravery and plain old stubbornness to damn well not give in.

When you find a way to pick yourself up and carry on you'll discover something really interesting; the mid-project slump is your friend. You'll look back at the hurdle you just vaulted, burrowed under or ran around and see all the other people who balked and quit. Then you'll understand that coming up with ideas is easy but few people have the drive to actually make them happen. And that makes those of us who do all the more valuable.

Psychologists are just starting to realise the importance of this ability to persist in the face of challenges. American psychologist Angela Duckworth has termed it 'grit' and has been studying its impact for 13 years. She has concluded that, 'If it's important for you to become one of the best people in your

field, you are going to have to stick with it when it's hard ...
Grit may be as essential as talent to high accomplishment.'

If your grit seems to have gone missing right now, let's get
you back on track. Here are four tasks for today to help:

Today's tasks

- ## The instant procrastination fix

  'The real enemy of success isn't failure. It's inertia.'
  —Barbara Winter, author of *Making a Living Without a Job*

  The mid-project slump sometimes sneaks up on you. You
  find yourself getting distracted and doing something seemingly very important – updating all your apps, watering
  all your pot plants or perhaps tidying your sock drawer –
  instead of actually doing what is most important on your
  project. Perhaps you've found you've missed your microblock for a day or two and now you just can't face getting
  back into it. You're in procrastination town.

  What's the solution? It's not to wait for inspiration or
  even try to get yourself in the mood. It's to use the Swiss
  cheese approach:

  1. Just grab your kitchen timer or timer app and set it for
     ten minutes.
  2. Grab something related to your project, start the count-
     down and dive in.
  3. If you can't decide what's most important to do, start
     anywhere. If you want to clear your spare room piled
     with clutter, to turn it into your office, walk in and pick
     up the first five things you can find and deal with them.
  4. When the timer goes off, you have full permission to quit.
  5. Do the same again tomorrow and the next day until
     you're back into the swing of it.

Time-management specialist, Alan Lakein, named this the Swiss cheese approach; keep picking holes in any task no matter how large or unpleasant and eventually it will start to look more manageable.

When you don't know where to start, start anywhere

Sometimes those ten minutes will feel very unpleasant indeed – particularly if Top Dog chimes in with messages like, 'I should have done this ages ago' or 'This isn't going to work anyway' – but you'll usually find that once you've got over the pain of re-entry and worked for ten minutes (or several batches of ten minutes), the worst is over. I still use the Swiss cheese method for the tasks I feel the highest resistance to (either getting started on very large projects like redrafting an entire book or very dull projects like bookkeeping). Because sometimes, in the words of Ernest Hemingway, 'The shortest answer is doing the thing.'

- **Lost your drive? Get connected**

Often when you find yourself demotivated it's because you're disconnected. It's very hard to stay motivated on your own. If you're working on your project alone, find a community to plug into, learn from and get support from. Look on meetup.com for meet-ups related to your topic near you. Join a course that will teach you something while also placing you in a room with people on a similar path. Join the conversation with others following this book on social media – search for the hashtag #screwworkbreakfree. For more ways to get connected and to learn about my group programmes, such as The Screw Work 30-day Challenge, go to www.screwworkbreakfree.com.

- **Make it fun**

  If you're not enjoying yourself on your project right now, is there a way to make it more fun? Perhaps there's a way to change it to suit your personality better? If you're a people person who's found yourself stuck behind a computer, see if you can change your approach to give you more contact with others. What would make your project a little more fresh and enjoyable for you? As IBM founder Thomas Watson says, 'If you aren't playing well, the game isn't as much fun. When that happens I tell myself just to go out and play as I did when I was a kid.'

- **Engage others to do the bits you hate**

  Whether it's doing the figures, sorting the tech out, designing your brand or selling your service, there will be someone who actually loves doing that stuff. Perhaps it's a friend who can get involved with your project or you could hire someone at peopleperhour.com, fiverr.com or 99designs.com.

Player pointers

Whatever happens, always fall back to microblocking. Yes, it's good to do longer sessions of work on your project when you have time but when you're busy or your enthusiasm seems to have abandoned you, turn up and do 20 minutes regardless. That will prevent your project from stalling. To quote Confucius, 'It doesn't matter how slow you go as long as you do not stop.'

Workerbot thoughts to challenge

'This project isn't going well, I should switch to another one.' When you hit the slump, you may be tempted to switch project. After all, you have this other great idea, another Play Project that you could have or should have started, and it looks problem free! But don't fall for this. Every project turns into hard work at some point, even that shiny new one, and you've just got to get through it and produce something. WD40 is the famous water-displacement spray found in 80 per cent of homes in the US. If you've ever wondered what the name means, it was chosen by its inventor Norm Larsen back in 1953 for it being the fortieth attempt to create a water-displacement spray. It's fortunate they persisted; over 60 years later, the WD40 product range makes $378 million a year.

Paul Graham gave a talk to his cohort of fledgling startups at Y Combinator where he addressed the mid-project slump directly:

> So I'll tell you now: bad shit is coming. It always is in a startup. The odds of getting from launch to liquidity without some kind of disaster happening are one in a thousand. So don't get demoralized. When the disaster strikes, just say to yourself, ok, this was what Paul was talking about. What did he say to do? Oh, yeah. Don't give up.

Keep going and continually reflect and adapt your project to maximise the ENERGY, GENIUS and VALUE elements to make it both fun and successful. We'll learn more about this on Day 20.

The Perfectionist Challenge

*'Perfectionism is a 20-ton shield that we lug around
thinking it will protect us, when, in fact, it's the thing
that's really preventing us from taking flight.'*

– Brené Brown

Attention to detail is a great talent but when it strays into perfectionism that stops you finishing things and releasing them to the world, it is no longer helping you. Perfectionism is driven by the belief that if we get everything 'just right', then no one will be able to criticise it, least of all our own internal critic or Top Dog. The problem, of course, is that Top Dog always finds something to fault anyway! You could *always* have 'done it better'. Or it barks that you should have done it quicker. That's why author Anne Lamott says that, 'Perfectionism is the voice of the oppressor.'

Sometimes you just have to stop trying to placate your Top Dog and make friends with imperfection. Dare to dash something out that is good enough. When Top Dog growls, just sing out, 'Don't worry, be crappy!'

Version one is better than version none

If you have countless ideas and projects that you've never started or never finished because they weren't quite right, don't repeat the same pattern this time round. Get it done and get it out there. You can always improve on the next version or the next release. Remember, this is just version 1.0. As co-founder of LinkedIn, Reid Hoffman, says: 'If you're not embarrassed by the first version of your product, then you've launched too late.' The first version of LinkedIn launched in 2003 with limited functionality and attracted as few as 20 sign-ups a day. Ten years later it had 225 million members and is now growing at more than 150,000 a day. You have to start somewhere.

Whatever it is you're doing, your first version, first event, first performance or first project won't be perfect. Take your very best shot but get it done. Then you can iterate – go again and make it better. Kanye West's well-known perfectionist streak has previously delayed albums and even entire tours so for his 2016 album *Life of Pablo* he decided to release it online as a beta version, describing it on Twitter as a 'living breathing changing creative expression'. He has updated tracks on the album several times since then.

If you often hold back for a fear of not reaching perfection, why not try doing something different today and take my perfectionist challenge?

Today's task: the perfectionist challenge

'Done is better than perfect'
>   —poster on the walls of Facebook head office

- If your inner perfectionist is holding you to ransom I have a challenge for you today in two steps:
  1. Do something that you think is mediocre, rushed, imperfect, not good enough to show the world and then ...
  2. SHOW THE WORLD ANYWAY. Release it!

Have fun abandoning perfection for a day: go and take a hundred photos in an afternoon and put a bunch on Instagram, write a quick blog post and publish it without obsessing over it, take a video of yourself with your phone without planning out exactly what you're going to say or use a service like strikingly.com to build a one-page website in a couple of hours.

If you've made some good progress on your project but have held back from showing any of it until it's perfect, dare to clean it up just enough to share something of it *today*. You can always go back and improve whatever you share in another iteration or simply release more and more, watching your work get better as you go.

You might find you're surprised by just what you can create without trying to be perfect. Perhaps it will even be better than some of your more laboured work, just as musicians sometimes find that the professionally finished studio track loses some of the freshness and energy of the imperfect demo track. And the thing you dashed off in an hour or two sometimes gets more appreciation from your audience, users or market than the things you spent many weeks on! **Share it!**

Once you've got something ready today, share it with others – show your friends on Facebook or tweet it or Instagram it. You can share it with other people following this book by posting on Instagram or Twitter with the hashtag #screwworkbreakfree.

To inspire you, here's a fantastic example of ditching perfectionism and reaping the rewards:

The award-winning product company that started production under a street light

One of my favourite companies for fun gifts is Suck UK, the award-winning organisation founded by design graduates Sam Hurt and Jude Biddulph. Their range includes all sorts of quirky products, like an umbrella that changes colour in the rain, a laundry bag that doubles as a punch bag and corks that turn empty wine bottles into lamps.

Looking today at their flagship stores and beautifully packaged products, you would never guess the origins of the company back in 1999 when they had no money, no premises and no real plan. Sam told me the remarkable story of how they put aside perfectionism and worked with the little they had available:

Jude was working in a garden centre and I was working in a record shop when we ran into each other. Jude asked me, 'Do you really want to work in a record shop the rest of your life?' We never sat down and thought let's start a business. We just started getting together in pubs, drinking too much and talking about what we could do in design.

We quickly realised you can't sell a design, you have to make stuff. So we decided, let's make things and sell them. I guess you could call that our business plan! So then it was, 'OK, what should we make?' We can make soap. That's easy. You just buy buckets of liquid soap and mix it together and we'd make bars of soap in moulds. We can also make candles quite easily. The first 20 things we did failed. We spent days making Christmas tree decorations and then didn't sell a single one of them because to be honest they were kind of horrible.

We were working on all this in the evenings after our day job, often going late into the night. Our workshop was the kitchen floor in my shared flat. Some of our flatmates didn't take kindly to us using power tools in the kitchen at three o'clock in the morning. So we had to run an extension lead out of the kitchen window down on to the street so that we could crouch under a street light and continue to carve metal and drill holes in things.

The first product we thought had some potential to sell was an unusual design of waste-paper bin. It's a bit of a weird product to even consider launching a company on, which I guess was what we were doing in retrospect. The bin was made by wrapping the frame in a special kind of metallic foil and then sucking the air out using a machine we'd found while rifling through the classified ads – a vacuum machine normally used for vacuum-packing fish.

We knew we wanted to sell things in shops so we had to figure out how that works. We found out that shops have buyers, people who are responsible for buying in the stock and making decisions about what they do and don't want to sell. So we'd take our notebooks and go spend hours sitting on the floor of WHSmith going through magazines like Elle Decoration and Country Living. And we'd write down the names and addresses of the shop buyers which were in the back of the magazines – because we couldn't actually afford to buy the magazines.

Now we had a list of contacts that we wanted to try and sell these things to. And we'd drive around in the car and drop off samples, literally, just jump out of the car and run into reception and leave a couple of boxes with the bin in it and a little note saying, 'We thought you might be interested in this'.

The problem was the bin was universally hated by everyone we gave it to. Really, not a kind word to say from anybody. People phoned us and said 'Can you please take this thing away? It's offensive.' I admit it was a bit odd; it looked like some kind of bondage equipment!

We kept making things and finally we managed to sell one or two. But otherwise we had so little success that we decided to fork out 350 quid to get a tiny little booth at a design expo. We had 20-odd objects, things that we had made models or prototypes of by hand. We put our smartest clothes on, and we took all our prototypes to this exhibition stand that was like two metres by two metres that we had for three days, and we put them all up. And we put prices next to them. Then we stood there with clipboards and we tried to sell these products to people who had shops.

People assumed they were products we'd already produced and that were ready to buy when in fact they were just proto-types for things we hadn't manufactured yet. Strictly speaking we didn't lie, we just didn't mention it! People were like, 'How much are these?' And we'd be like, 'Well, they're 25 pounds each. How many do you want?' 'I'll take six.' 'Well, fantastic. We'll take your order for six of those.' But really we had noth-ing. It was like being an ice-cream salesman and not really having any ice cream! We had to rush back and actually start making the stuff.

That was the start of their business. Today, 17 years after their nights of welding under a street light, they now have an office in Hackney with 25 staff, a great range of products sold all over the world and stores in OXO Tower and Westfield. All this despite their only goal being, as Sam describes it, 'to get out of our day jobs'.

You can see all of Suck UK's innovative and playful products at www.suck.uk.com.

If Sam and Jude had waited until they had the perfect idea for a product or the means to build it perfectly they might still be working in dead-end jobs. Instead, they just kept making stuff over and over again, learning on the go, until they cracked it and produced products that people loved.

And it goes to show that if you take something that has ENERGY for you and use some of your GENIUS spots, then you can get to VALUE if you just keeping taking action and listening to feedback to improve what you're doing.

Create Your Website
in One Evening

*'Every first draft is perfect, because all a first draft has to
do is exist.'*

– Jane Smiley, Pulitzer Prize-winning novelist

By this point in your project you may be wanting your own blog or website – either as a promotional tool for what you're doing or as a central part of it (for example, a website you will charge to be a member of).

I meet a lot of people who have reached this point and they are often really stressed out about it. Perhaps you are too. You want to do your website properly – to get the design and content just right so you can give the right message. You may also be worrying about choosing the perfect name for your site. These are understandable concerns. And they can stop you in your tracks. I've met people who have gone without a website for years because they couldn't decide how to approach it all. How long have you been putting it off?

The problem with all this delaying is that meanwhile you have no website! That is a big mistake. As long as you don't have a website (or at least something I can point at), I can't easily refer people to you, I can't tweet the interesting project or client you told me about because you don't have anywhere for me to point people to.

So here is my clever solution for your website conundrums:

STICK THE DAMN THING UP NOW!

That's right, just get something up because here's the great thing about websites: they're editable! They're not written in stone or even paper. They're not the same as designing a brochure that you're going to print 10,000 copies of. You can't edit a poster after it's printed but you can edit a website.

What this means is that it's entirely OK to chuck your website up today and improve it tomorrow. Now, I'm not suggesting you throw up some mess of a site but the fact is that with the wonders of WordPress and cheap page builders, you can actually create something in a couple of hours that looks really good.

Here's my second top tip:

DO LESS BUT DO IT WELL

Don't lay out some sophisticated menu structure with 14 pages and sub-pages that you then have to fill in before you can go live with the site. You can simply choose four pages (for example, Home, Blog, About, Contact) with one or two paragraphs of text each and get it up. Beware in particular writing reams of prose in a word processor to paste into the site. Your pages will end up a mile long on screen and no one will want to plough through it.

Hide any pages you might have created where it currently says 'This page still under development' and go live with it right now!

Even easier, you could make it a one-page site. If you're looking to simply have something that describes you and the one thing you are launching right now, this is actually a very good option. Try using Strikingly.com, Instapage.com or another page builder that allows you to make a very good-looking site quickly and easily. What you end up with is a single long page that has sections covering everything you want to include – introduction, what you do, about you, contact details, social media links etc.

Here's an important reminder:

NO ONE WILL SEE YOUR EARLY SITE!

Another reason not to fret about your website at the beginning is that no one is actually going to see it when you first put it up (unless you point them to it). It won't even appear on Google for a while (until other people link to it).

Just make sure that if anyone did stumble across your site, it won't embarrass you. So delete the bit where you wrote, 'Insert some nonsense here' and then go live.

This is called a 'Soft Launch' in the website business – the site is visible but it doesn't matter too much if it's not perfect yet because you haven't pointed anyone to it.

Here's another surprising tip:

YOU WILL THROW THIS WEBSITE AWAY

At some point, much sooner than you imagine, you will change the design, content, focus and probably even the name of your website or blog. And you may even choose to dump it and start something else entirely.

This is particularly true when you are just starting out on your entrepreneurial or creative adventure because a huge amount of work at the beginning is to discover what it is you are actually trying to do. And that means your market, your message and even your business changes.

The business you start is never the business you end up succeeding with. It evolves. And that's even more reason to get something up as soon as possible.

The business you start is never the business you end up succeeding with. It evolves. And so will your website.

How to build your site

My recommended method for building your website or blog depends on how comfortable you are with using online systems. If you're really tech-phobic, the easiest blogging systems are probably WordPress.com or blogger.com (both free).

If you want something more like a website than a blog, there are several easy website builders available, like Squarespace and Weebly, but my favourite for quick websites is now the one-page website builders, like strikingly.com and instapage. com. Strikingly produces gorgeous sites very quickly. Instapage is similar but a little more business-oriented and better for building sales pages. Find my latest recommendations at www. screwworkbreakfree.com.

If you want complete ownership and control over your blog or website so that you can add anything you want to it and make it the centre of your business, my recommendation is self-hosted WordPress.

'Self-hosted' means that you pay for your own domain name and web-hosting (costing as little as $8 a month) and install a version of WordPress on it. Fortunately, that is not as complicated as it sounds because, if you use my recommended web-hosts, much of it is automatic. Read step-by-step instructions at www.screwworkbreakfree.com.

Today's tasks

- Do today's microblock and tick it off. Why not use it today to start your website – perhaps just a one-pager to get you started? Grab a coffee (or something stronger), check my latest recommendations and guides at www.screwwork-breakfree.com and dive in. You can make a real start in just 20 minutes.

Player pointers

What if I don't know the name of my business or website yet?
Accept that any name you choose now is likely to change somewhere down the line anyway so there's no point waiting for the perfect name. You can change the domain name (i.e. the website address) for your website later, when you think of a new one. Just register the new domain name and then there will be a couple of settings to change with your web-hosting company. Their support department should be able to help you. Worst-case scenario, you'll need to pay someone on peopleperhour. com $25–50 to change the domain over.

Workerbot thoughts to challenge

'I had better put my formal voice on for writing my website text.' Please don't switch into business-speak when describing yourself and your project. Write as you speak. And don't pretend you're a giant corporation when it's just you – don't write, 'We have five years of experience' when what you actually mean is, '*I* have five years of experience'.

Feedback, Critics and Trolls

'By the time I was 14, the nail in my wall would no longer support the weight of the rejection slips impaled upon it. I replaced the nail with a spike and went on writing.'

—Stephen King, bestselling author

Fun with feedback

'Knowledge speaks but wisdom listens.'

—Jimi Hendrix, rock icon

If you want to create something successful you need to not just be open to feedback, but actively seek it out. It's feedback and responses from your target market or audience that feed the Play Cycle and allow you to keep improving what you're doing.

Each time you work with a client, look carefully at the responses you're getting. When you publish blog and social media posts, notice which ones get the biggest response. Feedback is a natural result of playing in public but if you're feeling brave, you can actively seek it out by opening up a direct channel of communication with your users, readers, listeners or buyers.

As valuable as feedback is, it can be difficult to hear. As Gloria Steinem said, 'The truth will set you free, but first it will piss you off.' Opening yourself up to feedback from all and sundry too early in the process could be demotivating but as you get more confident you can start to invite more feedback. In order to be able to hear feedback on your project you must separate your self-worth from how your project is received. You are more than this project. If you've entered a new area you're passionate about and the feedback at first is not good, that doesn't mean you should immediately give up and change to something else. Be willing to invest the time and energy to improve.

Separate your self-worth from how your project is received

There is also no point evaluating the output of your project in progress on the same terms as a finished product. Right now you're working on version 1.0. Don't expect it to match up to more established products and services. This goes for books too. I developed my own rule while writing this book: 'Never compare your first draft to anyone's final draft (even your own)'.

Never compare your first draft to anyone's final draft (even your own)

If you're ready for more feedback take inspiration from cartoonist Scott Adams who took the dramatic step of publishing his private email address in newspapers:

The spark in the gasoline for the *Dilbert* comic strip

Scott Adams' *Dilbert* comic strip sold to a few dozen newspapers at its launch but within a year sales to newspapers had stalled. Scott felt he needed a direct communication channel with his readers, something normally not available to newspaper cartoonists. So he took the surprising decision in the early 1990s to publish his email address right in the margins of each strip, allowing any reader to give their opinion to him directly.

The feedback from readers was eye-opening, as he describes in his book, *How to Fail at Almost Everything and Still Win Big*:

> *The turning point for Dilbert came in 1993 after I started printing my e-mail address in the margins of the strip. It was the first time I could see unfiltered opinions about my work. Until then I'd relied on the opinions of friends and business associates, and that had limited value because that group of folks rarely offered criticism.*
>
> *But wow, the general public doesn't hold back. They were savage about my art skills—no surprise—and that was just the tip of the hateberg. But I noticed a consistent theme that held for both the fans and the haters: They all preferred the comics in which Dilbert was in the office. So I changed the focus of the strip to the workplace, and that turned out to be the spark in the gasoline.*

Dilbert went on to be sold into 2,000 newspapers in 57 countries.

Scott got some very blunt feedback because he was already well known and the public tends to be hardest on the people who are most successful. As a beginner or fledgling business, you're unlikely to hear such harsh words but it can still be painful to hear what people have to say, no matter how carefully it is phrased. If you can hear and act on feedback, though, you'll be able to steer your project for the limelight.

The tumbleweed moment

Sometimes the worst feedback is silence. You do your big launch, drop your biggest gag or announce your exciting new direction. Then you stand back to be greeted by ... well, nothing but tumbleweeds rolling by.

Paul Graham of Y Combinator gave some great advice on the tumbleweed moment in a speech to the group of startups on Y Combinator's legendary accelerator programme. Although it's aimed at tech startups it's actually great advice for any venture:

> Another feeling that seems alarming but is in fact normal in a startup is the feeling that what you're doing isn't working. The reason you can expect to feel this is that what you do probably won't work. Startups almost never get it right the first time. Much more commonly you launch something, and no one cares. Don't assume when this happens that you've failed. That's normal for startups. But don't sit around doing nothing. Iterate.

Your aim, Paul says, should be to try to

> make something that at least someone really loves. As long as you've made something that a few users are ecstatic about, you're on the right track ... So when you release something and it seems like no one cares, look more closely. Are there zero users who really love you, or is there at least some little group that does?

And if it really is zero the solution is simply to REFLECT, ADAPT and then ACT again. Sometimes you'll realise you need to get better at what you're doing. Sometimes you'll recognise a need to bring in some extra expertise. Or perhaps you've been aiming at the wrong audience. We'll look at what the problem is and how to fix it tomorrow.

Dealing with critics and haters

'If nobody hates you, you're doing something wrong.'
—Hugh Laurie as Gregory House, in the TV series *House MD*

Some kinds of feedback are particularly difficult to hear. One is a critical review: a considered but negative review or a complaint by someone who has experienced your service or product.

Your first response, no matter how calm and collected you consider yourself, is likely to be a mix of anger, defensiveness and hurt. The most important thing is not to respond while in the first flush of emotion. Resist the temptation to immediately hit reply and start furiously typing to angrily defend yourself (or even to acquiesce to all their criticism). Leave it a few hours, talk to some other people about it, then see what might be useful for you to absorb. Is there a piece of truth within this? If so, sometimes the best response is to admit that you could have done better and take steps to make amends.

Complaints and negative reviews are sometimes the results of a mismatch of expectations. Someone buys a product or a book from Amazon and then writes a scathing review because they'd assumed the product to be useful for a purpose for which it wasn't intended.

Check your marketing and messaging around your product or service; have you made it clear who it is for and what they can expect out of it? When you've done this you may wish to respond to the critical review, acknowledging any points that you consider to have some value but also clarifying what someone should expect from your product.

Then there are the haters – a whole different species of animal. These are people who do not leave considered reviews but instead are utterly damning of your product or service and usually hide behind anonymity. If someone writes nothing positive and seems full of anger, then you have a hater. Never try to change a hater's mind as they are often driven by a desire for attention – 'don't feed the trolls', as the Internet forum maxim goes. It is usually best to stay out of the way and let the positive reviews from other people outnumber the small number of negative ones. If someone misrepresents your work, however, or says something defamatory it can be worth responding in case other prospective buyers assume the critical review is accurate.

Remember this about haters: it isn't personal. They might be saying bad things about you but if their response seems extreme, it's because something they see in you or your project has triggered one of their issues. If you have any sensitivity a hateful comment, review or complaint is going to feel bad to receive. You may be disturbed or distracted for a few hours or more but think on this: people who are regularly damning in their criticism do that not just with others but with themselves. You live with their negativity for a moment, they have to live with it every hour of every day. They are often, in fact, blocked creatives who channel all their creative energy into anonymously taking down others' work instead of being brave enough to create their own. You may be tempted to say something to hurt them back but there is no need; haters are their own punishment.

Haters are their own punishment

You tend not to see any nasty reviews or haters in the beginning. You only attract them once you've made a mark. So when you see your first hater, congratulations, you've arrived!

Steve Jobs and the ultimate putdown for critics

The greater your impact on the world the more criticism you'll experience. No one writes hate pieces about unknown novels and albums, only about the famous ones.

So just imagine how much criticism came Steve Jobs' way at Apple.

While he valued feedback from customers and often passed their emails around to others in Apple, he had less patience for opinionated critics. In 2010 Ryan Tate, a writer at gossip blog Gawker, was irritated late one night by watching an Apple ad describing the iPad as 'a revolution'. With a cocktail by his side, he shot off a spiky email to Steve Jobs' personal email address (which was fairly well known to the press at the time).

As Ryan tells the story on Gawker.com, three hours later, at nearly one am, Jobs replied and the two got into a heated email debate about the iPad being a closed system tightly controlled by Apple.

Steve passionately defended his philosophy on the iPad and the reasoning behind it during the course of a ten-email exchange. Finally he ended the conversation with this line:

By the way, what have you done that's so great?
Do you create anything, or just criticize others' work and belittle their motivations?

It's always easier to critique than to create. Feedback is valuable but you don't have to bow to every person with an opinion.

Today's tasks

- Pay attention to the feedback you're already getting – the responses to social media and blog posts, the spontaneous comments from readers/clients/customers. What is it telling you about how to adapt your project?
- If you're ready to hear more feedback you can accelerate the Play Cycle by seeking it out. Share more of your project publicly and notice the reactions. Give a talk about your

ideas. Put an early prototype in front of some friendly users. Share some of your book as blog posts and see what response you get. Ask people who have used your product or service how they liked it. No need for elaborate surveys; a quick but personal email will often get more responses.

Player pointers

Your customers can tell you what's working and what's not working but take their advice on how to fix it with a pinch of salt. How you solve the problems they identify with your project is really up to you.

Remember the best feedback of all is people paying for what you do. That's great if it's actual monetary payment but it could also be paying with their time and energy or by recommending you. They'll only do that if they see the value.

How to Get Traction

*'Success in most things depends on knowing how
long it takes to succeed.'*

—Montesquieu, French philosopher

I
f you've been diligently microblocking and producing stuff
and putting it out but all you're getting back is a giant, collective 'meh', today you're going to see how to make your idea
click into place and finally get traction.

What's traction? It's that moment when your wheels have
been spinning, you've been going nowhere and then suddenly
the rubber bites the road and you're off. So, if you feel like
you're still spinning your wheels, let's debug what's happening
using the Playcheque Formula.

Check the foundations

Traction happens when you hit the VALUE element of the
Playcheque Formula. So, if you don't feel like you're getting anywhere, we need to work out why you haven't yet found that element.

Let's start at the bottom; how much ENERGY are you
putting into it? You can't do one blog post a month, halfheart-
edly mention your service to a few people or put an unenticing
listing of your event up and expect the world to throw themselves
at your feet. You have to put the work in. Sorry, but even Tim
Ferriss doesn't work four hours a week. If you're not putting
lots of ENERGY into something you can't expect to get a lot of
energy back from people.

But what if you're slogging away and still nothing is happening? Then we need to check, are you using your spots of GENIUS? If you're starting something new, that's quite different from your previous work, you need time to get good at what you're doing. Keep producing, keep shipping, keep working for free if necessary, until you get there. Even better, if you can find a way to include in your project some of the skills and knowledge you've built up over the years, that can make a big difference.

So what if you're putting in the effort and you're bringing some real skills, talent or knowledge to your project and still no one is biting? Well, then you might not be far off. Let's dive in and see if with a little tweaking we can hit the VALUE element and send you shooting off into the distance.

Four questions to help tweak your project to get traction

A common mistake beginning entrepreneurs make is that they offer something that appears to be somewhere in an area of need but the actual offer they're promoting is vague and doesn't hit a real need or desire that people have, so they don't hit the VALUE element. Often the beginner's response is to try to throw more traffic at the failing offer – with advertising, social media or Search Engine Optimisation (SEO) tweaks to get found on Google. But if zero per cent of people care about what you're offering, throwing a million new visitors at it isn't going to help.

Here are four questions to explore that will help you get really specific about where the value is in what you're doing and how to adjust your project to hit the bullseye. Not all of them are relevant to all projects. Some suit practical products and services, others are more applicable to art and experiences. See which ones resonate with you for your project.

1. Who's your avatar?

Some business experts would criticise me for not talking about who your target market is until halfway through this book. Seth Godin says 'Don't find customers for your products, find products for your customers.' This is true once you've got into the swing of entrepreneurship, you've clarified your market and you know what to create next that they will love.

However, in my experience, most people at the beginning of the entrepreneurial journey don't have a clear conception of their customer, client, buyer or reader. They just have an idea they want to pursue. (Or if they don't even have that, they want to *find* an idea to pursue.)

Now that you're up and running on your project it is worth starting to turn your thoughts to your potential customer. The easiest way to do this is to imagine an actual person who represents the person you think you would most benefit (and that you would be happy to get into a business relationship with). This is your *customer avatar*. Give them a name – Dave the Designer or Patty the Partygoer. Think about what they wear. What newspaper do they read? What social media do they use? What TV do they watch? What books do they read? Alternatively, if you're approaching companies, name the company and their values. You might have two or three avatars representing the different types of people who could benefit from what you do. Give them names and describe them separately.

Imagine a bike shop selling bicycles and accessories and doing repairs. One avatar might be Newbie Nadia who's buying a bike because she wants to cycle to work and get more exercise. Another could be Sporty Spencer who's been cycling a while and wants to buy a triathlon bike. You can quickly see how they want different things. Which one you focus on will affect everything you do – what you stock and how you market it.

Think about your avatar whenever you're making decisions about your project or writing any marketing material. That way you can ensure you're creating something they would appreciate.

2. What's the precipitating event?

Think about *when* someone is most likely to contact you, buy from you or search for your website. You might think they could buy at any time but often there is a precipitating event that tips them over the edge. People could join a gym at any point in the year but when do most join? In January. The *precipitating event* here is the start of a new year and its accompanying resolutions. That makes it a great time of year for a gym to gear up for higher numbers and to write blog and social media content around getting fit in the new year.

My book sales go up on a Monday morning and drop on a Friday afternoon. What's the precipitating event here? Returning to work in a job you hate! Logically, Friday afternoon would be the best time to buy a book; you'd have all weekend to read it then. But purchases are emotional not logical. People buy when they feel most strongly about their situation.

Purchases are emotional not logical. People buy when they feel most strongly about their situation.

What might be the precipitating event that brings people to your blog, event, website or app listing? The more you understand about this, the clearer you'll get on what your buyers' needs are and the better you can tune your project and your marketing.

3. What's the job to be done? An introduction to 'Milkshake Marketing'

Harvard professor Clayton Christensen has another way of focusing in on what prompts people to buy. He says that, 'Customers don't buy products, they hire products to do a job.'

Clayton developed this idea when his team was trying to help a fast-food chain sell more milkshakes. The company had already conducted market research with customers to ask them if they wanted the shakes to be creamier or thicker or chocolatier (and so on). The customers gave great feedback, the company altered the milkshakes, but sales didn't actually increase.

So a member of Clayton's team went and stood in one of the restaurants for 18 hours with this question in his head: 'What job are the customers hiring the milkshake to do for them?' After many hours, he could see that nearly half the milkshakes were bought early in the morning by lone customers who then drove off with their purchase. The researcher then started asking the customers questions to try to determine the job the milkshake was doing for them. And he discovered that they all had a long and boring drive to work, they wanted something to do while driving and they needed to have eaten by the time they got to work. The milkshake was therefore performing a very specific job – to fill them up on the go and alleviate the boredom of a long drive.

And the customer 'hired' the milkshake because it was better at this job than a doughnut or a bacon sandwich; it fits in the cup holder, lasts a long time and is easy to consume without making a mess of your work clothes. That means a promotion on breakfast shakes is going to get you a lot better results than tweaking the flavour.

You can use this 'jobs to be done' approach, or 'Milkshake marketing', as it's also become known, to make your product or service more attractive. What's the job that people hire your product or service to do? If you haven't started selling anything yet, what job do you think your product, service or content could be good at?

4. Is it aspirational?

This question is about exploring whether you've created something that people will aspire to be part of. Part of this is down to quality – how well you've executed on your idea. When Sean Rowley had the idea for a Guilty Pleasures club night, he didn't just turn up at the first available venue and play some old records; he created a remarkable and decadent experience with circus performers and celebrity guest appearances. Similarly, Apple didn't just make another smartphone, they created something beautiful, elegant and incredibly easy to use that people aspire to own.

Often the way to answer this is to look around at how your competitors present and package what they do. Is there something you can learn from them and put into your project? What can you do with your project to make it sexier – something people want to tell others about?

How to find answers

It's unlikely you have clear answers (if any at all) to these questions right now. That's OK. These are for you to hold in mind as you play out your project and interact with people.

If you're ready for it, there are things you can do to get some answers quickly. Try them out in today's tasks.

Today's tasks

- Go where there are people of the kind you think will be interested in your project. Look for questions about your topic on Quora, Reddit or forums on Facebook and other sites. Then see if you can help people out by answering their questions.

  Here's an even more direct way to get into contact with people. Sign up for an appointment-scheduling app like TimeTrade or ScheduleOnce, mark out an entire day with 20-minute slots and share the link around, offering people to book themselves into your diary to get 20 minutes of free help from you. I've done this myself multiple times and I can tell you this: you will be amazed how much you'll know at the end of a day spent learning about your customers' needs and wants and seeing if you can help them.

If you're selling to organisations, call up a bunch, say what you're working on and ask to meet them for 20 minutes purely for research (no pitching allowed!). When you meet, ask what their biggest headache is in the area you're helping with. Your only aim is to explore what their pain is so that you can create something to help with it. If you can do five of these research meetings you will have a much clearer picture of what you can sell.

If you're writing a blog, drawing a comic or doing a podcast you can simply pay attention to which content gets the strongest responses. You can also ask your readers or fans what they'd like you to write about next or who they'd like you to interview.

Your goal: product/market fit

The point of the four questions above and of this process of enquiry in general is to help you reach the goal of product/market fit. This is a term from the tech startup world that represents the first milestone for a functioning business – you've created something that meets a real need that a particular market has.

Product/market fit is an important goal even if your project feels a long way from a startup or a serious business. It's really just about knowing for sure that you have made something that some group of people wants. That applies whether you're creating an app, writing a comic strip or developing a new method of stress management.

This is an important milestone to recognise because what you spend your days doing before product/market fit and what you spend your days doing after product/market fit are completely different. Before product/market fit your only focus is on working out how to make something people want. That means you're creating stuff or working with clients and seeing what resonates with people. Nothing else matters.

Before product/market fit, there is no point worrying about getting tons of sales or getting lots of people to come to your website. You only need enough traffic for you to be able to test whether you've achieved a fit. And you only need enough sales to prove that people are willing to spend money on what you've created.

Once you've got there, *then* you can go crazy getting website traffic, running Facebook ads, performing Search Engine Optimisation and running a big marketing promotion.

You know you've arrived at product/market fit when people would be really disappointed if you stopped doing what you are doing for them. If you get to the point where you've tried everything but still can't see how to get a fit, then on Day 20 you'll see how to pivot your project in a new direction.

Workerbot thoughts to challenge

Lottery thinking. Our workerbot training can get in the way here. Instead of diligently focusing on getting traction by creating VALUE for people, we are drawn towards a set of behaviours that seem well intentioned but subtly hand over the responsibility for success to someone else. I label these behaviours and beliefs 'lottery thinking'. Some examples are:

- Pinning all your hopes on getting your one idea for a TV programme commissioned by a major channel – rather than just starting to make programmes and putting them out online (or collaborating with someone who is already doing this).
- Sending a hundred identical emails to people asking them to hire you rather than building a relationship with the five people you most admire and finding out how you can help them.

- Focusing on how to get a book deal from a standing start rather than doing interesting projects so that you start to build a profile – then publishers and agents approach *you* to ask you to write a book (this is how almost every non-fiction author I know got their book deals).
- Asking 'How do I get lots of traffic to my website?' before you have anything on your website of value to people.

Our training is to wait for others to give us the opportunity to do what we want. We haven't quite woken up to the fact that we don't need it anymore. Yes a book deal or TV deal can be very beneficial but you don't have to wait for one. You can create something of VALUE now. And doing so is more likely to get you noticed by the publishers and channels you're seeking. As advertising legend Sir John Hegarty once said, 'Do interesting things and interesting things will happen to you.'

When we realise that we are in fact in control and do now have the means to create something and release it to the world, life becomes very exciting indeed. Now we can publish our own book, market our own creative output, launch our own business in our spare time or start our own campaign to change some piece of the world for the better. That's a lot better than waiting a lifetime to get picked.

Pivot! Or 'What to Do When It Just Ain't Working'

'Life is pretty simple: You do some stuff. Most fails. Some works. You do more of what works. If it works big, others quickly copy it. Then you do something else. The trick is the doing something else.'

—Tom Peters, management guru and author of *In Search of Excellence*

We're now ten days from launching your project so I want to take a moment today to talk about what to do in the worst-case scenario, if your project doesn't work out. That might sound negative but I think you'll find it reassuring to know that, if you don't get the result you want, it's not the end of the story.

What to do if it doesn't work out

The worst-case scenario is that you launch something and people simply don't respond as you'd hoped. You've failed to unlock the VALUE element. The good news is you don't necessarily have to throw the entire idea in the bin and start from scratch. Instead, you can do what's known in the world of tech startups as a *pivot*.

Pivoting is about taking the part of your idea that still has value and discarding the rest. Here are five ways to do this:

1. Continue with the same idea but direct it at an audience that will value it more – for instance, aiming at a new niche

that can better afford what you're offering or moving from focusing on selling to consumers to selling to businesses.

2. Change the way you deliver what you do – run online courses instead of in person if that's what the feedback you're getting suggests.

3. Change the business model – instead of charging a one-off fee, make your service available for a lower monthly fee or sell your product to shops instead of direct to the public.

4. If you're doing well in connecting with a particular market but your idea is still not taking off, you could find something else to offer to them. Is there a more pressing problem or desire they have that you could address instead?

5. Take the component of your product or service that people are responding to and make it the central offer, discarding or minimising the rest – like the example below.

About-turn! The history of successful pivots

Many of the world's most successful companies started out with an idea that performed so poorly that they had to make a radical change of direction. In fact, for innovative businesses like tech startups this happens more often than sticking with the original idea.

Many of the world's most successful companies had to make a radical change of direction from their original idea

---

In 1998, Peter Thiel and his co-founders launched a company called Confinity. They raised $4.8 million in funding to create a service to beam money between mobile devices, which at that point meant primarily the Palm Pilot, an early personal organiser. The idea was that you installed the app, then you could beam money to another Palm Pilot owner, as long as they also had the app. Then you went home, synced your Palm Pilot to your PC and dialled up to the Internet to complete the transaction. Handy, huh? Unsurprisingly, the service was not a huge hit.

Rather than give up, the two founders had a rethink and realised that perhaps mobile devices were not the thing to be focusing on at that point in time. Instead, they noticed that buying and selling on the Internet was just starting to take off even though there was no effective means of online payment. Even sales on eBay were still being paid for by cheques and money orders sent through the mail. Our startup founders realised that what electronic business needed was a simple, convenient payment system tailored specifically to the web – a system that would enable a person to email money to someone else. So they created it. And they used all the expertise they'd developed in secure payments to make it trustworthy.

The result was PayPal, which within just a couple of years went on to be sold to eBay for $1.5 billion. The PayPal service now handles over $600 million in payments every day.

This process of radical adaptation is actually the norm. As I said at the beginning of our journey, the business you start is rarely the business you end up succeeding with. And the same goes for creative projects like a book, movie or social movement.

There are many other successful companies that made a radical about-turn:

- YouTube was originally a video-dating site which faltered before they changed into a video-sharing site, eventually selling to Google for $1.65 billion.
- Groupon emerged from a 'social good' funding site called ThePoint.
- Pinterest, the visual bookmarking and discovery platform with over 100 million monthly active users, started life as

Tote, a site for people to browse retailers and be told when their favourite items went on sale. The founders pivoted when they realised that the users were mostly interested in building 'collections' of their favourite items and sharing them with friends.

- Flickr grew out of a multi-player online game called *Game Neverending*, as a way for players to drop photos into text messages.
- Nintendo started out selling playing cards (and many other household items) before getting into gaming consoles.
- William Wrigley Jr started out as a soap and baking-powder salesman and offered free chewing gum with purchases. The gum turned out to be more popular than the cleaning products and the William Wrigley Jr Company now makes billions annually out of it.
- When Steve Jobs acquired Pixar it was a computer and animation technology company; its wonderful animations were primarily demonstration material for the computers. But Pixar only ended up selling a few computers. Steve decided it was time for a pivot away from hardware and did a deal with Disney to produce a full-length feature film. That film was *Toy Story* which went on to gross more than $362 million worldwide.

Pivot or switch?

'If at first you don't succeed, try, try again. Then quit. There's no point in being a damn fool about it.'

—W. C. Fields, comedian and writer

Sometimes you realise your idea really isn't going to fly in any form and you have to let it go to make way for something completely different. A pivot implies keeping one foot in the place you started and moving the other to point you in a new direction. Sometimes though you just have to walk away altogether. Then you can switch your attention to something new.

Twitter grew out of a podcasting business called Odeo. But the introduction of Apple's iTunes threatened to kill it off. It was time to switch to a new idea.

The founders gave employees two weeks to come up with ideas. Jack Dorsey, working with Biz Stone, sketched out the idea for something new in Jack's notepad. It was called status and was originally expected to be used to keep close friends updated with your whereabouts. (The founders apparently even considered calling it 'Friend Stalker'.) Once it was launched, the Twitter founders constantly reflected on how the service was being used and adapted it accordingly.

Seven years later Twitter has over 300 million monthly active users and floated on the New York Stock Exchange at a valuation of approximately $25 billion. Twitter has experienced slow growth recently and problems with bullying on the platform. As a result, CEO Jack Dorsey is once again looking to adapt Twitter to reinvigorate growth.

When to pivot

The only way to tell if you need to pivot is after you've released your project into the world. Although you'll be doing that for the first time on the thirtieth day, many projects will take longer than that to know for sure.

If, whatever you do, you can't get your audience or market to invest their attention, time or money in your project it could well be time to pivot. If that happens, consider one of five ways to pivot listed above.

How a pivot led to a billion-dollar app

In 2009, 27-year-old Stanford University graduate Kevin Systrom was working in marketing at Nextstop, a travel recommendations startup. Kevin had no formal training in computer science but he started to learn to code at nights and on weekends. He put his new skills into starting a social media and check-in app called Burbn. He met some people from venture capital firms at a party and, encouraged by their response, he decided to leave his job to see if he could make Burbn into a real company.

Within two weeks of leaving he'd raised $500,000 and started work on finding a team. When his co-founder Mike Krieger joined they took a step back to review where they were with the app. Burbn allowed users to check in to locations, make plans, earn points for hanging out with friends, post pictures and more. But despite check-in apps being all the rage at the time, it didn't look like Burbn was going to take off. It was time to pivot.

Kevin tells the story on Quora:

We decided that if we were going to build a company, we wanted to focus on being really good at one thing. We saw mobile photos as an awesome opportunity to try out some new ideas ... We actually got an entire version of Burbn done as an iPhone app, but it felt cluttered, and overrun with features. It was really difficult to decide to start from scratch, but we went out on a limb, and basically cut everything in the Burbn app except for its photo, comment, and like capabilities.

They renamed the new simplified app to Instagram.

We renamed because we felt it better captured what you were doing—an instant telegram of sorts. It also sounded camera-y.

It took them just eight weeks to create version one of Instagram providing just photo sharing, filters and 'Likes'. They then gave it to their friends to test out. When they'd fixed the bugs that came up they were ready to go live on the App Store.

Kevin and the team describe what happened next in a post on the Instagram blog in 2010:

It was 12:15am, October 6th and we had been working on the app non-stop, day and night for 8 weeks. With a bit of hesitation, I clicked the button that launched 'Instagram' live to the Apple App Store. We figured we'd have at least 6 hours before anyone discovered the app so we could grab some shut-eye. No problem, we figured.

Within a few minutes, they started pouring in. People from places like Japan, France, New York, started signing up in droves. The night of sleep we were hoping for turned into a few meager hours before we rushed into the office to add capacity to the service.

Now, only a couple months later, we're happy to announce that our community consists of more than a million registered users. But why is this important?

We believe it's the beginning of something bigger.

They were right. Instagram now has 400 million users and was bought by Facebook for a billion dollars in 2013. For Kevin, Mike and their team, less really did turn out to be more.

Today's task

- You can only tell whether you need to pivot once you've launched and have persisted at trying to make it work. However, something you can do before then is to check how well this project suits *you*. That means looking at how much you're hitting the ENERGY and GENIUS elements of the Playcheque Formula and adapting your project accordingly. This gives you a better chance of ensuring your project will have VALUE to others so you won't need to pivot. You'll have the chance to look at this tomorrow.

Workerbot thoughts to challenge

'If this doesn't work out, I'll have to go back to the day job.' As you've seen, many successful companies have risen out of a failed project. Just because one idea doesn't work out it doesn't mean you should give up. Commit to the iterative process of finding an idea you love that works rather than getting fixated on this current idea. If you're willing to adapt and pivot you will be able to find something that works.

Week 3 Check-in: Tuning In to What People Really Want

'I don't need time, I need a deadline.'
—Duke Ellington, jazz legend

There are nine days to go until you launch on Day 30, so it's time to check in on your commitments and see what you learned in Week 3 and what you can do to make the most of your remaining time.

This is your last check-in of the project – there is no check-in on Day 28 because we'll do a full review after you've finished the project.

REFLECT: What happened and what have you learned?

Take a moment to reflect on the last week so that you can learn from it. Write the answers to the following questions in your Playbook:

- Over the last week, on how many days did you do a micro-block of at least 20 minutes on your project? Remember the aim is to do a minimum of a 20-minute microblock 6 days a week – and tick them all off on the ticksheet.
- In your last check-in a week ago you wrote a list of tasks you were committing to doing. How many did you complete?

- If you didn't do all your tasks or didn't do six microblocks of time on your project, what happened? Be curious, not critical. Did you forget? Did you hit the mid-project slump? If you skipped a microblock what did you do with the 20 minutes instead?
- What are the most interesting things you've learned over the week, whether it's from working on your project or from reading the last seven days' lessons?
- How well has your project has been hitting the ENERGY and GENIUS elements from the Playcheque Formula this week: how much does this project excite you (ENERGY)? How much does it use your spots of GENIUS?
- What have you learned about the VALUE you're creating from listening to feedback and looking into getting traction?

When reviewing your own performance, be curious not critical

ADAPT: How can you use what you've discovered?

- If you didn't do all your microblocks or meet all your commitments, what can you do differently over the next nine days?
- Fine tune your project: given what you've learned over the last seven days about your project, creating a website, getting traction and the willingness to pivot, how can you tune your project to create something of real interest or use to people?

Get ready to ACT again

Your focus now should be on delivering something by the end of Day 30. No excuses; no 'I'll finish it next week'!

Concentrate on doing the real work behind your Play Project. It's better to have one rough five-minute movie shot on your iPhone that reflects the spirit of your idea than to have a beautifully laid-out plan for a feature film you'll make 'one day'.

In a moment we'll create another list of actions to focus on. But first, what is the end result of your project? It's to have something to share.

What will you share?

Remember that on Day 30 you need to share something, to deliver something of value to a client or to friends or to share something publicly online.

What might that be for you?

- If you're doing a photography project, it might be the best of your last 30 days of photos in an album on your site, Facebook or elsewhere. Or perhaps even in an exhibition.
- If you're working with clients, it's to have worked with your first client (most likely a friend or friend of a friend) – even if it was for free or at a token price – and sharing a quote from them on your work.
- If you're creating an app, it's a full interactive mock-up of the app created in something like the Pop app, and the results of sharing it with some people you think would like it.
- If you're writing a non-fiction book, it's a chapter and outline of the book or a bunch of blog posts exploring the themes.
- And, if you're presold a product or service, it's a picture of the payment!

Whatever it is, the point is to actually have done, delivered or produced something and not just planned it, researched it online or written a business plan.

Decide now what you'll share that represents the heart of what you've been creating. If you're running out of time, you might have to temporarily set aside a huge amount of what you originally planned and deliver something simpler; for example, one blog post, one page of your novel, your favourite three photos, the rough demo take of your song, a client's quote or thank you letter or a screenshot of the PayPal payment for your first bit of business.

And if you're ready for a real challenge, see if this week you can step up the pace for a big finish and deliver something you're really proud of. Get up early to work on your project (or go to bed late if you're a night owl). Whatever you can do in the final days, go for it and produce something that makes you smile when you look back on it.

Commitments to take you to the deadline

Let's get your commitments written down for the remaining nine days. Open your Playbook and write the following:

- *'By Day 30 I will ... '* and then list the things you are absolutely committed to doing by the end of your 30-day Play Project.
- *'I also want to ... '* List the things you'd like to do but can't guarantee you'll manage. It's particularly important now to be clear which things are definite commitments and which are not.
- Check your diary to make sure that you can do what you've promised yourself and write in the time for your microblocks.
- Also write, *'On the 30th day of my project I will share* [my deliverable] *with* [the audience you're sharing it with].' If it feels like very early days for your project, just commit to sharing it with a buddy, a group of friends, your writing group or a supportive entrepreneurial colleague. If you're ready to share it more widely, you might place it on your website, Facebook, Twitter, YouTube, Instagram etc.

- Share your commitments with others – declare them on Facebook to your friends or post your top commitments to Twitter or Instagram with the hashtag #screwworkbreak-free (and take a look to see what others are committing to).

The startup that went from idea to paying customer in seven weeks

Tech startups are one of the more difficult businesses to launch quickly. And yet it can be done if you're smart about it.

Joel Gascoigne is co-founder of Buffer, the wonderfully simple yet effective social media-scheduling system. He explains on the Buffer blog how he came up with the idea and what happened next:

It was a tiny idea. I wanted to take the scheduling feature of many Twitter clients and apps and make that single feature awesome. I believed that single feature was worthy of its own application. The aim was to create something genuinely useful with a delightful experience. The fundamental idea was to create a way to queue up tweets without scheduling each tweet individually. This is an idea I had after using other Twitter scheduling applications for the purpose of ensuring I didn't flood people with 5 tweets at once whilst reading my tech & startup news in the morning. I couldn't get it out of my head, and I'd suggested it to existing apps and they hadn't implemented it. It was time to build it myself.

Joel thought about what the Minimum Viable Product could be for his idea. He read the advice by Eric Ries, founder of the Lean Startup movement, answering the question 'How minimal should your Minimum Viable Product be?' Ries' answer was 'Probably much more minimum than you think'.

So Joel took this to heart and came up with a way to test whether people saw VALUE in his idea before he even built it. Without doing any development on the app at all, he set up an attractive one-page website. It described in three lines what the app would do and then had one button labelled 'Plans and pricing'. But when people clicked to find out more it simply said 'Hello! You caught us before we're ready' and asked them to enter their email to be notified when the app was available. His plan was to find out if people who read the description would be interested enough to click to find out more ...

I simply tweeted the link and asked people what they thought of the idea. After a few people used it to give me their email and I got some useful feedback via email and Twitter, I considered it 'validated'.

Then Joel decided to go a stage further: would people be willing to pay for this service? He modified his simple website to show three pricing plans for the app, at different price points from free to $20/month. He again shared the website link around and enough people clicked on the paid options to tell him people were willing to pay for the app – he'd proved to himself that the app was worth building. He built the first very basic (but still elegant) version in the evenings and weekends over a period of seven weeks. Within four days of launching the working Buffer app he had his first paying client.

Since that launch five years ago the Buffer team has added features and support for more social networks while keeping the core product beautifully straightforward. Today they have more than 2 million registered users.

Check out the app at buffer.com.

Player pointers

The most important thing that you can do for your own success is to get something out into the world. It doesn't matter whether you are part of a tech startup or you're making jewellery by hand – you need to do the actual work and avoid wasting too much time at this stage fiddling with your website and other distractions. Do what you need to do, and make sure that you have something to share by Day 30.

WEEK 4

Make Your Idea Take Off

This week we get into the juicy stuff of modern market-ing, making money and all the things that can make your idea really take off. You might not yet be ready to put some of the things you learn this week into action. That's OK; I want you, by the end of 30 days, to at least understand all these great strategies you can use to successfully launch a money-making idea.

Get Ready to Hustle

'Good things come to those who hustle.'

—Anaïs Nin, novelist and short-story writer

There are just eight days left to finish your 30-day Play Project. Now would be a good time to start to hustle. There comes a point in building a business or any other creative project where you simply have to go for it – pull out all the stops, throw yourself into your work and be bold in your mission to get your stuff done and out into the world.

You've made a commitment to launch on the 30th – to release *something* to the world, even if it's more modest than you'd originally hoped. You can call yourself a creative or an entrepreneur but if you don't finish and actually *ship* something it doesn't count. 'Real artists ship', as Steve Jobs used to say to the Apple team. This is the point where you decide that the commitment you made to yourself at the beginning of these 30 days is important enough that it's worth doing whatever it takes to meet it. This might mean working all day (or even all night) on your project to finish it off.

Hustling might also mean doing whatever it takes to get customers or clients, even if your first ones are just testing your service or product out for free.

Even the most successful companies have had to hustle. Airbnb has revolutionised the market for travel accommodation by allowing people to rent out their spare rooms. The company has over 2 million listings in 190 countries and has raised more than $2 billion in funding. But when they started, the founders went door to door in New York, recruiting new users and helping existing ones improve their listings. Then they started flying all over the US to do the same. Paul Graham whose incubator, Y Combinator, was an early-stage investor reported that, 'When I remember the Airbnbs [then], I picture them with rolly bags, because, when they showed up for Tuesday dinners, they'd always just flown back from somewhere.'

Paul recommends that even in a tech startup you hope will one day have millions of users, you must be willing to 'do things that don't scale'. That means in the early days, personally walking customers through the sale or adoption process or delivering part of your solution personally if you haven't yet hired someone or built a system to do it. Businesses don't take off automatically, they take off because the founders hustle to *make* them take off.

Hustling can mean getting out on the frontline to find out what your prospective customers really want and what their concerns are. You might want to have others do sales or support for you later but right now you should go out there and do it yourself. You'll get invaluable feedback.

When I meet people who are worried about a lack of sales, whether it's for an event, workshop, product or some enterprise software, I ask them why people aren't buying. Despite their constant anxiety about the situation, they usually admit they don't know why. Here's what I advise them to do: install a live chat window on your website (particularly on the page for buying) that allows visitors to ask you questions, and personally answer every query. Or if you have some prospects who have expressed an interest but not paid yet, go call them all up and ask them what would need to change for them to be able to commit. Do this and you'll know within just a few days what's stopping people buying – and you can then set about addressing it.

I installed a live chat pop-up on the website for one of my programmes and I personally answered the questions on the chat system from website visitors for 12 hours a day. I found that more than 80 per cent of people's questions came down to one of just four concerns (for example, 'Do I need to be in London to take part?'). As soon as I realised this, I wrote my answers to these four concerns prominently on the website for everyone to read. Sales, which were already doing well, immediately increased.

I've seen entrepreneurs fail on a business that was already starting to make money simply because they weren't willing to hustle like this. They wanted to be CEO, but they weren't willing to be founder.

If you want to be CEO, *you have to be willing to be founder*

Elon Musk hustles $500 million of sales

Sometimes even a successful and well-established company will run into trouble and will have to revert to hustling to save the company. Elon Musk is CEO of two multi-billion-dollar companies and yet is known to step into any job he deems necessary at critical moments, including machining rocket parts on the factory floor at SpaceX.

He's not afraid to bring everyone else in the company in to the hustle too. Ashlee Vance tells the story in his biography, *Elon Musk: How the Billionaire CEO of SpaceX and Tesla is Shaping our Future*, of when Elon's pioneering electric car company Tesla hit a crisis point in 2013. Many customers had paid deposits but they weren't completing their purchase of the cars. Elon responded by pulling 500 people from recruiting, design, engineering and finance and turned them into car salespeople:

[Musk] ordered them to get on the phone, call people with reservations, and close deals. 'If we don't deliver these cars, we

are fucked,' Musk told the employees. 'So, I don't care what job you were doing. Your new job is delivering cars.'

Elon then worked flat out on making big changes in the company to fix the issues that were holding people back from buying. At the same time, he hurriedly met with Larry Page to hammer out a fallback plan to sell the company to Google if the worst came to the worst, ensuring Tesla wouldn't collapse. Fortunately, it never came to that:

The five hundred or so people whom Musk had turned into car salesmen quickly sold a huge volume of cars. Tesla, which only had a couple weeks of cash left in the bank, moved enough cars in the span of about fourteen days to end up with a blowout first fiscal quarter. Tesla stunned Wall Street on May 8, 2013, by posting its first-ever profit as a public company—$11 million—on $562 million in sales. It delivered 4,900 Model S sedans during the period.

The lesson: do whatever it takes and never get too proud to hustle.

This doesn't just apply to business and entrepreneurship. There's plenty of hard slog in creative work after all the fun brainstorming is done. Ernest Hemingway once advised a younger writer

Don't get discouraged because there's a lot of mechanical work to writing. There is, and you can't get out of it. I rewrote *A Farewell to Arms* at least fifty times. You've got to work it over. The first draft of anything is shit.

This dogged determination to get the results you want is within us all, even if it's been squashed and bruised a little along the way. It's what got you to stand up and walk for the very first time, even though you fell over more than you stood up. And it's still there today if you reach inside to find it.

Today's tasks

What do you need to do? Here are some ways you can start to hustle today:

- Clear your diary for the next eight days so that you can work on your project.
- Send a whole bunch of emails to help your project succeed.
- If you're ready for customers, find out why people aren't buying or engaging: speak to them directly or try out a live chat window on your website.
- Go call people who have said they're interested in what you're doing but haven't taken action yet.
- Reach out to a leader in your field to ask for something.
- Go to meetup.com and announce your first event.
- Call someone who can promote your product or book or online shop.
- Call someone who might stock your product in a shop.
- Write yet another draft of the book you're working on to really make it shine.
- Go meet someone who inspires you and interview them over coffee for your podcast or blog.

Whatever it is for you, go do it now. 'Build your hustle muscle' as Academy Award-winning actor Jamie Foxx advised in an interview on *The Tim Ferriss Show* podcast.

Player pointers

You have to launch on the 30th – no excuses! If necessary, reduce the scope of what you were planning to do. The Pareto Principle suggests that, whatever you are doing, 80 per cent of your results come from 20 per cent of your activities. So focus on the 20 per cent of tasks that will get you 80 per cent of the results you want from your project.

Workerbot thoughts to challenge

'I'm CEO; I shouldn't have to do this' or 'I'm an artist; I don't do sales.' It's time to get over yourself, roll up your sleeves and get your hands dirty.

'This was supposed to be fun.' Even if you've chosen a project that excites you, not all of it is going to be fun. You need to be willing to do whatever is required to make it a success. At the end of the 30 days you can adapt what you're doing or pivot entirely. But you have to finish. Remember: dabblers don't get rich. And they don't get to make a positive impact or make a name for themselves or find real meaning in their work.

Dabblers don't get rich

What's Your Story? Or 'How to Find the Words to Sell Your Idea to the World'

'Those who tell the stories rule the world.'

—Hopi proverb

So you've been hustling and putting stuff out and you're getting good feedback. Perhaps you've worked directly with some clients and they rave about what you do or you've got some early adopters of your app or service and they're loving it. Congratulations! You've unlocked the VALUE element, the most important one of all. But for some reason you're not getting enough people turning from website visitors into subscribers or buyers. You're great but people don't know it until after they've used you. When you reach this point it's time to unlock the fourth element of the Playcheque Formula, STORY. STORY is about capturing what you do in a simple message that instantly communicates its VALUE to the people who can benefit.

Now we're into the realm of marketing and, specifically, the message you want to communicate. One of the world's greatest marketing experts, Seth Godin, says that, 'Marketing is telling a story about your value that resonates enough with people that they want to give you money.'

Marketing is different in this connected world than it was in earlier days of TV, radio and magazines. In the last century you could simply describe your product, broadcast it to millions of people and guarantee you'd get sales. But today that doesn't work so well. Your opinion of a product is probably based more on what you hear from friends and social media than on broadcast TV ads. Therefore, as Seth puts it, 'Marketing is no longer about the stuff that you make but about the stories you tell.'

What is a story?

A story is simply the most effective way to communicate information and make it stick in people's minds. Stories are how we think, how we make sense of the world. The difference between information and a story is emotion. An effective story makes you *feel* something. And as Maya Angelou once said, 'I've learned that people will forget what you said, people will forget what you did, but people will never forget how you made them feel.'

Stories are how we think, how we make sense of the world. The difference between information and a story is emotion.

What makes a story emotionally powerful is a sense of change over time. At the start you are one thing, by the end you are something (or someone) quite different. In the *Harry Potter* story, Harry starts as an orphan living in a cupboard and ends the first novel as a wizard and a hero.

Don't imagine though that a story has to be as elaborate as a novel or film. *Screw Work Break Free* is a story even if it is only four words. It speaks to the desire to throw in the towel on a boring job and escape to freedom. Think of it like a before and after. Before, you're in work you want to say 'screw it' to. After, you're free to do whatever you want. For both the before and after, an image is brought to mind and it's the transition between these two images that generates the emotion – in this case, excitement.

To create a story around your idea, answer these questions:

1. **Who is your protagonist?** Who is the person who is going to most resonate with your story, i.e. who can best benefit from what you do?

2. **What is their situation now?** This is the 'before' – they're bored on a Friday night, or frustrated with their unhelpful web-hosting company, or worried about their diet but fear they don't have the self-discipline to eat healthily or they're spending too much time on social media for their business and not getting any real results. Be sure to include, not just their situation, but how they feel about it: for example, worried about it, frustrated by it, fed up with it.

3. **Where will they be (or *who* will they be) after they've benefited from what you do?** They're someone with exciting plans for the weekend, they have a hosting company who helps them and puts their mind at rest, they've surprised themselves by how healthily they are now eating or they're relieved to have their social media activities taken off their hands and to see tangible results. Once again, include not just their situation now, but how they feel about it: relieved, at ease, delighted, excited.

4. **What did you provide that made the difference?** This is where you describe what you actually do and what it is in particular that contributes to the results people get.

If you struggle to answer these questions try thinking about a customer, client or fan who gave you great feedback. How would you describe them? What situation were they in before and where are they now that's so different? What did they say they appreciate about what you do?

If you know people are referring you to their friends and colleagues, ask what they said when they referred you – how did they explain why their friend should use you? If they say you go above and beyond to give people good service, or you're the best designer of multi-language websites or that Episode 12 of your comedy podcast made them snort coffee out of their nose, that's your story.

When you have a good story, you can use it everywhere – in your website copy, in your marketing emails or when you answer the question 'What do you do?' It might even show up in some form in the title or strapline for your business.

Let's start at the end

At this stage your story, if you have one at all, is likely to be pretty hazy. That's OK. I find that nailing down the perfect story is something you have to play out. Keep working on your project, playing in public and providing VALUE, while trying out different ways to describe yourself. Over time playing out your project will clarify your story and, as you try different stories, it will help clarify your project – until both eventually crystallise.

It's worthwhile taking a shot now at a first draft of what your final story might be. You can do this even at the start of a project. As you become more experienced in bringing ideas to fruition you will find it easier to know what the final story is in advance and guide your business or creative project to fit.

Amazon uses this principle and calls it 'working backwards'. Ian McAllister, a former director at Amazon, explains on Quora that when someone in the company wants to add a new feature or service to Amazon's systems, they don't start developing the software. They don't even write a project plan. Instead, they write a press release imagining the addition has already been made and describing how exciting it is. Then they distribute the press release (which is never more than a page and a half) internally to the people within Amazon most likely to be interested.

If no one is excited about the suggested addition, the originator has to go back and rework the press release until the benefits sound like something worth having. As Ian says, 'Iterating on a press release is a lot less expensive than iterating on the product itself (and quicker!).' Only when people agree that they want what is described does development begin. And as the team develops it, they make sure they stick to what they promised and don't waste time on any unnecessary extras.

Working backwards can be good for creative arts projects too. Some years ago I had an idea for a documentary about the science of optimism and how it impacts health. I wrote a proposal for BBC Radio 4 and was excited to get the programme shortlisted. Unfortunately it didn't get picked up in the end. Instead, I turned my attention to the possibility of it being made as a TV documentary. My first choice for someone to make the programme for TV was a director who had won an award for a superb and moving documentary about someone with a terminal disease.

I looked up the director's contact details and emailed him my programme proposal. The next day I called him to follow up. He was wonderfully helpful and he gave me what I can only describe as a 15-minute documentary masterclass. (I am deliberately not naming him to avoid every aspiring documentary maker cold-calling him!) The most important thing he told me was to write the programme listing that would appear in newspapers when the programme was already finished and scheduled for broadcast. These listings simply contain the title (usually in no more than five words) and a description of fewer than 35 words.

Can you describe your creative project in fewer than 35 words and make it compelling? If not, you may have a problem with the project itself. The ultimate success in television is to create something that is 'an appointment to view' – that is something that is so attractive that when you read about it you don't just say to yourself, 'That sounds good,' you say 'Wow, I have *got* to see that!' and you organise your life around watching it live. That's the difference between good and irresistible.

In trying to write my TV listing I realised that there was no easy way to describe my documentary in 35 words. The story was, as the documentary maker warned me, too complex to grasp quickly. I parked the idea but took away many important lessons from the experience.

You can apply a similar principle to write the Google Adwords ad for your product or business idea. Can you write a title of no more than 25 characters with a description of no more than 70 characters that makes the right person want to click to find out more?

Alternatively, if you're writing a book, can you write a title and subtitle that make you want to read the book or at least read more about it? Think of it step by step. The title should make you want to read the subtitle. And the subtitle should make you want to turn the book over and read the blurb on the back cover. The blurb then should make you want to read the book.

What's the big idea?

Part of your story might be some grander mission behind your project. Do you want your project to play a part, no matter how small, in changing an area of life or business you feel really strongly about? Perhaps you want to see the end of hard-to-use websites, help minority entrepreneurs get the media attention they deserve or transform the comedy scene in your town.

What could it be for you? How would you like the world to be different in the particular area of your project? When you know what it is, you can include your big idea in your marketing copy on your website and elsewhere. This gives more meaning for you in your work and helps enlist others who believe in the same mission. That's good for your cause and good for your business. As artist and entrepreneur Hugh MacLeod says, 'The market for something to believe in is infinite.' It's also a lot more palatable for others when you shout about the change you want to see in the world rather than shout about yourself.

Taking on Google at their own game with a killer story

When Gabriel Weinberg had the idea to create a new search engine and compete against Google, even his wife thought he was crazy. Who competes with the world's leading search engine and a company valued at over $500 billion?

But Gabriel stuck to his guns and created DuckDuckGo. His aim wasn't to be as big as Google but he thought there was plenty of room for a search engine that was different, even better in some ways. What could he do that Google (and Bing and Yahoo) could not? He decided to make the search results page less cluttered with adverts, produce more instant answers within the results and provide greater privacy. Google, after all, tracks everything you search for, stores it and even passes some of it to the site you click on in the search results. In theory this should help return more relevant results but it also means Google knows a huge amount about you. And that information is a fundamental part of their business model.

Gabriel reckoned he could make a good search engine without storing anything about what you search for. That turned out to be very fortunate as people were becoming increasingly concerned about their online privacy. So the story he chose to tell was about privacy.

He decided to invest $7,000 to put up a single billboard in San Francisco for four weeks, knowing that many people in the startup world would see it on their daily commute. The billboard featured the company name and smiling duck logo and a simple message, 'Google tracks you. We don't.'

This marketing story really paid off when the Edward Snowden revelations showed how much access the government has to our private data, including search history. This brought a huge influx of new visitors to DuckDuckGo and the number of daily searches almost doubled to 3 million over the following 6 months. And the rapid growth continued; now DuckDuckGo delivers just under 10 million searches every day.

It goes to show that even when someone has the entire market sewn up, there is often a niche open if you have a STORY about your VALUE that is clear, simple and compelling.

Today's tasks

Here are some things to try today to start to create your story. Write the answers to the questions below in your Playbook.

- Try writing out the parts of your story as listed above – who is the protagonist, what is their situation before using you, what is their situation after, how did you help and what in particular made the difference?
- If anyone has given you a quote or testimonial, see how that helps inform your story. If it's short and punchy, consider using it on your website. The best testimonials show specific results – 'I lost 12 pounds!', 'I doubled my sales' – and/or have a strong emotive statement – 'I can't stop smiling at the new me', 'The sales training blew me away'.
- Similarly, if someone has recommended you to others, find out how they described you and write it down. That will often give you the best story of all!
- What's your status story? That's a couple of paragraphs that might feature in your about page or on your sales page that sum up why you or your team can live up to what you're promising. It might include qualifications, work experience

that's relevant or years of personal investigation and engagement in a particular area. If you've already worked for prestigious people or organisations and have permission to say so, include that too.

- Start at the end: what's the Google Ad for your product, press release for your project, TV listing for your programme or blurb for your book? If you were writing a sales page for an offer (i.e. a one-page website describing it in the most compelling way possible), what would it say? Can you create it now using something like Instapage.com? If it's not ready to sell yet, instead of a buy button, provide an email sign-up box for people who are interested.
- What's your big idea? Thinking about the area your project is in, what is it you'd love to see change? What's the transformation you could play some part in even if it's a small one right now?
- What's the story behind this project and why you are doing it? This can be useful for your about page on the website or, if it's a particularly engaging one, could make a good promotional article or press release.

Keep rewriting your story to cut out any fluff and make it succinct. If you can create a one-sentence version with fewer than 140 characters, tweet it for others to read with #screwworkbreakfree.

Workerbot thoughts to challenge

'If I'm writing a mission statement I'd better make it sound serious.' It isn't 1950, so there's no need anymore to write in formal language, or even worse, business-speak – 'The company endeavours to leverage our skills to achieve excellence in the field of dog-walking'. Seriously, no one likes that stuff. Just write it in normal, everyday language.

Keep it simple and straightforward. Richard Branson wrote on his blog at Virgin.com

> To this day I don't make formal business plans, but am always crystal clear on the concept of the business. We have a saying at Virgin, if your pitch can't fit on the back of an envelope, then it's too complicated. In fact, we have written many business plans on the back of beer mats and envelopes – they have gone on to become successful companies like Virgin Australia.

When you've got a great story, you might well find you can charge more. We'll look at how to play the money game tomorrow.

How to Play the Money Game

*'Being good in business is the most fascinating
kind of art. Making money is art and working
is art and good business is the best art.'*

—Andy Warhol, pop art pioneer

The money game is all about getting creative with that final element in the Playcheque Formula, MONEY. Because once you've got something valuable and have worked out how to communicate it, then you're able to make a return and get some money out of it.

A lot of people don't realise that the money game – finding the ideal way to monetise your idea – is just as creative as all the other parts of launching a successful idea. For instance, charge 99 pence for your Kindle book and you might find you make more than if you charged £9.99 because more than ten times as many people buy it (thriller writer John Locke proved this when he became the first self-published author to sell 1 million e-books, pricing most of his books at just 99 cents). Or giving away a free app and then charging for in-app upgrades might make more money than releasing it as a paid app.

---

*The money game – finding the ideal way
to monetise your idea – is just as creative
as all the other parts of launching
something successful*

When to make money

As you've seen, the best place to focus your attention is creating value – that is the foundation of a good business. However it's also worth thinking about how you will make money from your idea so that you can start to plan for it.

When is the right time to start charging? It depends on what kind of idea you're pursuing but it can be as soon as you can see that people value what you're doing. If you've been helping friends and colleagues for free and they're now recommending you to their friends, that's a clear sign you're doing something of real value and can start charging.

If you've been writing a blog regularly and getting great feedback and a lot of engagement (people commenting on posts, sharing them) then you could introduce a paid product, such as an offer for one-to-one consultations, a live event, a group pro-gramme, a one-day workshop or a corporate training package. Bear in mind that this might not happen within your first 30 days.

The best reason to start charging is not because you need the money (it's better to have another source of income to keep you afloat while you're getting going), but because you want to prove the value with more certainty – after all, you know people really like what you do when they're willing to pay for it.

The next question is how are you actually going to monetise this thing you've started?

What's your business model?

Any idea you can come up with will usually have multiple pos-sible ways to monetise it. Let's take blogging as an example. You can't charge people to read your blog. Well, you could, but you won't get many takers because people expect to read blogs for free.

However, there are many ways a blog can turn into an income stream indirectly. So if you've been regularly writing a blog and followed the guidelines in this book – choosing a subject you care about, using some of your genius spots to create very valuable content and superniching in a very specific area – then there are plenty of ways you can make money out of it. The same goes for other projects that you might have been doing for free until now.

Eleven ways to make money from your project

Once you've managed to engage people in what you're doing (for example, a blog, an event, a free taster app, free consultations) and they see the VALUE, here are 11 ways you can get paid:

1. Create a downloadable product – that means something people can pay for and download directly from your site. It might be a combination of PDFs, video, audio and other elements. So if you're writing a blog on how to use Instagram, you could create a crash course in marketing your brand on Instagram.
2. Sell services to consumers – for example, personal training, accounting, coaching, therapy, a domestic cleaning agency. One of the simplest ways to start with this is to offer paid consultations in person or over Skype and provide a PayPal button on your website for people to pay in advance. You can also list yourself on peopleperhour and the other marketplace sites mentioned in Day 3.
3. Sell services to businesses – once you've demonstrated your expertise on a topic in your blog, then you can engage with interested people and invite them to connect on LinkedIn or look for invitations to speak at conferences and to consult to companies.
4. Events and workshops – have a dedicated page about your event on your blog and link from there to your Eventbrite/ Meetup page. Also have a link in the margin on every page.

5. Online course or programme – you can deliver a course with participants all over the world by combining email lessons, videos and live webinars (online seminars when you share your computer screen or speak to camera and answer people's questions). You can also invite participants to a private Facebook group to continue the discussion. Or, alternatively, create the course as a series of video lessons and sell it on Udemy.com.

6. Mobile or web app – blog about the problem your app is trying to solve and the niche it addresses and link to your app on the App Store.

7. Software as a Service – if you've ever used an email news-letter system, online accounting or social media scheduler, you've used a SaaS (Software as a Service). This model is one of the most complex because it usually requires the greatest amount of time developing your solution before you can test it out with people. A popular SaaS business model is 'freemium', meaning free plus premium. You provide useful functionality for free and then offer a paid option with more features for serious users. Reaching enough consumers for your service can be challenging. Creating software for cor-porations can be easier to succeed at because you can charge more than consumers would pay, have a smaller number of users and still create a multi-million-dollar company.

8. Sell physical products – write about items for sale on your blog and link to your Etsy or eBay shop. Alternatively, you could create your entire site with the Shopify ecommerce system instead (which has the ability to include a blog with your online shop).

9. Sell books – people won't pay for blogs but they will pay for books. Blog out your book to promote it, then suggest people go get the book and link to it on Amazon. Self-published books can make significant income if you have built a large enough audience. Traditional publishing pays much smaller royalties but can help get your book publicity, press and promotion in bookshops and so sell more copies.

10. Affiliate marketing – many companies, online services and people with training programmes provide affiliate programmes – they're a way for you to get paid commission in exchange for promoting their products and services. If there's someone whose business you really respect, ask if they have an affiliate programme and register with them. Then talk about why you like them on your blog and include the affiliate link. Note that in some countries there are legal requirements to state that you have an affiliate relationship so check for yourself before using affiliate links.

11. Subscription or membership programme – subscriptions are great because, instead of paying you once, people pay you repeatedly! This is usually monthly, sometimes annually. If you're helping people with some area of their lives or businesses you could create a membership programme that gives them the opportunity to learn from you regularly each month for an ongoing charge. You might provide online group seminars, private Google hangouts, membership of a private Facebook group and the chance to put their questions to you. Alternatively, you could create a network for people in a particular industry and charge a monthly or annual membership fee for the ability to connect with others, learn more about their industry and attend members' events. Rik Spruyt's story on Day 11 is a great example.

Over to you

Think of three possible income streams for your idea. Which one do you want to begin with? You can add more later. You often will use a combination of channels in one package – for instance, you could combine a one-day workshop plus a one-to-one consultation and a downloadable product to make one premium product.

If you need ideas on which channels to use yourself, look around and see how others in your field do it. Steal the business model that seems to be working best. Be wary about innovating on business model. If no one else is trying to make money in the same way that probably means it's been tried and hasn't worked. If, for instance, you're thinking of going freelance to provide the same thing you do in your job but you don't see an active freelance market for this function, that's a sign that you're likely to struggle to get work. Similarly, there is a reason all successful gyms function on membership subscriptions and do not allow you to pay per visit – it's the only way they can make a profit.

One of the most common mistakes beginners make in choosing their business model is to hope that advertising alone will create an income for them. They create interesting content on a blog and hope that placing ads in the margins will make them enough to quit their job. While it is possible to make money from advertising (you'll see it on almost all the most popular blogs), it is a very hard thing to do for a beginner. Although advertisers will pay you every time a user clicks on their ad on your site, the payment is just 50 cents or so and the proportion of visitors who click on an ad might be less than 1 per cent. That means 10,000 visitors a month will probably make you less than $100. So you need millions of monthly visitors to make anything significant. If you're obsessed with doing whatever it takes to make your blog number one in its niche – whether it's writing the best content in the world, or becoming a Search Engine Optimisation ninja – then go for it but there are far easier ways to start earning money. For example, selling consultancy by the hour or day to consumers or companies – and it doesn't take a huge amount of traffic to make it work.

Don't know what to charge?

Beginning entrepreneurs often worry a lot about setting the right price. If you have no idea, look around at what others are charging. Notice though that there is a wide variation in pricing in any field. And remember that the majority of people who work for themselves undercharge. If you use the techniques here and make sure you superniche on your areas of genius and tell a good story, you can vastly improve on what others charge. Sometimes a slight shift in how you present what you do or how you package it can massively improve your income.

The good news is you can test pricing out. If you're providing a service as a freelancer, consultant or advisor, the first few people you sell to will likely be through personal conversations. You can quote a price – what you believe you're really worth – and see what their reaction is. If no one ever says 'That's too much' you're undercharging!

For an app or startup you can test pricing before you release and you can experiment with different prices afterwards.

Do the numbers

Pricing and business model will also be determined by how much you're aiming to make. At some point you'll need to do a back-of-an-envelope calculation to check you can make what you want. Take your desired income, allow for expenses and divide it by your unit price to see how many sales you'll need to make each year. Divide it by 12 and you have your monthly sales target.

At this point you might panic and wonder how you'll ever make this thing work. If so you need to understand what I call *iterative income building.* If you're looking for one idea to replace your salary that is not always going to be practical. This isn't necessarily reason to abandon what you've started. All successful businesses are created from multiple income streams. Instead of thinking of this idea as a full-time income, think of it as just one income stream. If you can create one income stream, you can create more. And when you create enough of them, you'll be ready to quit your job (if that's your goal). You'll find this a lot easier if all your income streams are closely related – for example, you freelance, do phone consultations and sell an app in your field of expertise.

Today's tasks

- Write three ways you could monetise your idea.
- Choose your favourite out of the three and take action on them today, even if it's just adding a button to your website to buy an hour of your time.

Player pointers

Know your Minimum Survivable Income. What's the minimum amount you would need to make personally out of your business every month to be able to survive? This level of income might not be very enjoyable to live on but you *could* do it for up to a year. Your Minimum Survivable Income is an important number because once your idea generates that amount every month you can quit your job and go full-time on your business. In the startup world this is known as 'ramen profitable', meaning the business makes enough to cover its expenses and pay you enough to survive, even if it's on instant noodles!

How to scale. Once your idea is working and making money you can scale your business in one of two ways: with people or systems. Systems means automating what you do, perhaps in an online course delivered automatically to buyers or with a Software as a Service. Scaling with people means training others in your methods so that they can work under your brand and you make a profit on what you charge the customer.

How to Make Your Idea Go Viral

'Ideas that spread, win.'
—Seth Godin

I've been fortunate to have a number of my projects – books, courses and live events – generate word of mouth and international press without actively seeking it. Today I'll share some of the principles I've used to help make this happen and what it takes to make something that truly goes viral.

Let's first understand what that means. Viral spread means that instead of people only hearing about your project directly from you, your message also spreads from person to person. When a proportion of people who use you or see your marketing start telling others about you, you multiply the exposure of your project.

The viral jackpot is when every person who uses your skills, downloads your app or watches your funny video brings at least one more person who does the same. That may not sound like much but what it actually results in is exponential growth – a doubling of your business every time it passes on. That means if you start off with ten users/fans, after just ten cycles of sharing you'll have 220,000. And after another ten cycles of sharing, you'll have nearly five billion.

In reality exponential growth is only attained by a very small number of businesses and projects – Psy's *Gangnam Style* with over 2 billion views, WhatsApp reaching a billion users in just 6 years. For most projects you can't rely on generating exponential growth but viral sharing at a more modest level is still a very important part of modern marketing.

Your aim should always be to build virality into your project from the start so today I'll show you the ten keys to making your project go viral.

Ten keys to going viral

1. Make it good

Start here: the smartest marketing in the world won't bring viral growth if what you're promoting isn't all that great. If you spent enough on advertising you might get an initial flush of sales but you wouldn't get any of those buyers recommending you to other people. Worse than that, the bad news would spread virally with people telling others how disappointing your stuff is.

So before you invest too much effort in trying to go viral, make sure you have something that has well and truly hit the VALUE element of the Playcheque Formula – that means you've got something people like so much that they are investing time, attention or money in it.

Then, people will share your stuff with their friends, not because they want to do *you* a favour but they want to do their friends a favour.

2. Make it relevant/useful

It's great if your project is not only good but clicks with a real need people have, i.e. it addresses a problem, pain or desire that they are conscious of.

There is a three-minute TED talk that has been watched over five million times. The subject? How to tie your shoe laces. Terry Moore shows in the short video that we have all learned to tie our shoes the wrong way. If you do it slightly differently, your laces will never accidentally come undone. If you're sick of your shoe laces coming undone regularly, you'll understand why the video is so popular.

Never underestimate the power of the most fundamental human desires – for more money, love, happiness, beauty, sex, status, acceptance, freedom, security, peace of mind. If you speak directly to any of these desires you will help your message and your project succeed.

On my @johnsw Twitter feed I share articles on work, entrepreneurship, creativity, technology and society. I like to think I have a pretty enlightened readership (that includes you!) but I still remember seeing one of my best click-through rates ever when I shared an amusing piece of research about sexual habits.

3. Make it clear

Make the message you want to spread simple and clear. Avoid clever product/ business names and taglines that can't be understood without explanation. If you see a successful book with an obscure title you'll see there will always be an explanatory subtitle immediately underneath.

Basecamp is one of many online project management tools and has numerous features but it manages to stand out with a simple message: 'World-famously-easy-to-use'. Many project management systems are bewildering to use so this simple message is an important one to differentiate Basecamp from all its competitors. The result is over 100,000 paying customers including NASA, Nike and the World Wildlife Fund.

4. Make it specific

As we saw on Day 13, it is a lot easier to get traction and spread virally when you narrow your focus to a very particular type of person or use case. When I ran a monthly live event called Scanners' Night it was very specifically aimed at people who have lots of interests and love to learn a new topic and then move on. That made it very compelling to people of that personality type and it spread quickly. It also attracted coverage in a national newspaper and several magazines without any PR activity. (Although I ended Scanners' Night after six years, I put everything I learned about helping scanners into my programmes like the 30-day Challenge.)

5. Make it fresh

People hunger for the new. Of course no idea is completely original but you can have a new take on an old idea. How is what you're doing different to what's gone before?

There are now many dating events where you can mix with other people and try to find someone you want to go out with. How do you do something different and get your event noticed? Well, Pheromone Parties certainly succeeded. These are dating events based on the idea that attraction is unconsciously influenced by differences in people's body odour.

To take part in a Pheromone Parties event, you bring a T-shirt you've slept in and place it in a sealed bag with a number on it. At the event people walk around with a drink in hand, sniff the bags and announce the numbers of the people whose odour they like. This very fresh take on dating attracted an enormous amount of publicity – CNN, *The Colbert Report* and many magazines.

6. Make a statement

This is an important one. If you want to stand out from the noise and spread quickly you need to make a strong statement. Be controversial, counterintuitive, funny or even shocking. When Sara Blakely invented her body-shaping pantyhose she could have chosen a normal brand name, as so many lingerie companies do. Instead she called it Spanx. As she has explained, 'The word "Spanx" was funny. It made people laugh. No one ever forgot it.'

John Parkin wrote the book *F**k It: The Ultimate Spiritual Way* in 2008. The juxtaposition of the F-word and spirituality is shocking to some but, as John explains, saying 'f**ck it' is, 'the perfect western expression of the eastern ideas of letting go, giving up and finding real freedom by realising that things don't matter so much (if at all)'.

You might think that having the F-word in the title of your book would hinder sales but in fact the opposite is true – the *F**k It* series of books has now sold over 500,000 copies and has been translated into 25 languages. The lesson? If you want to get talked about, say 'f**k it' to fitting in and don't pull your punches to avoid offending people.

If you're trying to make a point about the world, make a strong statement. What's the strongest statement you can make that is still accurate? Use that as the title of your book, headline for your article or subject of your press release. People who resonate with your message or the change you're trying to bring about will be all the more keen to help spread the message.

What's the strongest statement you can make that is still accurate?

You can also make a statement with price. The budget airlines in the UK generated a lot of publicity in their early days by selling their first few tickets for just a few pounds.

7. Make it timely

When a message references this moment in time it has all the more power to it. What are the hot topics of discussion right now? At the time of writing there is a lot of discussion around the overwhelm of modern life, the rise of powerful startups that are becoming monopolies, online privacy, private space travel and plenty of other topics. If you can insert your message into the public conversation you stand all the more chance of it spreading and attracting press – whether you're supporting the dominant thinking or taking a stand against it.

If you're writing a book, for instance, capturing the zeitgeist in your topic will make a huge difference to its success. This also works for writing your press release for an innovative business idea.

8. Make it personal

If you have a good story behind your project that explains *why* you're doing it that can help your message to spread. Jason Vale used to be a junk-food addict suffering from psoriasis, eczema, asthma, hay fever and weight problems. He discovered juicing and used it to clear his skin, lose weight and free himself of illness. He is now on a mission to 'Juice the World' and help people to turn their health around using natural means where possible. Although he is not a doctor or dietician, he calls himself the Juice Master and has sold approximately 500,000 books. He has also launched successful apps, seminars and juicing retreats. It's his personal story and his passion for his subject that makes it all work.

9. Make it quick to infect

You'll notice on Facebook, Twitter and elsewhere that the things that get 'Liked' and shared the most are images. That's because it's quick to absorb an image, have a reaction and pass it on. Similarly, TED talks often spread faster than the book by the same person. That's because you can absorb the TED talk and get the idea in 20 minutes whereas reading a book takes considerably longer.

What can you do to make your idea quick to get? Create an image, an infographic, a summary sheet or document, or perhaps give a talk at a TEDx event?

10. Make it easy and fun to share

Make it as easy as possible for people to share. Include a share button on your blog posts. If you send out an email newsletter, also include a link to a version that people can share with others on social media.

Make it not just easy but fun to share. Use humorous images as a means of spreading the message. Or, if you compensate people for promoting you, you can run a competition and give prizes to reward the people who send you the most business. Conventional businesses are so serious and dry that anything to make yours more warm, fun and friendly can really help.

If you promote courses or events, give people a badge they can put on their website (or even a badge for their shirt). If you run a 'Brilliant Baking' course, give people a website badge that says, 'I'm a Brilliant Baker!' The website badge can link directly to your courses to explain more and it will bring you customers.

Some companies make sharing the default. Think of how Apple add 'Sent from my iPhone' to every email. Hotmail used the same strategy to aid their growth – raising awareness and bringing in new users.

Rewarding sharing

Get the above ten keys right (or as many of them as you can), and you will find your project getting shared. But you can go one step further and directly reward people. In the startup world online storage app Dropbox gives you extra free storage when you convince a friend to join. Uber gives you money off a ride if you get a friend to use the app.

If you sell online products you can use an affiliate system to provide people with unique links to your website that automatically register when that person refers a sale. You can then pay them commission.

The ultimate reward is when the buyer's experience is directly improved by sharing. Snapchat, for instance, is a lot more fun if your friends join too so you're motivated to try to enlist them.

Unleashing your virus

If you follow these guidelines you will get unprompted sharing but you'll get much quicker results if you do a little 'seeding' – taking some initial actions to get the first shares happening. That might mean posting your video in a Facebook group or Reddit discussion on a related topic. Tweet influential people who you think will click with it. Or ask friends who have a following or lots of online friends to share your project. Of course, if you have your own email list or following on a social network, post it there too.

What's your target?

Before you go too far into your viral plan, consider what you want people to actually do once they've been 'infected'. There won't be much benefit if you spread something virally but there is no hook to bring people back to you! What's the action you want people to take as a result of discovering you? If you're sharing a video that might be to subscribe to your YouTube channel so that they see future ones. If you've got a great free download on your site, then it's a page where people can enter their email to get access to it so that you build an email list of interested people. And if you've got something ready to buy, it's a page describing your offer and a button to buy it (or at least the means to have a conversation about it with you).

When it all works

The primary aim here is to make your stuff *remarkable* in the purest sense of the word – people spontaneously remark on it to others. You know this is happening when people tell you that someone (who perhaps you don't even know) recommended you to them.

When you get all this just right you will find that, instead of feeling like you're pushing something uphill to make it succeed, it's more like you're chasing something that's rolling downhill, gathering speed and your only problem is how to keep up! But as entrepreneurs like to say, that's a good problem to have.

Today's task

- As you work on your project today, think about which of the ten keys to going viral you can apply to it.

How to Get Other People to Send You a Flood of Visitors, Followers and Sales

'Alone we can do so little; together we can do so much.'

—Helen Keller, author and political activist

One of the questions I get asked most by clients is, 'How do I get more traffic to my website?' If you are wondering the same thing, I'm going to answer that question for you today. But before I do, I want you to consider something: are you *ready* for traffic?

Sometimes people breathlessly ask me how to get lots of visitors to their website, but when I look at their site my first reaction is, 'You don't *want* any more people to see this thing!' That's because their website is a half-finished mess with mistakes and missing content. Or it isn't clear what it is they're promoting or what they want visitors to do. If I sent them a million fresh visitors they'd have nothing but a million confused people quickly leaving their site.

So before you worry about traffic-building strategies, make sure you have two things in place. Firstly, a decent-looking website. It doesn't matter if it's just one page, it just needs to look professional (which you can often achieve with a free or cheap website builder as we saw on Day 17).

Secondly, you need an action for people to take when they come to your site. What is it you want them to do? That should be either:

1. To buy something (or at least register interest in doing so) or
2. To opt in for updates from you (for example, join your email list, connect on LinkedIn, 'Like' your Facebook page).

You also need to know that this action 'converts' – i.e. when people land on a page describing why they should buy your product/service or why they should follow you, some of them actually do. In the early days you only need enough traffic to prove people like what you do enough to follow you or buy from you. And you can usually get that from your existing network of friends and colleagues. Once you've proven people are engaging you can look at strategies to bring more people to you.

Traffic hack: go where your buyers are

You can grow traffic organically by blogging regularly, sharing posts on social media and generally engaging with your market and playing your project out in public. However, the fastest way to get a big boost in traffic is to go where your buyers are. Answer the following three questions to put this hack to work for you:

1. **Who will find what you do most valuable?** People who have just lost their job? Design-conscious startups, app developers wanting more downloads, exhausted parents?
2. **Where are they?** Where do these people hang out online? What events do they go to? What websites do they frequent? Who do they follow on Facebook? What other services are they likely to be using at the moment?

3. **Who can put you in front of them?** Who runs an event these people are likely to attend? Who has a large email list or Facebook following of this kind of person? Who is already working with these people or organisations and can bring you in (or at least make an introduction)?
4. **What can you do of value for their audience?** Give a talk at their event? Write an article for their newsletter? Bring an extra skillset to their work with corporations?

So, for example, you might ...

- Go speak at an event which your target market is likely to attend and at the end pass round a sign-up sheet for people to give their details to get helpful free information from you.
- Write for someone's website and include a link back to your site or LinkedIn profile at the bottom with a one-sentence explanation capturing the value of clicking through.
- Cross-refer clients with other freelancers/service providers: if you offer hypnotherapy and you know a good massage therapist, arrange to pass clients to each other. That way, both of you win business.
- If you want to use your skills with corporations but you haven't consulted to them before, try partnering with someone who already has corporate clients but doesn't have your skills.
- It you want to get your blog posts read, you may get more readers, quicker, by blogging on medium.com or, if you're writing for employees or corporations, LinkedIn Pulse. Again, include a link to get more information from your own site or profile.
- If you interview someone who has a large following on your blog or invite them to speak at your event, they may be willing to share the news with all their followers.

Ensure you provide real value to both your partner and their audience and you could switch on a massive stream of traffic, email subscribers and even sales very quickly.

Open your mind: could your competitor be your best collaborator?

Sometimes, though, you will need to open your mind about who is a competitor and who is a collaborator, as I did at the beginning of my business. I wrote for free for careers sites that needed content and included a link to my careers toolkit on my own site. I also assisted at careers workshops and handed round a sign-up sheet on a clipboard at the end of the workshop. This gave me my first 2,000 people following me on email and at the same time gave me valuable experience writing and working on my subject of expertise. I could have considered these sites to be competitors but by working with them as collaborators everybody benefited – the websites got their blog content, I got traffic and subscribers and the readers got helpful advice.

How to make headlines

Getting national press, or even coverage on radio and TV can really put your project or business on the map.

To win press, you'll need to make sure you've got a good STORY, as we saw on Day 23, and that you've applied the ten keys to make it remarkable that we learned yesterday. You need a story that is clear, specific and a fresh, strong, or very personal, take on something.

The press additionally want to know three things before they will feature you:

1. **Why is it new?** I.e. what's different from what's come before? The press craves novelty. It is called the *news* after all.
2. **Does it fit the ongoing conversation?** Does your story mesh with the zeitgeist of the time? Right now, many publications

are talking about how to be more productive because so many people feel overwhelmed by their 'To Do' list. If what you offer helps people be more productive you can reference that in your story. Alternatively, if you run retreats, you can talk about how it's all the more important for people to unplug when life is so hectic. As an example, the book *Overwhelmed: How to Work, Love and Play When No One Has the Time* by Brigid Schulte received a huge amount of press when it was published, because the subject resonated with the mood of our times.

3. **Why now?** Why should they cover your story today and not next week, next month or next year? If a big brand just made a fool of themselves on social media and you help people manage their brand or provide customer service on social platforms, get a press release out quickly! Alternatively, you might be able to tie your story to the season – for example, Valentine's Day, spring, summer holidays, back to school etc. To increase the chance of being quoted in the press in general, try registering at HelpAReporter.com to receive a daily list of requests from journalists.

If you can come up with a remarkable and fresh take on something you could see multiple press stories that bring you a flood of new enquiries and business. That's what Jody Day managed to do in fewer than 30 days.

How Jody Day launched a global movement in 30 days

Jody Day was a freelance PR and marketing consultant when she joined The Screw Work 30-day Challenge. She had only a germ of an idea: to do something to help women who were childless not through choice. Many childless women (who didn't choose to be) report feeling undervalued by society, which is particularly painful if they are also having feelings of grief at not having had children. As a childless woman herself, Jody felt strongly about this and as a trainee psychotherapist she was keen to do something to help others. She coined the term Gateway Women – because a gateway is a threshold that can either be a block or an opening to something new.

Jody's goal within the 30 days was to set up the website, write her first blog post and find somewhere she could give a talk. She got her Gateway Women website set up and wrote her first blog. She then went out to a women's business networking event to ask if she could speak there. While at the event she met a woman who was also a blogger, who then referenced Jody's post on her blog the next day. This brought women from all over the world to read Jody's blog post. They started leaving comments like, 'Oh my God, I'm not the only one that feels like this!'

In the spring of 2011 Jody gave her first talk to eight people. One of them was a journalist and interviewed her for *The Guardian* newspaper. The article was entitled, 'I may not be a parent but I'm still a person'.

This generated lots of buzz and lots of traffic and women started asking Jody, 'Can you help us?' so she thought about the easiest way of testing a course out. She found a cheap venue near her and met with five women on Saturday mornings for ten weeks. The experience was a powerful one for the participants. Jody turned the syllabus she'd developed over the ten weeks into a weekend workshop and then into a self-published book that was crowdfunded by other Gateway Women.

Now Jody runs an online community for Gateway Women with 700 members around the world. She also runs weekend workshops and sees clients one to one in person and over Skype. She revised and updated her ideas when she got a book deal from a major publisher for *Living the Life Unexpected: 12 Weeks to Your Plan B for a Meaningful and Fulfilling Future Without Children*. The new book hit the number one slot in the infertility category on Amazon.

Gateway Women now has a global reach of 2 million across the website, mailing lists, Facebook 'Likes', Google Plus, Twitter followers and meet-up groups in the UK and Ireland, USA, Canada, Australia, New Zealand, South Africa and elsewhere.

Jody has been invited to speak at many prestigious events and has been selected by the BBC as one of a hundred women to represent feminism. More importantly, she has been able to make a real difference in the lives of women all over the world.

Learn more about Jody Day and Gateway Women at www. gateway-women.com.

How to buy traffic

You can, of course, simply pay for web traffic. Two of the most popular ways to do this is to pay for adverts on Facebook or Google which only charge you when someone clicks on them. Facebook in particular provides lots of different options to choose the people you want to see your ads. You can advertise only to people who have 'Liked' certain pages or who fit a certain demographic.

However, it's best not to pay for traffic to your site until you know you will get the money back in sales. That means that the amount you make on sales exceeds the amount you spend on advertising. Once you get to the point where every $10 spent on advertising makes you $20 in sales profit, you can spend as much money as you can on advertising. It's kind of like a slot machine that gives you $20 for every $10 – assuming there is no limit to how many sales you can cope with.

If it's too early to tell yet, you can spend small amounts on adverts to bring just enough traffic to test *whether* people will buy.

Getting adverts right is a skill. If you have a feel for marketing and you're not technophobic, it's a useful skill to learn. Otherwise, hire someone who is an expert from a site like upwork.com.

Today's task

- As you work on your project, consider the questions in the traffic hack and in how to make headlines. If you're ready for more traffic, can you take action on these in some way today?

Workerbot thoughts to challenge

'How do I get on the front page of Google?' When you first create your website you will probably find you won't even register on a Google search. In order to get noticed, you need to get other people to link to you. Search Engine Optimisation is the science of getting featured in search results. It includes making sure your website includes words that people are likely to search for in Google, writing regular good quality content and getting others to link to you in order to be seen as an important website by Google's search algorithm. SEO can be very effective but there isn't much point going beyond the basics until you're getting a really good response from people who visit your site.

How to Be Likeable: A Beginner's Guide to Social Media Success

'Maybe don't call it social media. Maybe don't call it anything. Just be human and tell your story.'

—Gary Vaynerchuck, CEO of VaynerMedia and author of four bestselling books on entrepreneurship and social media

I nternet users spend more time on social media than any other type of website. People are increasingly turning away from print, radio and TV and getting their news, media, entertainment and social contact from social networks.

So it makes sense that if you want to spread the word about your project, you need to be doing that on social media. However, many people are spending hours spraying updates on social networks with very little return. Done poorly, you can even damage any goodwill people have towards you.

Done well, you can get invaluable information about how you're being perceived, build a community of contributors and advocates, turn followers into fans and fans into buyers. Done really well, you can see explosive growth that is impossible by almost any other method.

Follow these five guidelines to approach social media the right way:

1. Connect, don't sell

The first big mistake people make on social media is to use it like a broadcast channel to advertise yourself. This will quickly lose you followers. Your model for social media is not a commercial break but a cocktail party.

Your model for social media is not a commercial break but a cocktail party

---

If you went up to every person at a party and told them how wonderful you are and suggested they buy your product or services, you'd quickly find yourself standing alone with a big, empty space around you! And you'd be unlikely to get invited back.

But if, instead, you took a real interest in the people at the party, listened to them, added to what *they* were talking about, shared something of yourself and told some interesting and amusing stories, you'd end up making some friends. Then they'd be more likely to ask what you do and a lot more interested in your answer.

Similarly, use social media to connect with people, take an interest in them, build relationships, be helpful, share all the amazing things you are learning, share other things that your audience will find interesting and tell the stories of your clients/customers. Then they might pay attention when you announce you're giving a free talk, online seminar or product sample or you're running a competition to win something cool. And when they absorb the free taster some of them will want more and will be happy to pay for it.

Even those followers who never buy anything from you might contribute something interesting to the discussion or share your updates with their networks, bringing you new fans.

Social media is also a great place to connect with influencers such as journalists, authors and leaders in your field. Follow the people you respect, take a genuine interest in what they're doing and interact with them. If you make a connection you could end up meeting them, interviewing them, collaborating with them or getting their help to promote your project. But if you simply jump in and ask someone to retweet your promotional message, expect a frosty response.

2. Be authentic

Social media has a more personal feel than traditional marketing in print, radio, TV and even perhaps your own website. That's because it's a place where you have an ongoing presence and engage in a two-way conversation.

People love to follow personalities. The official Virgin Group Twitter account has 212,000 followers. Richard Branson, over 7 million. That means Richard is about 3,500 times more interesting than the company he founded with a turnover of £15 billion.

Authenticity wins in the social world. Don't speak in impersonal business language. Show something of your personality and your passion for your subject. We want to know what you really care about, what you love and even what you hate. People and brands who try not to offend anyone end up boring everyone. If you can't decide on your project's Twitter name, you might be best off just making it your own name.

3. Promote the idea, not you

On Day 23 we touched on the big idea behind your project. If your project represents your belief in a better way, social media is the ideal place to build a tribe of believers who support your view. If you can become the standard-bearer for a cause – whether it's functional programming, better quality chocolate or the power of social enterprise in the developing world – you can play a part in furthering that cause and in the process raise your profile for your project.

How to sell a million books by starting a movement

Tim O'Reilly is the ultimate example of reaping the rewards of this strategy. Tim is the founder and CEO of O'Reilly Media Inc, considered by many to be the best computer book publisher in the world. O'Reilly has sold a lot of books over the last 32 years but, just as importantly, the company has been the standard-bearer for some of the most important technology movements of our time – including Open Source software, Web 2.0, the Maker Movement and even the Internet itself back in its early days.

In 1992 O'Reilly published the first popular book about the Internet, *The Whole Internet User's Guide And Catalog*, at a time when there was a grand total of about 200 websites in the world. They hired Brian Erwin, an expert in PR, marketing and activism to help market the book.

Tim tells the story on a LinkedIn post of what happened next:

'People don't care about your book,' I remember Brian saying to me. 'They care about the Internet itself.' Instead of marketing the book, we used the book to market the Internet. And we used the native tools of the Internet … to find people who were also evangelical about the power of the Internet, and offered them free copies of the book to help with their evangelism. The book sold over a million copies, and was selected by the New York Public Library as one of the most significant books of the 20th century.

O'Reilly applied the same philosophy to reignite enthusiasm in the computer industry after the dotcom crash of 2001 by coining the term Web 2.0 and running a conference around it. Tim wrote a white paper called *What is Web 2.0?* that was downloaded for free more than a million times. As he says

> *Our Web 2.0 events generated tens of millions of dollars in revenue, but our marketing was not about our products – it was about the people and technologies and ideas that we celebrated as the pathfinders of a way out of the wasteland that the web had become in the years leading up to the bust...*
>
> *In short, the secret of promotion in the age of social media isn't to promote yourself. It's to promote others. Success comes when your success depends on the success of your customers, your suppliers, your end-users and when you spend more of your time thinking about them than about yourself.*

So the question for you is, what's the cause you want to promote that your project plays a part in?

4. Make it good

At the risk of sounding like a broken record, no social media strategy will help you if you don't do something of VALUE for people. Yes, you can go out and follow 120,000 people on Twitter and many of them will follow you back but that won't move you forward very much.

Matt Inman, creator of the wonderful webcomic The Oatmeal, has half a million followers on Twitter and used social media to raise a million dollars in one day for a card game he helped to create. In his wonderful comic called *How to get more likes on Facebook* he makes fun of the desperate cries from people to 'Like my Facebook page' and sums up a better strategy, 'So how does one get more *likes*? Put your energy into making things that are LIKEABLE, not into some douchey social media strategy.' Rather than begging people to support you, 'Instead, create things that are hilarious, sad, beautiful, interesting, inspiring, or simply awesome.'

As he told Tech.co in 2013,

> Really, if you take all that energy you're putting into your social media campaign and just made your thing better, become a better writer, draw better pictures, make better software, you will probably see more success. I've never asked for a tweet in my life, and I never plan on it.

5. Learn the language

Every social network has its own demographic, culture and language (both verbal and visual). Instagram is artistic. Facebook is personal. LinkedIn is professional. Tumblr is young, visual and knowing. Snapchat is young, fast-moving and ephemeral.

Since every network has its own verbal and visual language, you can't post the same content to all networks or take your Twitter feed and pipe it into Facebook and expect to make friends. Choose one or two networks where your kind of people hang out, get into it as a user, follow people you respect, learn the culture and language, then start to interact and share.

If you want to consult to corporations, get into LinkedIn and Twitter. If you want to reach mothers, get into Pinterest and Facebook. If you want to reach young people, get on Snapchat, Tumblr, Instagram or YouTube.

Today's tasks

- Choose a social network to start with. It could be the one you are already spending the most time on personally.

Think about the people and brands you enjoy interacting with on it – the people who don't feel like they're marketing at you – and see what you can learn from them. You can search for me on Facebook, Twitter and Instagram – find the links on www.screwworkbreakfree.com.

- Think about the bigger idea, cause or mission you care about and be willing to talk about and share things related to it – even if it doesn't promote your project.
- Build a habit of posting daily and be sure to respond quickly to people.

Build a following and you might just find you have some people who want to buy from you – something we'll learn more about tomorrow.

DAY 28

How to Sell Your Stuff
(Before It's Even Ready)

*'What I discovered was that business was no great
mystery. It's not something like physics or medicine
that requires extensive study. You just try
to get people to pay you for stuff.'*

—Paul Graham

An idea, brand name, logo and website do not make a
business. What makes a business is sales. Whether it's a
product, service, membership, event, club, app, consulting, freelancing or software subscription, your first key milestone
in creating a business is to sell it. Once.

Now is not the time to worry about the colour of the curtains
in your future headquarters or which accounting package you
will run the company on. Just make an offer and get someone to
buy it. What do I mean by an offer? Let's find out …

Define your offer

An offer is simply a description of what you'll provide and how
much money you want in return. The large management consultancy I once worked in called that a 'value proposition' (but,
hey, they have to justify their rates somehow!).

For our purposes, it's really very simple. Here are some examples:

- 'I'll build you a simple modern website using one of 20
  templates and including a custom header and email sign-up
  box, all for £500.'

- 'I'll run a one-day workshop in your company for up to 15 people to cure email inbox overload for £1,500.'
- 'I'll create a logo, branding, website design guidelines, and business card design for £2,000.'
- 'I'll send you a framed artwork 1 metre by 1 metre for £1,000 including delivery.'
- 'I'll see you for therapy at my clinic at £75 per 50-minute session.'
- 'Join my exclusive dinner dating club for £150 per month.'
- 'My "Stop Smoking" programme will stop you smoking in eight weeks for £800 or I'll give you your money back.'
- 'Get full access to my time-management app for right-brain people for $10/month.'

Tomorrow we'll look at how to turn a simple statement like these into a promotion you can make a lot of money out of very quickly, but for your first few sales you can personally explain what you're providing and take payment.

Your first sales will usually come from your existing network of friends and colleagues (or friends of friends). One of the great challenges of selling is that people need to trust that you will deliver what you are promising. Your friends and colleagues already know and (hopefully) trust you, so you don't need to have all the things in place that convince a stranger that you're trustworthy – a professional website, slick ordering system, convincing marketing copy and so on.

Even with your existing network, you will still have to *sell* your offer. So that means explaining why you can fulfil on the promise – for example, 'I'm now putting my skills and experience from ten years in corporate marketing into helping small businesses and startups and I've already doubled traffic to one client's website.'

If you're still developing your skills you can offer a discount: 'The typical price for this kind of product/service is £500 but as I'm just starting out, I'm offering it at just £200 for my first ten clients.'

Make this description as clear and as tempting as you possibly can and email it to your friends or post on your social networks. Ask also that they share it or forward it on to anyone else who might find it interesting. Call people you know who you think can benefit and talk to them.

You might think that this kind of very personal selling doesn't apply if you're running a tech startup, but in fact it can be very valuable to approach your first test clients, explain the product and see if they're willing to pay. That way you can take note of every question they ask and if they say no, you can ask them what would need to change for them to say yes.

Remember, it's only a sale when they give you the money! (See below how you might be able to get paid in advance.)

Making your first sale for this project that excites you – your first Playcheque – is an important landmark. So celebrate it! Put a photo of the cheque on the wall, buy yourself a bottle of champagne or take a photo of your first project so that you can remember it in the years to come.

Sales, ew!

If you're queasy about sales, you have the wrong image in your head. Forget the dodgy secondhand-car salesman. Selling is something we all do every day: convincing someone to go out with you, persuading your friends to go for your choice of restaurant, encouraging your children to eat their greens, convincing your partner to get fit or your boss to give you a chance on a new project.

Selling is something we all do every day: encouraging your children to eat their greens, convincing your partner to get fit or your boss to give you a new opportunity

---

If you can provide something useful, interesting, or entertaining for people, then frankly it's time to get over yourself and go communicate the value you can provide. That's all that sales is in its simplest form: check whether the person you're talking to can benefit (that's called qualifying the sale) and, if so, communicate the value and ask for a commitment.

Remind yourself why you're doing this. Do you care about this idea? Will it make people's lives even a little better if they buy it? Then do everything you can to ensure that they do.

At its most basic, business is two steps:

1. Make something people want.
2. Sell it to them
   (repeat until rich).

Richard Branson is the ultimate example of how simple it can be to start a business.

How Richard Branson sold his first airline tickets

In the 1970s, Richard Branson was busy running Virgin Records but a problem at the airport while on holiday sowed the seed for a whole new business …

In '79, when Joan, my fiancée and I were on a holiday in the British Virgin Islands, we were trying to catch a flight to Puerto Rico; but the local Puerto Rican scheduled flight was cancelled. The airport terminal was full of stranded passengers. I made a few calls to charter companies and agreed to charter a plane for $2000 to Puerto Rico. Cheekily leaving out Joan's and my name, I divided the price by the remaining number of passengers, borrowed a blackboard and wrote: VIRGIN AIRWAYS: $39 for a single flight to Puerto Rico. I walked around the airport terminal and soon filled every seat on the charter plane.

As we landed at Puerto Rico, a passenger turned to me and said: 'Virgin Airways isn't too bad – smarten up the service a

---

little and you could be in business.' – From a speech in India by Richard Branson as reported by blogger Ravi J. Mevcha

Note that Richard cleverly made this inaugural flight of his makeshift airline profitable: by dividing the cost of the charter flight by the number of passengers *excluding* his fiancée and himself, he made his own tickets free.

(In case you think Richard shortchanged the other passengers, remember it was Richard who did the work to find a charter plane and sell the tickets and he took the risk that something might go wrong and cause him to lose out on the deal. In return he benefited a little financially.)

Within a few years Richard decided to start an airline for real, as he explained in *The Telegraph* in 2014:

So I called up Boeing and said I wanted to buy a second-hand 747. They asked what I did. I said I ran Virgin, and we had Sex Pistols, The Rolling Stones and Janet Jackson. When they saw I was serious they agreed to the deal.

I was very careful to protect the downside, with the key ruling being that we could hand back the plane in 12 months' time if Virgin didn't get off the ground. Many of my team at Virgin Records thought I was mad, but I believed the Virgin brand could expand.

How to sell your stuff before it's even ready

There are ways to get paid before you've even finished creating the thing you're selling (if you know for certain that you can create what you promise!). It reduces your risk to sell a product, package or programme before you invest the time to create it. After all, there's no point making something that nobody wants. And the only way to know for sure is to sell it!

Pre-selling your product is also great if you are doing something expensive, such as manufacturing a product or making a movie. Instead of taking a loan, you pre-sell the product to customers willing to trust you to deliver on it. Then you can use the money raised to produce your product.

There are now some superb platforms for this kind of crowdfunding as it's called. Kickstarter is one of the most well known. Kickstarter has received more than $2.2 billion in pledges from 10 million backers to fund over 100,000 projects, including films, music, stage shows, comics, journalism, video games, technology and food-related projects.

There are many other platforms. Indiegogo has an international user base that includes lots of music, film and creative projects. Pozible is a crowdfunding site in Australia. UK-based Unbound provides crowdfunding for books.

How to get paid for your art

A particularly interesting crowdfunding platform for artists and musicians is Patreon. Patreon allows members of the general public to become a small-scale patron of the arts. Patrons agree to pay as little as $1 every time their chosen artist releases a new work, whether it's a song, poem, animation, comedy video or podcast. Committing to a larger amount can bring larger rewards – all the way up to $1,000 or more, which might get you lunch with the artist!

How Matt Inman and his friends raised a million dollars in one day for a card game about exploding kittens

Matt Inman created the website The Oatmeal, featuring hilarious and sometimes educational comics about technology, cats, coffee, web design, English grammar and

---

zombies, in 2009. Matt's cartoons were so good that within a year or so he had more than 4 million unique visitors a month. He started making money from merchandising (books, posters and more) and some advertising and by 2012 he was making half a million dollars a year.

That same year, Matt decided to help save pioneering inventor Nicola Tesla's lab, called Wardenclyffe, and turn it into a Tesla museum. He ran a crowdfunding campaign on Indiegogo to raise $2 million for non-profit organisation Tesla Science Center at Wardenclyffe, with the promise of an extra million from Tesla Motors founder, Elon Musk.

Then things got really crazy. In 2015 Matt got together with a friend who had an idea for a card game. After a few hours' work they turned it into Exploding Kittens, 'The card game for people who are into kittens and explosions and lazer beams'. They decided to run a fund-raising campaign on Kickstarter to raise the money to produce the game.

The funding goal was $10,000. They reached that goal within eight minutes of Matt announcing it to his followers. And they went on to raise a staggering 1 million dollars in the first day. When they ended the campaign a few weeks later they'd raised over $8 million from 219,382 backers.

Matt and his friends created something simple, executed it extremely well and made it both funny and shocking. The result was that Exploding Kittens became the most funded game in Kickstarter history and the project with the largest-ever number of backers.

Throughout the history of The Oatmeal, Matt has cared about creating a high quality product and he's followed the kind of principles you saw in Day 25 – he writes and draws funny and shocking pieces that are quick to read and he manages to catch the mood of the time, saying what others are thinking but are afraid to say.

Crowdfunding sounds like a dream come true – get paid in advance and use the money to produce what you really want to create. But unfortunately it is not a magic cash machine. Running a crowdfunding campaign is a significant project in itself. You'll need a great story about your project (often shown as a video) and be willing to throw plenty of energy into drumming up support. On Kickstarter, you set a funding target and if you don't raise the entire amount you don't receive anything.

But if you have a strong track record or you are partnering with people who can deliver the product, crowdfunding can enable you to pursue projects that you otherwise couldn't afford.

Even if you aren't yet ready to go down the crowdfunding route, it is possible to get paid in advance. Remember that that can be as simple as sending a PayPal link to the people who say they want what you're offering!

Today's tasks

- If you have something that you think you are ready to provide, why not try getting your first sale today (if you haven't already)? You can provide a discount if you're still finding your feet.
- If you're nervous about charging, see if you can find someone who is at least willing to invest their time to use your product or service. Ask for feedback and a testimonial in return.

Launch Zone

Take your protein pills and put your helmet on because in these last two days we look at the art of launching a project that can make a lot of money in a short period of time and we finally ship something of your project! Then you'll find out what to do next.

The Fine Art of Launching or 'How to Make a Lot of Money Very Quickly'

'One more thing ... '

—Steve Jobs' famous phrase that marked the launch of
Apple's world-changing products in his keynote addresses

It's 24 hours to launch day. Get ready to share your project with a wider audience. That may be something grand, like releasing your app, or it may be just your first baby steps, like sharing your photos on your website or Instagram, releasing the first chapter of your book as a PDF, writing up a case study of your first client or announcing more widely that you are available for doing the stuff you've been practising all month. Your project launch is about sharing the value you've been creating over the last 30 days; it's putting a stake in the ground.

This can also be your first step towards a full *promotional launch*. A promotional launch is a marketing campaign to make a big splash and generate the largest possible number of sales of your product, service, book, event or app in a short time period. Get it right and you could make three months or more of revenue in just a few days. That could mean tens of thousands of pounds in your account. For established companies it can mean a lot more.

*Learn the art of launching and you
could make three months or more of
revenue in just a few days*

Tesla Motors demonstrate the power of a launch

On 1 April 2016 Elon Musk's company Tesla Motors launched the Model 3. It started taking orders on the $35,000 car with a deposit of $1,000. By the time Elon took to the stage at an event in Los Angeles to unveil the car itself, the company had already received 115,000 orders despite the buyers knowing little but the price of the car. By the end of the next day the orders totalled 276,000. That's $276 million of down payments for a car that wouldn't be delivered until the end of the following year at the earliest. That translates to over $10 billion for the company when the orders are completed. $10 billion of orders in two days is quite a launch!

While you might not earn billions, knowing how to run a promotional launch is a fundamental stepping stone to a successful business that allows you to escape your day job and have the biggest possible impact. So that's what you're going to learn today.

The art of the launch

Running a launch well is indeed an art. It takes practice. And when you've got good at it, it's one of the most exciting moments in running a business.

I remember the excitement of one of my first big launches. I was sitting with my assistant in my favourite café in front of our laptops. At exactly noon an email was automatically sent by my system to 14,000 people announcing that my new programme was on sale, with a link to the sales page.

Within a few seconds, there was a ping as the first sale of £200 came into my account. Then another. And another. For a while there was a £200 sale about every 60 seconds. By the end of the weekend I'd made £24,000. A few days later, the total was up to £48,000. And all this was for a programme that I was proud of, that participants raved about and that was a pure joy for my team and I to run.

That moment was the culmination of the many weeks of planning and marketing that go into a promotional launch. To run your own promotional launch you'll need the following five things.

1. An offer

We talked about the simplest kind of offer yesterday – a succinct description of what you do for people. But to make a really compelling offer you need to describe in detail what you're offering and why someone should buy it.

To do that you'll need a place to put your offer. This is usually on a single page of your website, known as a sales page. Your offer could be a post on a social network or even be sent directly by email but a page on your website is a good place to start. Then you can include the web address of this page in emails and social updates to everyone you think will be interested.

If your website is already rather cluttered or the design is not ideal, you can create a separate, single-page website for your sales page using a page builder like Instapage, LeadPages or Unbounce.

Describe your offer on your sales page including the following:

- **Headline and subheading** – this captures the name for your product/service/book and something of the promise, i.e. what this thing will give the buyer.

- **Name target market + problem** – for example, 'For people over 30 who really want to get back into shape but struggle to stick to a disciplined workout routine.'
- **Describe solution state** – remember the before and after message from Day 23? This is where you describe what life might be like after using your stuff. For example, 'You'll get fit at last – and have fun doing it.'
- **Give your status story, a success story and/or testimonial** – this is where to include anything that gives confidence in your abilities or the quality of your product.
- **Describe how it is delivered and any Unique Competitive Advantage (UCA)** that's relevant: this is where to describe how you do what you do. And if relevant, why your product is different to others.
- **Pre-empt any possible objections** – pre-empt the typical concerns that might stop people from buying and address them on the page. You can weave them into your text 'You don't need self-discipline with this method' or list them as questions 'What if I don't have much self-discipline?' and then answer them.
- **Name the price and limited time offer** – name what the normal offer is and then detail the discount or added benefits for buying within the launch period (see below). Make the deadline very clear.
- **Give a single, clear call to action** – most likely a buy button. More on this below. Don't include anything else on your offer page. This is not the place to put links to your blog or social media or other products and services. Your aim is to focus the attention of the reader.

2. A reason to buy now

A sale, launch or promotion is marked by the fact that it's for a limited time. That's what makes it so powerful – it has a deadline; a point when it ends. This creates an urgency for people to buy. And that's a very good thing because most of us hate making decisions and committing to spending money. Imagine for a moment that you could leave booking your holiday until the day you wanted to depart and know that it will definitely be available with no price increase. Wouldn't you be tempted to leave it to the last moment? The danger then is that, if you can book any time with no pressure, you never actually get around to doing so.

That's why the enemy of sales is the thought in the head of your potential buyer of, 'I'll decide about this later'. A good promotion therefore gives a reason to make up one's mind. We're not trying to get anyone to buy something they don't want or need, we just want people who could benefit to make a decision: in or out.

If we provide a reason to buy now, we can persuade people to make that decision. Your reason could be any of the following:

- Limited availability – for instance, you only have 50 tickets before your event is full or you only have time for 10 consultations a month.
- Discount for a limited time – for example, the first ten tickets are thirty per cent off, or get two tickets for the price of one when booking early, or people ordering from your Kickstarter campaign before the product is in the shops get it at a reduced price.
- Pilot group or beta testers – you might invite early users of your app or early members of your membership network to join at a discounted price for life in exchange for giving feedback on the product and influencing how it develops.
- Bonus if ordering early or if one of the first customers – for example, give an add-on product to the first ten buyers or the people who buy within the first seven days or invite people who buy your book on the day of publication to join a free live video conference with you. The bonus of ordering early in the Tesla Model 3 launch was that you would be further up the waiting list for your new car.

Don't make things up that aren't real – saying you only have a limited number of an e-book for instance is kind of ridiculous. But often there is a natural limit to what you do – the number of people you have time to help for instance. And there's nothing wrong with rewarding people who book early with a discount. Simply say something like: 'I'm rewarding people who book by the end of the month with a 20 per cent discount.'

3. An audience to market to

Now that you have an offer with a reason to buy now, you need someone to show it to. The amount you can make from a promotional launch is dependent on how many people you can reach. Bear in mind that the number of people willing to buy out of all those that follow you could be as low as two–five per cent.

At this stage you might not have access to a large email list that you can send messages to, but if you follow the principles laid out over the past few days of playing in public, creating a good story, helping it go viral, using social media wisely, getting others to send you visitors and followers and perhaps even winning some press, then you should have collected the details of some people who are interested in what you do.

You can of course also share your offer with the people in your own personal network – your Facebook friends, LinkedIn contacts, Twitter followers, emailing your friends and so on.

If your project is in an area you've been working in for a while then you hopefully should have built up a database of previous customers or clients. If you run a promotion just to people who have already bought from you (for instance, offering a discount on a second purchase for a limited time), you can generate a lot of sales quite easily. The people who have already paid you money are often your best prospects of all!

If you have very few people to market to here are two things you can do to help. Firstly, you can run a promotional launch around something that's free just to get people's contact details. Make something really tempting of genuine value to people (for example, a focused guide to some aspect of your topic) and then give it away in exchange for people entering their email address or 'Liking' your Facebook page. Also ask other people to send the link out to their followers.

Secondly, you could run a competition. If you have a valuable product or service to give, you could invite people to enter their contact details to be included in a prize draw. Once the competition is over, choose one person at random to receive a free product or session. All the other people who entered the competition have already said they are interested in what you're providing so you can then make them a separate offer.

4. A marketing campaign

Simply creating your sales page won't get many extra sales. You need a marketing campaign around it. This is a sequence of email and social media messages leading up to the launch and through to the end of it.

I often see people send a single email to announce something they've been working on for many weeks and then write it off as a failure when no one buys. That doesn't mean your offer is a failure, you may just need to communicate it more.

After all, when a new iPhone comes out, they don't just slap a photo of it on their website with a buy button. There is a whole performance around it – complete secrecy, followed by a teaser campaign about what might be coming, a big launch event and then an advertising campaign to follow up. This makes it into something beyond a simple sale and more like a piece of drama. Ever seen the *Jaws* movies from the 1970s? The shark didn't just pop out of the water with a little splash. There was a build-up of tension as the sinister music reached a peak before the climax of the shark appearing with its giant jaws open. The build-up draws you in and focuses your attention.

The shark in Jaws *didn't just pop out of the water with a little splash. It's the build-up that makes it dramatic. The same is true in marketing.*

You need to allow time for a marketing campaign – perhaps a month or more, depending on the size of what you're trying to achieve. And if it's for something like a live event, people need time to arrange their diary accordingly.

The best offer is one you co-create with the community of people you're trying to help. Listen to what people want, what their frustrations are and what language they use. You can then create something to fit what they want and even ask them to contribute to it.

Your marketing campaign might include some education element – a series of three or four emails or posts explaining the problem you're trying to solve. Then you can move into announcing your solution. Describe its benefits, what it will do for people, not just how it works. Make these the sole focus of your emails; don't mix it in with other news or stories.

Be willing in these early stages to answer all questions personally and move people towards making a decision. This is where the hustling comes in!

One of the most important parts of this sequence is to remind people of the deadline when your offer expires. So make sure you send an email or other message in the days running up to the deadline and on the day itself. Don't be surprised if you get up to 50 per cent of all your sales on that last day.

Avoid cheesy, overblown messages that make out you're more successful than you are. If you've got something valuable, that's enough. Your first launch might just do enough to get you beta testers, or a pilot group or feedback on your product. That's OK. You can then use the feedback to improve what you're doing and launch again using the positive comments of your test group in your marketing.

5. A call to action

It's important to make it clear what you want people to do after reading your offer. Sometimes I read descriptions of really interesting offers on people's websites and then I can't find the button to buy it or contact the person! I have to go search for it somewhere else on the page or on an entirely different part of the website.

When someone has finally decided to buy from you it's essential to remove all potential friction and barriers that might get in the way. One of the reasons Amazon is such a powerhouse in retail is their one-click ordering. It means that once you've decided to buy a product, ordering it is a single click – no searching for the buy button or entering lots of details before checking out. It's estimated that this feature alone has made Amazon billions of dollars.

The rule for the buying process and for website design in general is summed up by user-experience expert Steve Krug's maxim, 'Don't make me think!' So, want to know one of my greatest secrets to business success? Stick a big buy button at the end of your offer!

If you're selling something that isn't a simple purchase you might have a big button that says 'Apply now' or a simple, clear form that says 'Enter your name and email and I'll get straight back to you'. For Tesla's launch it was a simple page with a form to enter your credit card and contact details. Whatever it is for you, make it as frictionless as possible.

Today's tasks

- Today you probably have your mind on finishing your project as that is the number one priority. But, if you can steal a few minutes, see if you can put a simple version of your offer on a page on your website. Describe what you do and have a clear call to action to buy or to get in contact. You can always come back later and add to it.

- If you're more advanced in your project and already have something ready to sell, you might choose launch day tomorrow as the day you put up a full sales page and begin a promotional launch.
- If you don't yet have much of a following, consider creating a truly valuable offer that you give away for free in exchange for people's contact details.
- And think about what you're going to share tomorrow for your project launch. The most important thing is to share *something* – that's non-negotiable.
- Now get on with your project and get it finished! If you've got too much to do in the time available, apply the Pareto principle again and focus on completing the 20 per cent of the project that will give 80 per cent of the result. Then get ready to share it with the world!

DAY 30

Launch!

'Ship. Ship it out the door. Do things that frighten you and put them out there.'

—Seth Godin

Congratulations! You've done it. You've made it as far as the finish line and that alone makes you something special. But you haven't stepped over that line just yet – you've not launched until you've shared your project.

As you've learned over the past 30 days, the path to fame, fortune and impact is to create something of value and share it with others. You don't get rich or famous or change the world by writing a book that stays on your computer, making stuff that people never see or designing the perfect app that's never released. It's the point at which you share it with others that you start the journey to real impact.

Celebrate!

Whatever you are sharing today, whether you're surprised how much you've achieved and the reactions you've had or it feels like you could have done much more, it's cause for celebration.

Your results so far might seem rather modest. More likely than not you don't have a fully formed book, app, lucrative course or thriving consultancy practice ready to launch onto the world after just 30 days. More probably you have the seed of something – a first event you ran, the notes you made while helping a few people with something for free, a bunch of blog posts you've written with an emerging theme that excites you. That's fine! This seed is just the beginning.

What you're launching today is a seed;
this is just the beginning

You've seen from the stories over the last 30 days how tiny seeds can grow into bestselling books, thriving businesses and global brands. Wolfgang Wild's Retronaut began when he installed WordPress and started sharing some of his historical photos, Jody Day's Gateway Women project started when she published one blog post and talked about it to another blogger at a networking meeting, Sean Rowley's Guilty Pleasures started with a two-hour show of beloved old records, Craigslist started as an email to friends and Mark Zuckerberg launched the first, very basic version of Facebook in 30 days, having been inspired by a bunch of even smaller experiments in social collaboration.

None of these businesses, books and brands would exist if their creators hadn't been willing to share the things they were working on at an early stage. So that's what you're going to do today.

And when you've done that you should congratulate your-self. You are not one of those who merely sits and dreams. You are a *player* now. And that deserves celebrating.

What will you share?

You've been playing out your project daily for at least 20 minutes and hopefully you've also been sharing and interacting with others as you went along. So today is about going public with what you've already been doing and opening up to feed-back, support and new opportunities.

So the deal is that by the end of today you're going to share something of your project with a wider audience. That could be:

- The Eventbrite or Meetup page for your first paid event.
- A link to a site where people can buy a framed print of one of the best nine photos you've taken this month.
- Your Etsy shop or eBay listing with your first few hand-made goods.
- The story of how you helped someone with their marketing or time management or fitness or whatever it might be and what you learned from it.
- The beta version of your app released only to a test group or a mock-up of the app with a call for people to give you feedback.
- The link to your blog with your first ten posts or your YouTube channel with your first three guest interviews or tutorial videos.

And if you're ready for more, your launch might also include:

- An email to everyone you know to ask for people interested in what you're offering.
- A simple one-page sales page to sell what you've so far perhaps only done for friends or for a test audience at a reduced price (as we saw yesterday).
- An opt-in page where people can enter their email address to get updates about your project.

Today's tasks

- Finish your 30-day Play Project by the end of today. Pull out all the stops to make your project as good as you can before you launch it.
- Launch! Share something of your project with a wider audience – see below.
- Celebrate and then relax – you've earned it.

How to launch

Here's how to actually launch your project:

1. Choose what you're going to share (see the examples above).
2. Choose where you're going to share it. That might be multiple places – your social media accounts, emailing friends and people at work, perhaps volunteering to give a talk somewhere.
3. Go ahead and share what you've been doing. You can choose to make it a big announcement or you can simply say that you've been following the process in this book for the last 30 days, share your results and say that this is just the beginning. Email it to friends, show it to them in person or post it on Facebook.
4. Share with everyone else in the Screw Work tribe! Here's how …

Share it with the Screw Work tribe

This is where you get to share with everyone else following this journey. My intention is that this book will play a part in fostering a mass movement of people around the world breaking free of their workerbot conditioning, embracing the New Entrepreneurialism and creating amazing products, businesses, books, art, movements and startups.

And you can connect with them on social media – post your launch to Twitter, Instagram, Pinterest, LinkedIn, Facebook and elsewhere with #screwworkbreakfree, so that we can all see what you're doing. Be sure to tell us all if you get a good result come out of your project too. I'm always looking out for good news from the tribe that I can share.

Visit www.screwworkbreakfree.com to see some of the examples of what people have done with their Play Projects and find ways to connect more with the Screw Work tribe.

Ready to make some money today?

If you're ready for it, today could be the day you start making money from what you've started. To do that you can simply send a description of what you're offering to all your contacts and networks as we saw on Day 28. You could also take the time to place yourself or your products on a suitable marketplace, like peopleperhour, Etsy, the App Store or Meetup, depending on what you're offering.

Alternatively, you could make today the start of a full promotional launch, which we learned about yesterday: take some of the tribe-building actions described there and create a promotion you can send to them. If you're ready to make the launch right away, you can call it a launch-day offer and give a special discount or extra bonuses for buying from you today.

Avoid last-minute self-sabotage

There is a danger that this will be the moment when your Top Dog (or inner critic) barks the loudest. It might tell you there's no point sharing what you've got, that it isn't good enough to show anyone or that you should work on it a bit longer to make it just right.

If you've let these messages stop you in the past from following through, finishing what you're doing and sharing it with others, don't sabotage yourself this time.

Be willing to share what you've created even if you think it's too small or not that great. You only took a dozen decent photos all month? Fine. Stick them on Instagram or on Facebook for just your friends to see. That's your launch. No need to declare it with any more import than simply to say, 'I've been playing around with some photography this month. Here are some of the results.'

I'm not promising your output today is going to go viral and launch you onto the world stage but you will have broken the spell of your Top Dog and workerbot thoughts. And you will be building that habit of publication and interaction that leads to greater and greater things. You never know, you might be surprised just what a warm response you get from your friends and supporters.

Now is not the time for perfectionism. Sure, use your last few hours to make your project as impressive as you can but accept that it won't be everything you want. The deadline is your friend; it prevents you from fiddling forever with your project and suffocating it in the process. Leonardo da Vinci said, 'Art is never finished, only abandoned', and the same could be said of a software release, book manuscript or manifesto.

The deadline is your friend; it prevents you from fiddling forever with your project and suffocating it in the process

---

Sometimes your seemingly imperfect project will quickly lead on to amazing new opportunities. In which case try to remember the Amish proverb, 'If at first you succeed – try not to look too astonished.'

Workerbot thought to challenge

Here's your last workerbot thought of the book to catch and challenge:

'My results haven't lived up to my plans.' Making it to the thirtieth day deserves congratulations in itself. Perhaps, though, you are feeling disappointed that you haven't achieved as much as you would have liked? If so, don't give yourself a hard time but realise it's good to wish for more. Let the gap between your vision and what you managed to achieve drive you to keep going. Michelangelo said, 'Lord, grant that I may always desire more than I can accomplish.'

And remember that this isn't the end of our journey. We're just getting started. You'll see in the next chapter how to keep going ...

What Next?

'If you want a happy ending, that depends, of course, on where you stop your story.'

—Orson Welles, actor and director

Of course, we haven't finished yet. We're really just getting started. You've learned all the essential skills of the New Entrepreneurialism and can continue playing out your idea as far as you want to take it. Here's how to do that …

End of project check-in: How was it for you?

REFLECT and ADAPT– how did this 30-day Play Project go?

- ENERGY: How much did this project focus on the things that excite you? What could you change about it to make it even more fun for you?
- GENIUS: Did you get a chance to use your skills and talents in this project? How could you incorporate more of them into this and future projects?
- VALUE: How well are people responding to your launch? Which aspects of your project did they appreciate most? How can you make it even more interesting, useful or entertaining to people?
- STORY: How did people take to the name and story around your project? Did people respond better when you explained your project in person? If so, how can you make your title

and wording around it clearer and better at communicating the VALUE?

- MONEY: Have people asked whether they can hire you or buy your product? If you've put something on sale have you got any takers? Is the price point right for your market? Is there another way to monetise your project to make even more out of it?

STICK, PIVOT OR SWITCH?

Having reflected on your project, are you happy to continue it or take it to the next level? Or do you need to 'pivot' and change some aspect of your project significantly? Look back at Day 20 to help you decide. If you've now got an idea for a completely different project that has even more potential, you can of course switch altogether.

ACT – Get ready to go again

Whether it's a stick, pivot or switch, it's time to choose the project you want to dive into next. Now you've been through the process once you don't have to stick to 30 days. It could be six weeks or maybe even three months, according to what you're trying to do, but the more uncharted this territory is for you, the shorter the cycles should be. And make sure you keep doing regular check-ins throughout to reflect, adapt and act again.

Keep playing it out

I have an interesting perspective in my work; I get to help thousands of people go through the same processes to find an idea they love, to get the first version out, to develop it into something that makes them money, then to scale it and market it to create a successful business.

Of course, not every one makes it and I'm really keen to understand why. Even when I see someone with a really interesting idea, they still sometimes lose their way and just give up. That's maddening for me when I know that all you have to do is keep acting, reflecting, adapting and you will get something great. Then I realised what's happening.

It's all very well for me to sit here knowing that if you do the things I teach you'll achieve success, but even I didn't know this back when I was in a job I wanted to escape. All I could see was fog up ahead, the fog of not knowing where I was heading or how I would get there. It didn't matter that people told me that if I did the right things I'd get to my destination of freedom. All I could see was a suffocating greyness.

If that's where you are now, I want you to know this: if you keep shipping, keep tuning into the response you get, keep noticing your internal experience in what you're doing and keep adapting to get what you want – even if it means taking on a completely different project – you really cannot fail.

And when you keep on going, there will come a time when the fog clears. You'll see where you're going and how to get there. You'll see just how possible it is to have the things you want and you'll achieve things that surprise and even shock you. That's worth hanging in there for.

Pass it on!

'The function of freedom is to free someone else.'
—Toni Morrison, Nobel and Pulitzer Prize-winning novelist

If the last 30 days have had a big impact on you, and you believe, as I do, that everyone needs to know these ideas, go spread the word. Share the one thing you've learned that's made the most difference to you with other people who could benefit. Call some friends and encourage them to join you on their own Play Projects over the next 30 days. They can download tools to help them for free at www.screwworkbreakfree.com. (You can also check on the site for the latest developments from me and those who have completed this process.)

Life is too short for boring work.
Screw Work.
Break Free.
Create what only you can create.
Pass it on.

Acknowledgements

Bringing this book to fruition has been a long journey and owes a lot to the people I have learned from and been supported by.

Firstly, I'd like to thank Katy Denny at Penguin Random House for your enthusiasm for, and belief in, this book. Thanks also to my agent and friend Jacqueline Burns for sticking with me through five years of iteration (and a couple of pivots) and going far beyond the remit of an agent to help guide my writing and come up with the suggestion of a 30-day format.

Thank you to Jane Birch for your great editing work; it's wonderful to know I can trust someone sharper than me to spot the things I miss. Thanks also to Lindsay Brodin for helping to wrestle my original book notes into some sort of usable shape.

To Roger Hamilton for his mentoring over the past two years. And to Daniel Wagner and James Watson for their insights into the world of online marketing and thank you Daniel, in particular, for finally nailing the title for this book.

Thanks to John Parkin and the Barefoot Doctor for branding advice (and to John for many chats about the world of non-fiction books and the recommendation to 'go where the energy is').

Thank you to everyone I interviewed for this book: Wolfgang Wild, Sam Hurt of Suck UK, Sean Rowley, Betty Herbert, Rik Spruyt, Saskia Nelson and Jody Day.

To Selina Barker for her role as coach in the first five 30-day Challenges and Allison, Frank and Julia who also helped make the experience a great one for the challengers.

To my friends who never lost faith in me finishing this damn thing: James Lawn, Liz Rivers, Candy Newman, Natasha Curnock. To Alasdair Inglis for our business chats over coffee at Monmouth. To Stony Grunow for many intelligent (and some infuriating) conversations on entrepreneurship, marketing and life, and for reading the first draft.

Thanks to Jerry Hyde for his creative wisdom. And to the guys in my men's group for their support and, in particular, Ed Smerdon and Chris Boydell who bet on me finishing.

Love to my mum and also to my brother David who always embodies the 'cut the crap' attitude of an entrepreneur.

To all the people I have been inspired and informed by: Paul Graham, Seth Godin, Eric Ries, Steve Pavlina, Barbara Sher, Barbara Winter, Austin Kleon, Kirby Ferguson and QuoteInvestigator.com.

To my mastermind and mentorship clients and over a thousand enthusiastic participants of the Screw Work 30-day Challenge who inspired some of the ideas in this book.

Thanks to Sarah Lou Davies at sarahloudavies.com for the lovely Playcheque Formula and Play Cycle graphics.

And finally to Grace, for your love and encouragement and for inspiring the title of Day 14.

Download the free resources for the book

The associated website for this book has a whole suite of resources you can download for free. This includes the Idea Cheatsheets with details on five possible projects that are particularly good if you're still in the exploration stage, project choice worksheets to complement the Killer Idea Crash Course, a daily ticksheet to track your progress and my recommendations and guides on how to create your website.

Elsewhere on the website you'll find the references mentioned in each chapter, some audio and video interviews with people in the case studies, the interactive Playcheque Formula assessment, an app for timing your microblocks, the latest updates to the book, news of life-changing Kiva loans made from royalties of the book to entrepreneurs in the developing world ... and even my music playlist for getting you charged up for doing your project.

You can also read the latest information on how to connect with me and the rest of the Screw Work tribe following this book on social media.

Access it all, free of charge, at www.screwworkbreakfree.com.

The Screw Work 30-day Challenge

On the website you can also find out more about the Screw Work 30-day Challenge, the programme that inspired this book. On the Challenge, hundreds of people around the world are led by me through a process to launch an idea in 30 days.

Participants describe the experience as transformational and the Challenge has now launched numerous careers, businesses, books, blogs, events, apps and social movements.

Learn more about The Screw Work 30-day Challenge and when the next one is taking place at www.screwworkbreakfree .com.

Kiva – supporting entrepreneurs in the developing world

I donate ten per cent of ongoing worldwide royalties from this book through Kiva, a non-profit organisation that makes microloans to entrepreneurs in the developing world. Even a $25 loan can be life-changing for someone needing to buy a sewing machine to make clothes to sell or buy stock for a small shop in a remote location.

Kiva works with microfinance and social enterprise partners on five continents to provide loans to people without access to traditional banking systems. Since 2005 Kiva has lent over $850 million in 84 countries and they get a 98 per cent repayment rate.

Simply by buying this book you have already helped an entrepreneur to create opportunity for themselves and their family.

Follow the Kiva link on www.screwworkbreakfree.com to find out more and see the stories of the loans that have been made in the name of the book. Once each loan is repaid, it can be lent again to another individual so that it can continue to create benefit. (While normal Kiva account holders can withdraw their funds, I have arranged with Kiva that the account associated with these donated royalties is non-withdrawable and so will remain in the Kiva ecosystem permanently.)

Want to get more involved? Join the Screw Work lending team

If you wish to support Kiva's work further, you can join as a member yourself and make your own loans – read through the borrower stories from around the world on the Kiva site and choose who to help.

You can also join the Screw Work lending team and connect with me and other readers to share how we're making a difference in people's lives all over the world. Learn how to join us in the Screw Work lending team at www.screwworkbreakfree.com.

One hundred per cent of every dollar you lend on Kiva goes directly towards funding loans; Kiva does not take a cut. Furthermore, Kiva does not charge interest to their field partners who administer the loans.

Once your loan is repaid, you can empower another person by making a new loan, donate the money to help cover Kiva's running costs or withdraw it.

INDEX